DECLINING
INEQUALITY IN
LATIN AMERICA

D1564457

DECLINING INEQUALITY IN LATIN AMERICA

A Decade of Progress?

Luis F. López-Calva
Nora Lustig
editors

UNITED NATIONS DEVELOPMENT PROGRAMME
New York

BROOKINGS INSTITUTION PRESS
Washington, D.C.

Copyright © 2010
UNITED NATIONS DEVELOPMENT PROGRAMME
All rights reserved. No part of this publication may be reproduced or transmitted in any form or by any means without permission in writing from the Brookings Institution Press.

Declining Inequality in Latin America: A Decade of Progress? may be ordered from:
Brookings Institution Press, c/o HFS, P.O. Box 50370, Baltimore, MD 21211-4370
Tel.: 800/537-5487; 410/516-6956; Fax: 410/516-6998; Internet: www.brookings.edu

Library of Congress Cataloging-in-Publication data
Declining inequality in Latin America : a decade of progress? / Luis F. López-Calva and Nora Lustig, editors.
   p.   cm.
Includes bibliographical references and index.
ISBN 978-0-8157-0410-2 (pbk. : alk. paper)
   1. Income distribution—Latin America.   2. Latin America—Economic policy—21st century.   3. Latin America—social policy—21st century.   4. Equality—Latin America.   I. López-Calva, Luis Felipe   II. Lustig, Nora.   III. Title.
   HC130.I5D43 2010
   339.2'2098—dc22   2010008554

9 8 7 6 5 4 3 2 1

Printed on acid-free paper

Composition by R. Lynn Rivenbark
Macon, Georgia

Printed by R. R. Donnelley
Harrisonburg, Virginia.

Contents

Foreword

One of the key strategic objectives of the United National Development Programme is to strengthen the capabilities of governments to reduce poverty and inequality and promote social inclusion, engaging and empowering the people for whom development policies are meant. This objective is particularly relevant in Latin America and the Caribbean, a region characterized by persistently high levels of inequality. Because of inequality, although many countries are on track to meet the MDGs at the national level, poor regions and excluded groups within middle-income Latin American countries most likely may not. At present the international community is focused in providing support to the poorest countries of the world in their efforts to achieve the Millennium Development Goals (MDGs). This emphasis is undoubtedly correct. However, if we shift our concern from poor countries to poor people, it is immediately apparent that this emphasis must be complemented with an equally active effort to address poverty in middle-income countries with high levels of inequality.

To address this concern, the UNDP's Bureau of Development Policy (BDP) and the Regional Bureau of Latin America and the Caribbean (RBLAC) launched in 2007 the project "Markets, the State and the Dynamics of Inequality in Latin America." Similar initiatives were launched in other regions of the world. The project's main objective was to identify and propose policy actions that governments could institute to ensure that the millions who live in stark poverty today in unequal middle-income countries reach the levels of well-being consistent with the social norms adopted by the international community in the MDGs.

Declining Inequality in Latin America: A Decade of Progress? is one of the project's key outputs. The volume focuses on an unusual period of declining inequality in Latin America: of the seventeen countries for which comparable data are available, twelve experienced a decline since 2000 in particular. Through in-depth analyses of Argentina, Brazil, Mexico, and Peru, this book suggests that two main factors account for the decline in inequality—namely, a fall in the earnings gap between skilled and low-skilled workers and an increase in government transfers targeted to the poor.

The fall in the earnings gap is mainly the result of the expansion of coverage in basic and secondary education during the last couple of decades. Thus, two important policy lessons emerge: indeed, broad-based access to education and targeted government transfers can be effective in reducing inequality. However, in the context of Latin America, it may be difficult to keep the redistributive momentum. While broad-based access to primary and secondary education has been achieved (or seems achievable within a reasonable period of time), such access to tertiary education (the next phase in educational upgrading) will not be easy to achieve—mainly due to the low-quality education that the poor receive in basic and secondary levels. Thus, the decline in inequality is not likely to continue. In addition, despite the progress in making public policy more pro-poor, a large share of government spending continues to be focused on specific programs, rather than integrated social protection schemes, while the collection of taxes on personal income and wealth is very low. Making public spending and taxes more progressive and improving the quality of public services for the poor to avoid further segregation—basic services such as education and health—are key to continue on the path toward more equitable societies. In addition, rising food prices and macroeconomic contractions—unless the affected groups are protected from such events—will slow down the progress in reducing inequality and poverty.

The experience of advanced countries analyzed in this volume shows that sustaining equity over time requires a permanent redistributive effort through progressive income and wealth taxation of the very top incomes in particular. In this regard, Latin America is still far behind, especially when compared with industrialized countries. Deepening and consolidating the redistributive momentum will require stronger democratic institutions. Despite the undeniable progress in terms of democracy experienced in the region, clientelism and state capture on the part of predatory elites are still a challenge for policy effectiveness. Sustained reductions in inequality in Latin America will demand more actions on the part of policymakers and polities alike.

REBECA GRYNSPAN
Associate Administrator

United Nations Development Programme
March 31, 2010

Acknowledgments

This book is based on a project of the United Nations Development Programme, "Markets, the State and the Dynamics of Inequality in Latin America," coordinated by Luis F. López-Calva and Nora Lustig.

The project was a joint initiative of the Poverty Cluster/Regional Bureau of Latin America and the Caribbean and the Poverty Group/Bureau of Development Policy (PG/BDP), undertaken under the leadership of Rebeca Grynspan and Olav Kjorven, the bureaus' respective directors, and Selim Jahan, director of PG/BDP. Project managers in PG/BDP included, at various times, Selim Jahan (director, Poverty Practice), Rathin Roy (director, International Policy Centre for Inclusive Growth), and Shantanu Mukherjee (policy advisor, Microeconomics).

The editors are greatly indebted to Fedora Carbajal and Alexandra Solano for their excellent research assistance and to Maria Fernanda Lopez-Portillo for her excellent administrative support in the preparation of this book. They also would like to thank Marina Blinova, Elia Carrasco, Patrice Chiwota, Queenee Choudhury, and Jacqueline Estevez for their support in the administration of the project. Last but not least, they are greatly indebted to Eileen Hughes and Mary Kwak from the Brookings Institution Press for their terrific editorial recommendations and to an anonymous referee for the invaluable suggestions to an earlier draft.

1

Explaining the Decline in Inequality in Latin America: Technological Change, Educational Upgrading, and Democracy

LUIS F. LÓPEZ-CALVA AND NORA LUSTIG

Latin America often is singled out because of its high and persistent income inequality. With a Gini coefficient of 0.53 in the mid-2000s,[1] Latin America was 18 percent more unequal than Sub-Saharan Africa, 36 percent more unequal than East Asia and the Pacific, and 65 percent more unequal than the high-income countries (figure 1-1). However, after rising in the 1990s, inequality in Latin America declined between 2000 and 2007. Of the seventeen countries for which comparable data are available, twelve experienced a decline in their Gini coefficient (figure 1-2). The average decline for the twelve countries was 1.1 percent a year.[2]

The decline in inequality was quite widespread. Inequality declined in high-inequality countries (Brazil) and low-inequality—by Latin American standards—countries (Argentina); fast-growing countries (Chile and Peru) and slow-growing countries (Brazil and Mexico); macroeconomically stable countries (Chile and

The authors thank Raquel Fernandez for her invaluable suggestions as well as Alan Barreca, Mary Kwak, and an anonymous referee for very useful comments on an earlier draft; they also are very grateful to Fedora Carbajal for her excellent research assistance.

1. Named after its originator, Corrado Gini, the Gini coefficient is commonly used to measure inequality. The Gini coefficient is an index that can take values between zero and one; the closer it is to zero, the less unequal the distribution in question. Ginis are usually never above 0.65 or below 0.20. The figure is for 2004.

2. All the declines except that for Venezuela were statistically significant.

Figure 1-1. *Gini Coefficient by Region, 2004*

Percent

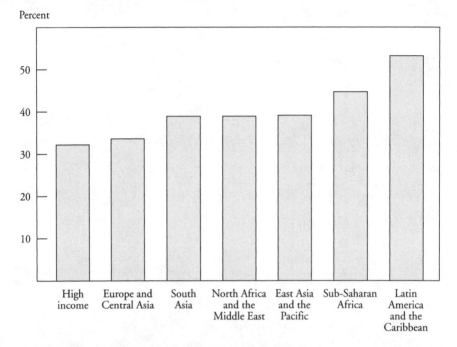

Source: Authors' calculations based on Ferreira and Ravallion (2008).

Peru) and countries recovering from economic crisis (Argentina and Venezuela); countries with a large share of indigenous groups (Bolivia, Ecuador, and Peru) and countries with a low share (Argentina); in countries governed by leftist regimes (Brazil and Chile) and in countries governed by non-leftist regimes (Mexico and Peru); in countries with a universalistic social policy (Argentina and Chile) and in countries with a historically exclusionary state (Bolivia and El Salvador).[3] Inequality in Latin America is the result of state capture by elites, capital market imperfections, inequality of opportunity (in particular, of access to good-quality education), labor market segmentation, and discrimination against women and nonwhites.[4] Hence, the observed fall in inequality is good news.

This book is among the first attempts to address the question of why inequality has declined in Latin America during the last decade, through in-depth analyses of Argentina, Brazil, Mexico, and Peru.[5] In all four cases, the data come from

3. This may be changing given the leftist-leaning characteristics of the regimes now in power.
4. See, for example, Atal, Ñopo, and Winders (2009); Barros and others (2009); Levy and Walton (2009); and De Ferranti and others (2004).
5. Readers interested in other countries can refer to the UNDP-sponsored studies Bruni, Fuentes, and Rosada (2009), for Guatemala; Eberhard and Engel (2008), for Chile; and Gray Molina, and Yañez (2009), for Bolivia.

Figure 1-2. *Change in Gini Coefficient by Country, circa 2000–06*[a]

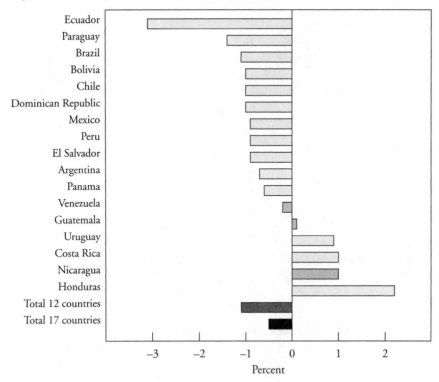

Percent

Source: Authors' calculations based on data from SEDLAC, July 2009 (www.depeco.econo.unlp.edu.ar/sedlac/eng/).

a. Data for Argentina and Uruguay are for urban areas only. In Uruguay, urban areas covered by the survey represent 80 percent of the total population; in Argentina, they represent 66 percent. The average change in the Gini for each country is calculated as the percentage change between the end year and the initial year divided by the number of years; the average for the total is the simple average of the changes by country (twelve countries in which inequality fell). The years used to estimate the percentage change are as follows: Argentina (2006–00), Bolivia (2007–00), Brazil (2006–01), Chile (2006–00), Costa Rica (2007–00), Dominican Republic (2007–00), Ecuador (2007–03), El Salvador (2005–00), Guatemala (2006–00), Honduras (2005–01), Mexico (2006–00), Nicaragua (2005–01), Panama (2006–01), Paraguay (2007–02), Peru (2007–01), Uruguay (2007–00), and Venezuela (2006–00).Using the bootstrap method, with a 95 percent significance level, the changes were not found to be statistically significant for the following countries: Guatemala, Nicaragua, and Venezuela (represented by horizontal lines in bars in the figure).

country-based household surveys and the analyses focus primarily on changes in labor income inequality and changes in the size and distribution of government transfers (and remittances when relevant).[6]

The four countries analyzed here can be considered a representative sample of middle-income countries in Latin America. The sample includes one of the five

6. The reason for this focus is the tendency to underreport property income in household surveys. In Latin America, in contrast to the United States, top incomes come primarily from property, not wages. Therefore, household surveys do not provide reliable data for measuring overall inequality. That fact can

Figure 1-3. *Latin America: Gini Coefficient by Country, circa 2007*[a]

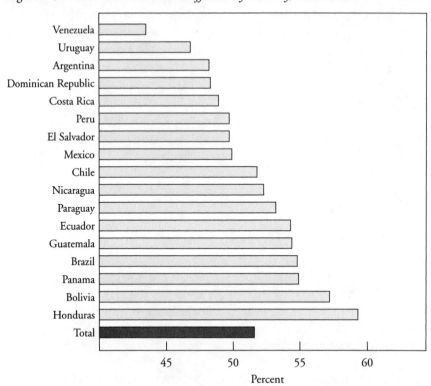

Percent

Source: Authors' calculations based on data from SEDLAC, July 2009 (www.depeco.econo.unlp.edu.ar/sedlac/eng/).

a. In order to make the differences in the Gini coefficients easier to compare, the vertical axis starts at 40 percent instead of zero. The years used to estimate the Gini coefficient are as follows: Argentina (2006), Bolivia (2007), Brazil (2006), Chile (2006), Costa Rica (2007), Dominican Republic (2007), Ecuador (2007), El Salvador (2005), Guatemala (2006), Honduras (2005), Mexico (2006), Nicaragua (2005), Panama (2006), Paraguay (2007), Peru (2007), Uruguay (2007), and Venezuela (2006). The difference between figure 1-1 and this figure in the average for the region is due to the fact that figure 1-1 uses the Gini coefficients for circa 2005 and the coefficients used here correspond to later years.

most unequal countries in Latin America (Brazil) (figure 1-3); a traditionally low-inequality country, which witnessed the largest increase in inequality of the region in the past three decades (Argentina); three of the largest countries in the region in terms of population and GDP (Argentina, Brazil, and Mexico); two countries

---

be observed, for example, by looking at the average income of the two "richest" households for each country in this book as recorded in the household surveys used for the analyses. In 2006, the average monthly *total* household income in current U.S. dollars was $70,357 for Brazil, $43,148 for Mexico, $17,563 for Peru, and $14,779 for Argentina. Clearly, those numbers indicate that the incomes of the rich are not included.

where innovative, large-scale conditional cash transfers have been implemented (Brazil and Mexico); and one country with a large indigenous population (Peru).[7]

All four countries experienced substantial market-oriented reforms in the 1990s (in the case of Mexico, since the 1980s). In particular, trade and foreign investment were liberalized, many state-owned enterprises were privatized, and, more generally, markets were deregulated. The four countries also faced significant macroeconomic crises between 1995 and 2006 and, except for Argentina, have pursued broadly prudent fiscal and monetary policies in particular since 2000. In 2003, following the boom in commodity prices, Argentina and Peru began to benefit from very favorable terms of trade; as a result, both countries enjoyed high per capita growth rates between 2003 and 2006 (7.8 and 5.2 percent a year, respectively). In contrast, GDP per capita growth was modest in Brazil and Mexico (2.7 and 2.8 percent a year, respectively).[8]

Two leading factors seem to account for the decline in inequality in Argentina, Brazil, Mexico, and Peru during the last decade: a decrease in the earnings gap between skilled and low-skilled workers and an increase in government transfers to the poor. The decrease in the earnings gap, in turn, seems to be mainly the result of the expansion of basic education during the last couple of decades;[9] it might also be a consequence of the petering out of the one-time unequalizing effect of skill-biased technical change in the 1990s associated with the opening up of trade and investment. In any case, in the race between skill-biased technical change and educational upgrading, in the past ten years the latter has taken the lead.[10] The equalizing contribution of government transfers seems to be associated with the implementation or expansion of large-scale conditional cash transfer programs in Argentina (Jefes y Jefas de Hogar),[11] Brazil (Bolsa Escola/Bolsa Familia and BPC), and Mexico (Progresa/Oportunidades) and with in-kind transfers in Peru.[12]

---

7. Based on Maldonado and Rios (2006); in 2001 around 37 percent of Peru's population was indigenous (30 percent Quechua).

8. The GDP data are from World Development Indicators (WDI) database, World Bank, January 2009. Annual GDP per capita growth was based on GDP per capita at purchasing power parity (PPP) prices in constant 2005 international dollars. The income per capita calculated from household surveys is considerably lower than the GDP per capita, in part because the concept of GDP includes more than personal income. However, surveys also underestimate average income per capita because of underreporting of income at the very top of the distribution, a well-known problem that has plagued household surveys in Latin America since the surveys were first conducted.

9. Basic education includes grades 1–9 in Argentina and Mexico; 1–8 in Brazil; and 1–11 in Peru. The number of grades includes what countries call basic primary and secondary education.

10. Tinbergen (1975) was among the first studies to use the expression "race between education and technology"; more recently, it was the central theme of Goldin and Katz's illuminating analysis of the United States (Goldin and Katz 2008).

11. Bolsa Familia and Progresa/Oportunidades are briefly described in chapters 6 and 7, respectively. Also, see Fiszbein and others (2009).

12. See chapter 8 by Miguel Jaramillo and Jaime Saavedra in this volume.

In this chapter, we discuss the evolution of inequality and its determinants and present a synthesis of the main findings of the chapters included in this book.

Rising Inequality: The 1980s and Early 1990s

Income inequality increased in most Latin American countries during the so-called "lost decade" of the 1980s and structural reforms of the early 1990s.[13] Although data availability constrains comprehensive comparison,[14] the evidence suggests that the effects of the debt crisis during the 1980s were unequalizing. In particular, because the poor were less able to protect themselves from high and runaway inflation and orthodox adjustment programs frequently resulted in overkill,[15] those in the poor and the middle-income ranges were hurt disproportionately while the income share of the top 10 percent rose.[16] The unequalizing effect of the crisis was compounded because safety nets for the poor and vulnerable were conspicuously absent (or poorly designed and inadequate) in the Washington-led structural adjustment programs in the 1980s.[17]

The pattern of inequality for the four countries analyzed here is shown in figure 1-4. Both Argentina and Mexico show a clear inverted U. That is not the case for Brazil, and comparable data for Peru do not go far enough (Ginis for 1984 and 1991 are not strictly comparable). However, as Jaramillo and Saavedra argue in chapter 8 of this volume, there are indications that income inequality increased during the period of reforms in the early 1990s (1991–93 in figure 1-4).

In the early 1990s, as governments turned to market-oriented reforms to pull their economies out of crisis, inequality continued to increase, driven in part by a significant increase in the relative returns to tertiary education (figure 1-5). What was behind the sharp increase in returns to education? Figure 1-6 shows that the supply of skilled and semi-skilled workers rose in the 1980s and 1990s; therefore the increase in returns to education must have been driven by skill-biased changes in the composition of demand for labor. There is evidence that both the sectoral

13. See, for example, Altimir (2008) and Londoño and Szekely (2000).

14. Before-and-after analysis of inequality in the 1980s could be done at the national level for few countries. Eleven countries had at least one national-level survey in the 1980s. Among those, a strict before-and-after adjustment comparison could be made for only four: Brazil, Costa Rica, Panama, and Venezuela. Surveys from Argentina, Bolivia, Colombia, Ecuador, El Salvador, Paraguay, and Uruguay did not include the rural sector. Only three countries had at least one survey that recorded total income (including nonwage and nonmonetary income): Chile, Mexico, and Uruguay (Lustig 1995, table 1A-1, p. 37). It should be mentioned that even in the countries in which surveys collect information on nonwage income, there is every reason to believe that there are gross underestimations, particularly with respect to property income. A quick look at the top income levels recorded in the surveys demonstrates that the rich are not counted. Hence, existing measures may underestimate the true level of inequality in a nontrivial way.

15. That is, the reduction of fiscal deficits went beyond what was necessary to restore equilibrium in the external accounts and that over-adjustment had counterproductive effects on stabilization itself. For a discussion of overkill in Mexico see, for example, Lustig (1998).

16. See Lustig (1995).

17. Lustig (1995).

Figure 1-4. *Gini Coefficients for Argentina, Brazil, Mexico, and Peru, 1981–2006*[a]

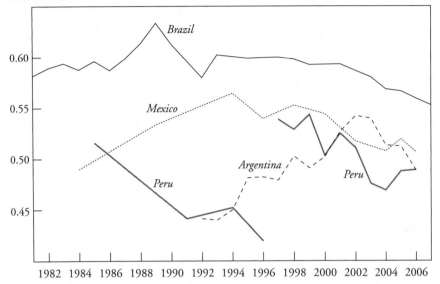

Gini coefficient

Sources: Argentina: Gasparini and Cruces, chapter 5 in this volume; Brazil: Barros and others, chapter 6; Mexico: Esquivel, Lustig, and Scott, chapter 7; and Peru: Jaramillo and Saavedra, chapter 8. Gini coefficients for Peru in 1985–96 and 1997–2006 are not comparable.

a. Data for Argentina include urban areas only, representing about two-thirds of the population. Ginis are calculated for total current household income per capita. The income concept used is as follows:

—Argentina: current monetary income (does not include imputed value of owner-occupied housing or auto-consumption), after taxes for wage earners and before taxes for other categories and after monetary government transfers.

—Brazil: current monetary plus imputed value of income in kind (but does not include imputed value of owner-occupied housing), before taxes and after monetary government transfers.

—Mexico: current monetary income (does not include imputed value of owner-occupied housing or auto-consumption), after taxes and after monetary government transfers.

—Peru: current total income (includes imputed value of income in kind, auto-consumption, owner-occupied housing, and some in-kind government transfers such as food and health care services), after taxes and after monetary government transfers.

reallocation of production and employment and the skill intensity within sectors changed in favor of skilled workers, in particular college graduates. Results, therefore, are consistent with the presence of skill-biased technological change, in particular after the opening up of the economies in the 1980s and 1990s. While for Argentina (Gasparini and Cruces, chapter 5 in this volume), Mexico (Cragg and Eppelbaum 1996 and Esquivel and Rodríguez-López 2003), and Peru (Jaramillo and Saavedra, chapter 8 in this volume) there is evidence that the direct effect of trade liberalization on wage inequality seems to have been small, the indirect effect of trade and of capital account liberalization through their impact on adoption of new skill-intensive technologies of production and organization might have been

Figure 1-5. *Ratio of Returns to Education for Argentina, Brazil, Mexico and Peru*[a]

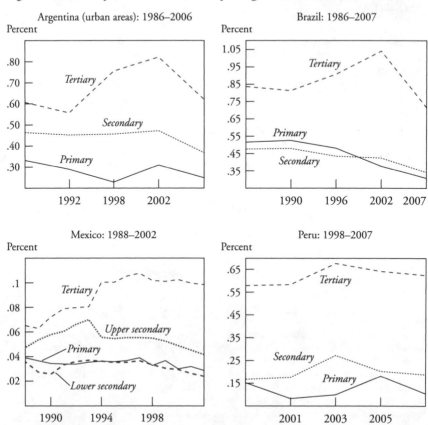

Source: Ratios for Argentina, Brazil, and Peru are from authors' calculations based on data from SEDLAC, July 2009 (www.depeco.econo.unlp.edu.ar/sedlac/eng/); ratios for Mexico are based on Lopez-Acevedo (2006).

a. Ratios for returns to education were calculated from educational dummy coefficients of Mincer equations, using wages from main occupation for men only. Variables of education level (college, secondary school, and primary school), potential experience, and geographic regions were included. Omitted variable was no schooling or incomplete primary school. Remunerations for men are for all workers, including wage earners, self-employed workers, and employers. Population considered was the age group from 25 years to 55 years. Data for Argentina are for urban areas only; urban areas covered by the survey represented 66 percent of the total population. Surveys before 1991 covered Gran Buenos Aires; surveys from 1992 to 1997 covered fifteen cities; and surveys from 1998 to 2006 covered twenty-eight cities.

substantial. That is not the case for Brazil, where trade liberalization seems to have caused a reduction in skill premiums and wage inequality, as suggested by Ferreira, Leite, and Wai-Poi (2007). That may be the main reason why inequality in Brazil did not increase during the reform period and did not show the inverted U found in other countries.[18]

18. The inverted U pattern in reference to the evolution of income inequality was first posited by Kuznets (1955).

Figure 1-6. *Composition of Adult Population by Educational Level for Argentina, Brazil, Mexico, and Peru*[a]

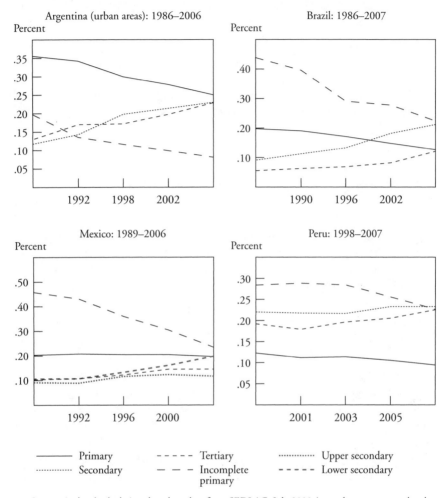

Source: Authors' calculations based on data from SEDLAC, July 2009 (www.depeco.econo.unlp.edu. ar/sedlac/eng/).

a. Skill groups are formed by level of formal education. Educational levels correspond to completed primary school, lower- and upper-secondary school, and tertiary education. In Argentina, complete primary school is achieved at 7 years, complete secondary school at 12 years, and tertiary education at 15 or more years of formal education; incomplete primary includes 6 years or less of education and no education. In Brazil, complete primary is achieved at 4 years, complete secondary at 11 years, and tertiary at 15 or more years of formal education; incomplete primary includes 3 years or less of education and no education. In Mexico, complete primary is achieved at 6 years, complete lower secondary at 9 years, complete upper secondary at 12 years, and tertiary at 15 or more years of formal education; incomplete primary includes 5 years or less of education and no schooling. In Peru, complete primary is achieved at 5 years, complete secondary at 11 years, and tertiary at 14 or more years of formal education; incomplete primary includes 4 years or less of education and no schooling. For 1997 completed secondary school in Peru is achieved at 10 years. Shares were calculated for adults only (the age group from 25 years to 65 years).

Declining Inequality: The Mid-1990s Onward

The rising trend in inequality came to a halt in the second half of the 1990s or in the early 2000s, depending on the country (figure 1-4). From then until the global financial crisis in 2008–09 (for which data on income distribution are not yet available), inequality declined in most countries in Latin America. In particular, inequality declined in the four countries analyzed here, beginning in 1994 in Mexico, 1997 in Brazil, 1999 in Peru, and 2002 in Argentina (figure 1-4). Income inequality as measured by the Gini coefficient fell by 5.9 percentage points in Mexico (1994–2006), 5.4 percentage points in urban Argentina (2002–06), 5 percentage points in Peru (1999–2006), and 4.8 percentage points in Brazil (1997–2007).[19]

Why did inequality decline in these four countries during the last decade? Have the changes in inequality been driven by market forces, such as the demand for and supply of labor with different skills? Have labor market institutions such as the strength of unions or minimum wages changed? Or have governments redistributed more income than they used to? We attempt to answer those questions here.

Specifically, the studies for Argentina, Brazil, Mexico, and Peru ask what the contribution was of demographic factors (changes in the proportion of adults in the household, for example) to the observed change in inequality in household per capita income. Were changes in the distribution of labor income an important equalizing factor? If so, were those changes, in turn, driven by changes in the distribution of personal characteristics (in particular, in the distribution of educational attainment), changes in returns to personal characteristics (returns to education, in particular), or changes in employment, hours worked, or occupational choice (wage labor or self-employment, for example)? If changes in all three were relevant, what caused them to change in turn? Was it increased coverage of basic education, the mix of production skills generated by technological change, macroeconomic conditions, or stronger labor unions? What has been the role of changes in the distribution of nonlabor income? Do changes in government transfers account for a significant part of the change in inequality in nonlabor and overall income inequality?

In each chapter, the authors estimate the contribution of proximate causes,[20] relying on parametric and nonparametric methods to decompose changes in

19. The Gini coefficients are equal to .564 and .505 (Mexico 1994 and 2006); .541 and .487 (Argentina 2002 and 2006); .54 and .49 (Peru 1999 and 2006); and .600 and .552 (Brazil 1997 and 2007). The declines are statistically significant at the 95 percent level of significance. According to Gasparini and Cruces in chapter 5, trends in urban Argentina are representative of changes for the country as a whole. Those Ginis may differ from those presented in the individual chapters because of rounding or because the chapters use a different concept of income or a different data source. Discrepancies among inequality indicators depending on the source are a fairly common phenomenon.

20. Typical proximate causes are changes in the distribution of educational attainment, returns to personal characteristics, access to employment, and hours worked. For example, inequality may fall because

household income inequality.[21] The empirical analysis is combined with circumstantial (that is, indirect) evidence and historical narratives to put together the multidimensional "jigsaw puzzle" of the fundamental determinants of inequality over time.

Several patterns recur throughout the four case studies. First, in all four countries changes in the distribution of the dependency ratio were equalizing. The proportion of dependents fell more in poorer households, but the contribution of that factor was far less important than the contributions of the reductions in labor income inequality and nonlabor income inequality. Also, the equalizing contribution of demographic changes was already under way in the 1990s, reflecting the reduction in fertility rates that has characterized the region in the past two or three decades. It is not a new phenomenon. The two most important differences between the 2000s and the 1990s (and 1980s too, depending on the country) are the observed declines in both labor income inequality[22] and nonlabor income inequality.

Determinants of the Decline in Labor Income Inequality: The Race between Education and Technology

Declines in labor income inequality appear to be associated with the educational upgrading of the labor force, which resulted in a more equal distribution of schooling attainment in the four countries, above all in Brazil, Mexico, and Peru. Figure 1-7 shows the Gini coefficients for years of schooling of the population between 25 and 55 years of age. The Gini for educational attainment declined by 5 percentage points in Brazil (1998–2007), 7 percentage points in Mexico (1996–2006), and 4 percentage points in Peru (2001–07). In Argentina, the decline was almost negligible for the period in which earnings inequality began to fall (2003–06). However, that should come as no surprise since the period was much shorter and Argentina's population had more years of schooling to begin with.

Thus, the quantity effect of education on labor income inequality resulting from a more equal distribution of the stock of education (years of schooling) was

---

the skill premium—return to education—declines. That is a proximate cause that can result from both demand (a relative expansion of labor-intensive industries) and supply factors (a change in the composition of the labor force by skill). Changes in output in labor-intensive industries, in turn, can be associated with a depreciation of the currency, which is the fundamental cause. Changes in the composition of the labor supply by skill can result from government policy to increase coverage in education and from individuals' decision to acquire more years of schooling in response to the higher earnings that more years of schooling commands. The political economy dynamics that shape public policy and individuals' response to incentives are examples of fundamental causes.

21. The methods vary across chapters. More formal descriptions of the methods can be found in the sources cited in the chapters.

22. In the case of Peru, the result is found at the individual but not at the household level, indicating that assortative matching dampens the equalizing effect at the individual earnings level.

Figure 1-7. *Gini Coefficients for Education for Argentina, Brazil, Mexico, and Peru*[a]

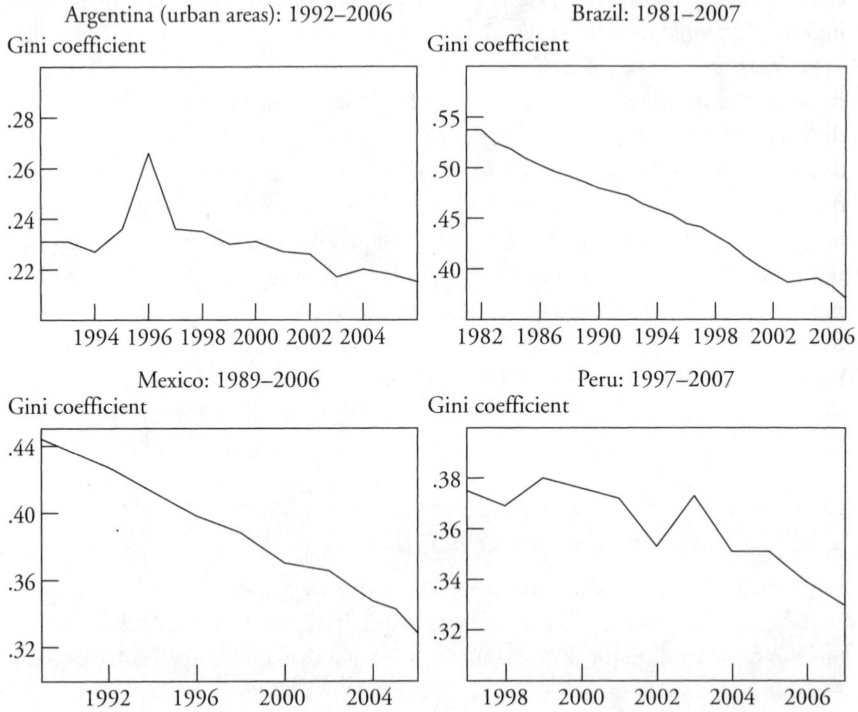

Source: Authors' calculations based on data from SEDLAC, July 2009 (www.depeco.econo.unlp.edu.ar/sedlac/eng/).

a. Data are for the age group from 25 years to 55 years. Data for Argentina are for urban areas only; urban areas covered by the survey represent 66 percent of total population. Surveys for Argentina from 1992 to 1997 covered fifteen cities; surveys from 1998 to 2006 covered twenty-eight cities. Education is measured in years of formal schooling.

an equalizing factor. However, the Gini for years of schooling had been falling for quite some time before labor earnings inequality started to decline. In fact, in Argentina and Mexico previous studies observed that the Gini for educational attainment declined while earnings inequality increased (!).[23] As discussed in Bourguignon, Ferreira, and Lustig (2005), that apparently paradoxical result is a consequence of the fact that the returns to education curve exhibits increasing returns: that is, additional years or levels of education command a proportionately higher return.[24] Did returns to schooling become less steep during the period in

23. During the 1980s and early 1990s, that happened in Argentina (Gasparini, Marchionni, and Sosa Escudero 2005) and Mexico (Legovini, Bouillón, and Lustig 2005).

24. Note that when the returns to education are convex (the returns increase proportionately more for higher levels of schooling), an equalization of the distribution of years of schooling does not necessarily translate into an equalization in the distribution of earnings. Bourguignon, Ferreira, and Lustig (2005) called that the "paradox of progress."

which inequality declined? The answer is yes: the returns to tertiary education as a ratio of the returns to incomplete (and in some cases complete) primary schooling or no schooling declined (figure 1-5)

That is big news because it signals a reversal of a trend. As can be observed in figure 1-5 also, in the previous decade returns to skill had been on the rise. Why did the reversal take place—did the relative supply of unskilled labor shrink or did the demand for skilled workers subside? The chapters do not analyze that question in the context of a full model of labor demand and labor supply. However, as shown in figure 1-8, in the period of declining (increasing) inequality, an increase in the relative supply of workers with tertiary education was accompanied by a decline (increase) in the relative returns to tertiary education (relative to primary levels), except for in Mexico, where the relative returns to schooling for tertiary levels continued to rise during the period of declining inequality, albeit at a slower pace than during the period of rising inequality.[25] Thus the data suggest that while during the 1990s the demand for skills dominated the effect, in the last ten years the growth in the supply of skills outpaced demand and the college premium consequently shrank. Or, to use Tinbergen's language, in the race between skill-biased technological change and educational upgrading, the latter took the lead.

Did the returns to schooling change because educational upgrading caught up with the increase in the demand for skilled labor or because the demand for skilled labor subsided as the effects of technological change petered off?[26] As Jaime Kahhat shows in chapter 2, in theory the presence of either factor can result in a decline in wage inequality. A review of existing models of exogenous and endogenous technological change reveals that more often than not, the effects of technological change are unequalizing at first but not in the long run. For example, after the learning phase is over and workers become fully efficient in using the new technology, firms substitute relatively expensive skilled labor with more economical unskilled labor.[27] These models assume perfect capital markets, allowing the supply of skills to adjust to increases in demand. Even if the demand for skilled labor did not decline, wage inequality would fall if the supply of skilled

25. Results for Argentina, Brazil, and Peru are from authors' calculations based on estimates on returns to education from SEDLAC, July 2009 (www.depeco.econo.unlp.edu.ar/sedlac/eng/). For Mexico, results are from authors' calculations based on estimates on returns to education from López-Acevedo (2006). Ratios for returns to education were calculated from educational dummy coefficients of Mincer equations (using wages from main occupation for men only). Variables of education level (college, secondary school, and primary school), potential experience, and geographic regions were included. An omitted variable was no schooling or incomplete primary school. Remunerations for men are for all workers including wage earners, self-employed workers, and employers. Population considered was the age group from 25 years to 55 years.

26. That does not need to be an "either/or" question. It is quite possible that both were present.

27. Other models assume different processes of adjustment but the results are similar: earnings inequality follows an inverted U.

Figure 1-8. *Changes in Supply of Workers with Tertiary Education and Returns to Tertiary Education (Relative to Primary Education) for Argentina, Brazil, Mexico, and Peru*[a]

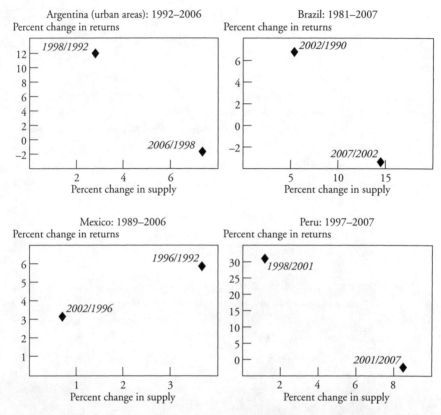

Source: Results for Argentina, Brazil, and Peru are from authors' calculations based on data from SEDLAC, July 2009 (www.depeco.econo.unlp.edu.ar/sedlac/eng/); results for Mexico are based on Lopez-Acevedo (2006).

a. Ratios for returns to education were calculated from educational dummy coefficients of Mincer equations using wages from main occupation for men only. Variables of education level (college, secondary school, and primary school), potential experience, and geographic regions were included. Omitted variable was no schooling or incomplete primary school. Remunerations for men are for all workers including wage earners, self-employed workers, and employers. Population considered was the age group from 25 years to 55 years. Ratios for education supply groups are formed by level of formal education. Educational levels correspond to completed primary, secondary, and tertiary education. Complete primary school is achieved at 6 years, complete upper-secondary school at 12 years, and complete tertiary education at 15 or more years of formal education. Incomplete primary includes 5 years or less of education and no schooling. Population considered was the age group from 25 years to 65 years. Percentage changes were divided by the number of years for each period. Years considered for calculations were those included in the figure. Data for Argentina are for urban areas only; urban areas covered by the survey represent 66 percent of total population. Surveys for Argentina from 1992 to 1997 covered fifteen cities; surveys from 1998 to 2006 covered twenty-eight cities.

workers caught up with demand. But what would happen if capital market imperfections impede or slow down the acquisition of skills?

Using a stylized model of capital market imperfections, Kahhat shows that when unskilled workers cannot borrow all that they want to invest in acquiring more skills, the share of skilled workers in the steady state is suboptimal: income per capita is lower than it would be if capital markets were perfect and no credit constraints existed. More important for our analysis, in the steady state with capital market imperfections, an economy that starts with an unequal distribution of wealth (and binding credit constraints) will have wealth inequality in the long-run equilibrium. In such a world, a redistributive policy that increases the share of skilled workers (for example, a substantial expansion in educational access that leads to an increase in the supply of skills) would increase the relative wage for unskilled labor. In turn, the higher wage for unskilled labor would provide greater opportunity for unskilled workers to invest in education. Consequently, both the wage premium and the inequality in educational attainment fall, reducing labor earnings inequality. Therefore, policies that enhance equality of opportunity in the present by extending subsidized educational services to underserved areas (rural areas and urban slums), improving the quality of education, and/or establishing conditional cash transfer programs (such as Brazil's Bolsa Familia or Mexico's Progresa/Oportunidades) allow larger fraction of the population to accumulate enough wealth to invest in upgrading its skills and improve its earnings in the future. That process can generate a virtuous circle leading to greater equity and growth in the long run.

We do not have precise estimates of the extent to which the observed reduction in the skill premium in Argentina, Brazil, Mexico, and Peru is the result of supply-side or demand-side factors.[28] Nonetheless, it is clear that during the last 20 years, educational upgrading received a push, particularly as democracy returned to countries in the region[29] and macroeconomic disequilibria disappeared or became more manageable. As a result there was a significant increase in coverage of basic education, and as low-skilled workers became relatively scarce (figure 1-6), they were able to command relatively higher wages. As Barros and others; Esquivel, Lustig, and Scott; and Jaramillo and Saavedra suggest in chapters 6, 7, and 8 of this volume respectively, higher spending per student in basic education and an effort to make education accessible in rural areas in Brazil, Mexico, and Peru eased supply-side constraints. In Argentina the picture is more mixed. Gasparini and Cruces argue that the reduction in the wage gap between low-skilled and skilled labor seems to be associated with several events: the post-2002 commodity boom, which increased total employment; the 2002 devaluation of the peso, which shifted demand in favor of intensive low-skilled labor sectors; government-mandated wage

28. In addition, there are no empirical studies that show whether the acquisition of skills is constrained by credit supply.

29. For a discussion, see James Robinson, chapter 3 in this volume.

increases (including the minimum wage); and stronger labor unions. In Brazil, higher minimum wages appeared to play a role as well. However, that was not the case in Mexico and Peru.

Before we turn to the analysis of changes in the distribution of nonlabor income, one interesting question remains to be answered. A decline in earnings inequality does not necessarily translate into a decline in the inequality of labor at the household level. In the cases of Argentina, Brazil, and Mexico, both moved in the same direction: that is, both earnings and per capita household labor income inequality declined. However, that was not the case in Peru. Although the changes in returns to schooling were equalizing at the level of the individual worker, they were unequalizing at the household level. That means that in Peru there probably was a change in assortative matching (more educated women increasingly marrying more educated men, for example) that increased labor income inequality in the household.

Determinants of the Decline in Nonlabor Income Inequality: The Political Economy of Redistribution

The reduction in the inequality of nonlabor income was the second major factor in the fall in inequality. Nonlabor income includes quite disparate income sources: returns to physical and financial capital (interest, profit, and rent); private transfers (for example, remittances); and public transfers (monetary and, in the case of Peru, some public transfers in kind). The contribution of changes in returns to physical and financial capital tended to be small and unequalizing. However, as mentioned above and shown by Alvaredo and Piketty in chapter 4 of this volume, incomes from property are grossly underestimated, so those results cannot be taken at face value.[30] It is hard to know what happened with properd-tied incomes, so the case studies do not delve into that issue. In terms of private transfers, remittances in Mexico, for example, were equalizing and became even more so in the 2000s because they closed the gap between rural and urban household per capita incomes.

As mentioned previously, the four case studies found a significant increase in the importance of the equalizing contribution of public transfers in the 2000s. In the four countries, government spending on transfers (monetary and in-kind) became more progressive in the 2000s. The contribution of programs such as Bolsa Família (Brazil) and Progresa/Oportunidades (Mexico) shows the remarkable power of well-targeted cash transfers to the poor in redistributing income and reducing inequality (and, of course, poverty). Those programs are a small share of total government redistributive spending (and GDP),[31] but they go a long way

30. See, for example, the comparison of Gini with and without top incomes presented by Alvaredo and Piketty for Argentina.
31. In the case of Oportunidades, for example, the budget is around 0.5 percent of GDP.

toward redistributing income to the bottom of the distribution. In the last ten years, the generosity and coverage of cash transfers increased; the design of the programs, particularly in Brazil and Mexico, improved; and targeting methods were fine tuned. Those efforts have clearly paid off in both Brazil and Mexico in terms of reducing income inequality and poverty. As shown by Esquivel, Lustig, and Scott in chapter 7, impact evaluation studies of Progresa/Oportunidades suggest that the program also had a positive impact in improving health outcomes and educational attainment. The trend toward more progressive public spending went beyond targeted cash transfers: as the analyses for Argentina, Mexico, and Peru suggest, the relative progressivity of spending on health, education, nutrition, and basic infrastructure (electricity and water and sanitation, for example) increased.[32]

Why has public spending in Latin America become more progressive in the last ten years? The analysis presented by James Robinson in chapter 3 on the political economy of redistribution may provide some clues. If political power is concentrated among a small group of elites, the political system will tend to generate unequalizing forces. Democratization should reduce the concentration of power. The last two decades in Latin America were characterized by a return to and strengthening of democracy. In advanced nations, democratization had a large effect on labor market institutions and redistributive policies and played a key role in reducing inequality over more than a century. While still imperfect in many Latin American countries, democracy also has been accompanied by a transition from clientelistic toward nonclientelistic politics.[33] In addition, transfers that targeted the poor may also have given traditionally disenfranchised groups more voice in the political process.

Furthermore, there is evidence that suggests that social democratic left-leaning governments (for example, in Brazil and Chile)—after controlling for factors such as terms of trade and income per capita—have been more redistributive than non-left or populist and radical-left governments.[34] While the relationship is not automatic, the emergence of more democratic institutions and a social democratic agenda may explain why government spending has become more progressive. At the same time, the surge of populist or more radical-left regimes in other countries (Argentina, Bolivia, Ecuador, Nicaragua, and Venezuela) may make elites in countries in which they exercise oligarchic control more willing to pay more taxes and support initiatives that make government spending more redistributive to the poor as "insurance" against the emergence of such regimes.

32. There are no data on the distribution of in-kind transfers for Brazil.
33. See, for example, Diaz-Cayeros, Estevez, and Magaloni (forthcoming).
34. See Lustig (2009) and Lustig and McLeod (2009). Lustig and McLeod (2009) documents the econometric results reported in Lustig (2009). See also Cornia (2009).

Will Inequality Continue to Decline?

The results presented above suggest that in a number of countries in Latin America, the government has been moving in the right redistributive direction—that is, allocating more of its public spending to the poor than it did before. In particular, governments have been making a greater effort to correct for inequality in the distribution of opportunities such as access to basic education. Moreover, governments have actively reduced poverty through direct transfers to the poor, thus making distributive outcomes, not just opportunities, more equal. Changes in the labor market—partly a result of governments' greater emphasis on expanding basic education—have contributed to a decline in earnings inequality and, except for Peru, in household per capita income inequality. Thus, for a few years (a decade or more in Brazil and Mexico and less in the case of Argentina and Peru), there was progress in making these countries more equitable.

However, the good news may not last. The redistributive momentum is likely to face obstacles. The upgrading of the educational attainment of the labor force will face a tough barrier in terms of postsecondary education. While educational attainment undoubtedly has become significantly more equal, the same cannot be said regarding the distribution of the quality of education. The poor and middle ranges of the distribution receive an education of significantly lower quality than the top 10 percent, members of which usually attend better-quality private schools. That reduces the probability that poor children—even those who complete secondary education—will be able to access tertiary education, because they cannot compete with the better-prepared children from richer households. In addition, compensating for the opportunity cost for poor children of attending postsecondary school is more expensive than compensating for the opportunity cost for children attending lower-level schools. If the state wants to continue equalizing opportunities through education as a way to equalize the distribution of income, it must give priority in the public policy agenda to addressing the inequality in quality of basic education and to finding ways to compensate for the opportunity costs of young people from poor backgrounds so that they can attend tertiary schools.

In addition, the incidence analyses presented in the country studies and elsewhere reveal that a large share of public spending is still neutral or regressive from the distributive point of view. It also reveals that taxes, in particular personal income taxes, are severely underused as an instrument of redistribution in a region characterized by having a substantial number of ultra-high net worth (that is, super-rich) individuals.[35]

---

35. See, for example, Breceda, Rigolini, and Saavedra (2008) and Goñi, López, and Servén (2008).

In other words, the extent of redistribution so far has been small, especially in comparison with redistribution through taxes and transfers in advanced countries. That may be due to state capture by Latin America's wealthy and powerful elites, who historically have been able to tilt government interventions in their favor more often than not. Proof of such capture is seen in the low level of taxes—personal income and wealth taxes in particular—prevalent in most Latin American countries and in regulations that create artificial monopolies and concomitant rents in key sectors of the economy.[36] Wealthy elites are hard to combat. Whether fear of the surge of Chavez-like figures in other countries or the power of the newly enfranchised might change the extent of state capture is unknown.

The entrenched power of elites might be a problem for the redistributive agenda even under democracy.[37] In chapter 4, Alvaredo and Piketty suggest that the large decline in inequality in advanced countries throughout most of the twentieth century was due to two factors: the Great Depression and war. Income inequality fell because capital owners—the very top tier of the wealthy in particular—were hurt by major shocks to their capital holdings (destruction, inflation, bankruptcy, the manner in which war debts were financed). Those were historical accidents as far as the fate of income inequality was concerned, not the result of deliberate policy. It is important to stress that the decline in the concentration of capital in advanced countries during the period between the world wars does not seem to have had negative effects on growth. On the contrary, it coincided with a period in which growth rates were substantially higher than in the previous century. It would seem that the shocks that occurred over 1914–45 allowed a new generation of "modern" entrepreneurs to replace old-style capitalist, rent-seeking dynasties. But what prevented the large fortunes from recovering after World War II? Alvaredo and Piketty attribute that to the introduction of high and progressive income and estate taxes, which prevented powerful elites from recapturing the state. The authors note that more equality, again, was consistent with prosperity, as the postwar period was characterized by especially high growth.

The lesson from advanced countries discussed in Alvaredo and Piketty appears to be that persistent and high levels of inequality will not necessarily be reversed without including substantial tax reform—in particular, progressive taxation—on the menu of redistributive policies. Progressive income taxation and estate taxation are two of the least distortionary ways to raise badly needed additional resources for the provision of public goods and to redistribute the gains from growth. This has an important implication for policymakers in Latin America: the agenda for tax reform needs to include more progressive tax systems and to ensure that they are enforced.[38]

36. See, for example, Levy and Walton (2009).

37. For a discussion of how, even after democratization, social welfare policies in Latin America evolved under exclusionary lines, see Haggard and Kaufman (2008).

38. For the case of Mexico, see the recommendations from Sobarzo (2010).

Organization of the Book

In addition to this chapter, this volume comprises two conceptual chapters; a chapter on the evolution of top incomes in advanced and developing countries; and four chapters on country case studies: Argentina, Brazil, Mexico and Peru.

In chapter 2, Jaime Kahhat presents an analysis of how the evolution of labor earnings inequality is heavily influenced by the pace of technological progress and the rate of growth of educational attainment. While new technologies tend to increase employers' demand for skills, improvements in educational attainment increase the supply of skills. Hence, earnings inequality tends to increase when the pace of technological progress exceeds the rate of growth of educational attainment and to decrease when the pace of technological progress falls below the rate of growth of educational attainment. The chapter reviews the literature exploring the role of technological progress on the demand for skills. Subsequently, using a stylized model, it examines how the interaction between capital market imperfections and wealth inequality may influence the allocation of investments in education in households and the supply of skills. Finally, it briefly discusses the effects of other factors, such as population growth and discrimination, on the supply of skills. The theoretical framework in this chapter fits the empirical findings on the evolution of earnings inequality in the four country case studies.

In chapter 3, James Robinson delves into how the proximate determinants of inequality—the distribution of assets and their rates of return—are heavily determined by a society's institutions and policies. From a comparative politics perspective, Robinson explains some salient cross-national patterns of inequality in middle-income countries, discussing in particular how they depend on differences in political institutions. The author argues that the advent and strengthening of democracy presents a potentially optimistic scenario in which middle-income countries finally move on to the virtuous circle of falling inequality and rapid growth that characterized advanced countries for most of the past century. This seems to have occurred with respect to education and targeted transfers in the country case studies included here. However, Robinson also sees the danger of an alternative scenario—one in which elites continue to control policy outcomes—in which that does not continue to happen. The author argues that to avoid the latter, international institutions have much to do in terms of strengthening grassroots democratic movements and promoting equality.

Chapter 4, by Alvaredo and Piketty, offers an overview of the main findings of a collective research project on the long-run dynamics of top incomes in developed and developing countries. The authors argue that the decline in income concentration that took place during the first half of the twentieth century in advanced countries was mostly accidental and does not seem to have much connection with a Kuznets-type process. Top capital incomes were hit by major shocks between 1914 and 1945 (World War I, the Great Depression, World

War II), and they were not able to recover fully in the postwar decades primarily because of progressive taxation. The pattern among rich countries diverged in the latter part of the twentieth century. In continental Europe and Japan, top income shares remained relatively stable while in the English-speaking countries there was a substantial increase in top shares beginning in the 1980s. As for developing countries, the authors found substantial heterogeneity among the countries for which top share estimates have been produced. No systematic patterns emerged. One important lesson for Latin America is that to make the reduction in equality sustainable, progressive income and wealth taxes were key.

In chapter 5, Leonardo Gasparini and Guillermo Cruces analyze the changes in Argentina's income distribution from the mid-1970s to the mid-2000s, a period of substantial increase in inequality. The authors argue that the upward trend was shaped by deep macroeconomic crises and periods of rapid opening up of the economy to external trade and investment flows. In the 1990s, economic openness led to a shift in resource allocation away from unskilled labor–intensive sectors and to skilled-biased technological change within most sectors. Those two factors—resource reallocation and skilled-biased technological change—pushed up the returns to skills, and they seem to be associated with a sizable increase in overall inequality. The depth and speed of economic reforms and the absence of public policies to ease the transition contributed to the severity of the income distribution changes. Later, a series of macroeconomic crises and subsequent recoveries contributed to the volatility of inequality along the upward trend. The latest macroeconomic crisis, in 2001–02, triggered a large jump in inequality, but income disparities returned to pre-crisis levels because the economy recovered quickly and large cash transfer programs were implemented. In addition, Gasparini and Cruces find that after a period of rising returns to skill, the trend was reversed. The petering off of the unequalizing effects of skill-biased technological change and economic openness combined with changes in labor demand and institutions to diminish the returns to skill.

Chapter 6, by Ricardo Barros, Mirela de Carvalho, Samuel Franco, and Rosane Mendonça, seeks to estimate the contribution of key aspects of Brazilian public policy and labor market performance to reducing income inequality. The chapter focuses on government transfers; earnings differentials by educational level; spatial and sector labor market integration; and minimum wage. The decomposition analysis suggests that the decline in inequality observed in Brazil since the end of last decade can be accounted for by a sharp fall in earnings inequality and nonlabor income inequality. The authors suggest that half of the decline in labor earnings inequality was caused by the acceleration of educational progress that occurred over the last decade in Brazil and that the other half resulted from labor market integration. The decline in nonlabor income inequality was driven by changes in its various components, in particular, public transfers. The authors find that increases in the coverage and generosity of the transfers as well as improvements in targeting cash transfers were key contributors to the decline in nonlabor income inequality.

In chapter 7, Gerardo Esquivel, Nora Lustig, and John Scott use decomposition techniques to identify the factors behind the decline in inequality in Mexico since the mid-1990s. The authors argue that the higher relative wages of low-skilled workers, a rise in the share of remittances, and expansion of government monetary transfers to the poor are the main factors. In turn, the fall in the skill premium appears to be associated with a reduction in the share of unskilled workers in Mexico's labor force. That change in the composition of the labor force coincided with—and probably was caused by—a significant expansion of government spending on basic education. In addition, the equalizing effect of transfers, driven mainly by the conditional cash transfer program Progresa/Oportunidades, rose over time. Benefits incidence analysis demonstrates that government redistributive spending on education, health, and nutrition also became more progressive over the last decade. In order for inequality to continue to fall in the future, Mexico needs to phase out regressive transfers and improve the quality of education, particularly for the poor.

Finally, chapter 8, by Miguel Jaramillo and Jaime Saavedra, attempts to identify the proximate determinants of the decline in inequality between 1996 and 2007 and discusses the market and policy forces behind them. Using a parametric decomposition method, the authors find that returns to experience, educational structure, and unobservable factors had an equalizing effect, while returns to urban residence and hours worked had an opposite effect. Returns to education had an equalizing effect at the individual level but were unequalizing at the household level. Market dynamics have kept returns to education on hold and, aided by demographic factors, have also caused a decline in returns to experience. They also suggest that the decline in inequality is associated with a fall in nonlabor income inequality, a reflection of the expansion of government transfers to the poor. Past and present policies have played a key role in the expansion of access to basic education and the consequent rise of overall educational attainment, and they have contributed to reducing the urban-rural gap in access to basic infrastructure. Jaramillo and Saavedra recommend that government actions in the future foster inclusive growth in three areas: improving the quality of education, promoting small businesses, and developing rural infrastructure.

References

Altimir, Oscar. 2008. "Distribución del ingreso e incidencia de la pobreza a lo largo del ajuste." *Revista de la CEPAL* 96 (December).

Atal, Juan Pablo, Hugo Ñopo, and Natalia Winder. 2009. "Gender and Ethnic Wage Gaps in Latin America and the Caribbean: An Extensive Review of the Literature and Contemporary Estimates for the Region." Unpublished paper. Washington: Inter-American Development Bank.

Barros, Ricardo, and others. 2009. *Measuring Inequality of Opportunities in Latin America and the Caribbean*. Washington: Palgrave Macmillan and World Bank.

Bourguignon, François, Francisco Ferreira, and Nora Lustig, eds. 2005. *The Microeconomics of Income Distribution Dynamics in East Asia and Latin America*. Washington: World Bank and Oxford University Press.

Breceda, K., J. Rigolini, and J. Saavedra. 2008. "Latin America and the Social Contract: Patterns of Social Spending and Taxation." Policy Research Working Paper 4604. Washington: World Bank (http://go.worldbank.org/BWBRP91A50).

Bruni, Lucilla, Alberto Fuentes, and Tomas Rosada. 2009. "Dynamics of Inequality in Guatemala." Paper prepared for the UNDP project "Markets, the State, and the Dynamics of Inequality: How to Advance Inclusive Growth," coordinated by Luis Felipe López-Calva and Nora Lustig (http://undp.economiccluster-lac.org/).

Cornia, Giovanni Andrea. 2009. "Income Distribution under Latin America's New Left Regimes." Mimeo.

Cragg, Michael, and Mario Epelbaum. 1996. "Why Has Wage Dispersion Grown in Mexico? Is It the Incidence of Reforms or the Growing Demand for Skills?" *Journal of Development Economics* 51, no. 1: 99–116.

De Ferranti, David, and others. 2004. *Inequality in Latin America and the Caribbean: Breaking with History?* Washington: World Bank.

Diaz-Cayeros, Alberto, Federico Estevez, and Beatriz Magaloni. Forthcoming. *Strategies of Vote Buying: Social Transfers, Democracy, and Welfare in Mexico*. Stanford University Press.

Eberhard, Juan, and Eduardo Engel. 2008. "Decreasing Wage Inequality in Chile." Paper prepared for the UNDP project "Markets, the State, and the Dynamics of Inequality: How to Advance Inclusive Growth," coordinated by Luis Felipe López-Calva and Nora Lustig (http://undp.economiccluster-lac.org/).

Esquivel, Gerardo, and José Antonio Rodríguez-López. 2003. "Technology, Trade, and Wage Inequality in Mexico before and after NAFTA." *Journal of Development Economics* 72, no. 2: 543–65.

Ferreira, Francisco H. G., Phillipe G. Leite, and Julie A. Litchfield. 2007. "The Rise and Fall of Brazilian Inequality: 1981–2004." *Macroeconomic Dynamics* (June): 1–32.

Ferreira, Francisco H. G., Phillippe G. Leite, and Matthew Wai-Poi. 2007. "Trade Liberalization, Employment Flows, and Wage Inequality in Brazil." Policy Research Working Paper 4108. Washington: World Bank (http://go.worldbank.org/BWBRP91A50).

Ferreira, Francisco H. G., and Martin Ravallion. 2008. "Global Poverty and Inequality: A Review of the Evidence." Policy Research Working Paper 4623. Washington: World Bank (http://go.worldbank.org/BWBRP91A50).

Fiszbein, Ariel, and others. 2009. *Conditional Cash Transfers: Reducing Present and Future Poverty*. Policy Research Report. Washington: World Bank.

Gasparini, Leonardo, Mariana Marchionni, and Walter Sosa Escudero. 2005. "Characterization of Inequality Changes through Microeconometric Decompositions: The Case of Greater Buenos Aires." In *The Microeconomics of Income Distribution Dynamics,* edited by François Bourguignon, Francisco H. G. Ferreira, and Nora Lustig. Washington: World Bank and Oxford University Press.

Goldin, Claudia, and Lawrence Katz. 2008. *The Race between Education and Technology.* Belknap Press of Harvard University Press.

Goñi, E., J. H. López, and L. Servén. 2008. "Fiscal Redistribution and Income Inequality in Latin America." Policy Research Working Paper 4487. Washington: World Bank (http://go.worldbank.org/BWBRP91A50).

Gray Molina, George, and Ernesto Yañez. 2009. "The Dynamics of Inequality in the Best and Worst Times: Bolivia 1997–2007." Paper prepared for the UNDP project "Markets, the State, and the Dynamics of Inequality: How to Advance Inclusive Growth," coordinated by Luis Felipe López-Calva and Nora Lustig (http://undp.economiccluster-lac.org/).

Haggard, Stephan, and Robert Kaufman. 2008. *Development, Democracy, and the Welfare States: Latin America, East Asia, and Eastern Europe.* Princeton University Press.

Kuznets, Simon. 1955. "Economic Growth and Income Inequality." *American Economic Review* 45, no. 1: 1–28.

Legovini, Arianna, César Bouillón, and Nora Lustig. 2005. "Can Education Explain Changes in Income Inequality in Mexico?" In *The Microeconomics of Income Distribution Dynamics,* edited by François Bourguignon, Francisco H. G. Ferreira, and Nora Lustig, pp. 1–38. Washington: World Bank and Oxford University Press.

Levy, Santiago, and Michael Walton, eds. 2009. *No Growth without Equity? Inequality, Interests, and Competition in Mexico.* Palgrave Macmillan and World Bank.

Londoño, Juan Luis, and Miguel Szekely. 2000. "Persistent Poverty and Excess Inequality: Latin America, 1970–1995" *Journal of Applied Economics* (May): 93–134.

López-Acevedo, Gladys. 2006. "Mexico: Two Decades of the Evolution of Education and Inequality." Policy Research Working Paper 3919. Washington: World Bank (http://go.worldbank.org/BWBRP91A50).

Lustig, Nora. 1995. *Coping with Austerity: Poverty and Inequality in Latin America.* Brookings Institution.

———. 1998. *Mexico: The Remaking of an Economy,* 2nd ed. Brookings.

———. 2009. "Poverty, Inequality, and the New Left in Latin America." Working Paper. Latin American Program. Washington: Woodrow Wilson Center for Scholars (www.wilsoncenter.org/events/docs/LUSTIG_INEQ%20POV%20&%20LEFT%20GOV%20LAT_JULY%2025_09_Revised.pdf).

Lustig, Nora, and Darryl McLeod. 2009. "Are Latin America's New Left Regimes Reducing Inequality Faster? Addendum to Nora Lustig, 'Poverty, Inequality, and the New Left in Latin America.'" Washington: Woodrow Wilson International Center for Scholars (July).

Maldonado, Stanislao, and Vanessa Ríos. 2006. "Más allá de la igualdad de oportunidades: Desigualdad de ingresos, responsabilidad individual, y movilidad social en el Perú." Informe Final. Lima: CIES (Consorcio de Investigación Económica y Social)/CEDEP (Centro de Estudios para el Desarrollo y la Participación).

Sobarzo, Horacio. 2010. "Reforma fiscal y relaciones fiscales intergubernamentales en México." In *México 2010: Volumen de Economía,* edited by Alejandro Castañeda, Nora Lustig, and Antonio Yúnez. Mexico City: El Colegio de México.

Tinbergen, Jan. 1975. *Income Distribution: Analyses and Policies.* Amsterdam: North-Holland.

2

Labor Earnings Inequality: The Demand for and Supply of Skills

JAIME KAHHAT

The distribution of income in Latin American countries has experienced substantial change over the last two decades. Income inequality rose in most countries in Latin America in the 1990s, but that trend was reversed in the 2000s. One of the main factors explaining the changes in the distribution of income is changes in labor earnings inequality. As the case studies in this volume show, labor earnings inequality followed a trend similar to that of income inequality in most countries in the region, rising in the 1990s and then falling in the 2000s. This chapter discusses the main economic factors accounting for changes in labor earnings inequality.

What are the main determinants of labor earnings inequality? Tinbergen (1975) argued that relative wages are the outcome of a "race" between technological progress, which increases the demand for skills, and educational attainment, which increases the supply of skills. That idea has guided much of the literature on labor earnings inequality. This chapter first reviews the theoretical literature exploring the role of technological change on the demand for skills. The main premise of this literature is that new technologies favor skilled labor because skilled workers are more able than unskilled workers to deal with the changes involved in the adoption and operation of those technologies. Moreover, new

I would like to thank Nora Lustig for her invaluable suggestions as well as Luis Felipe López-Calva and an anonymous referee for their helpful comments. I also am grateful to participants at the United Nations Development Programme meetings in New York and Mexico City for useful discussions.

technologies often replace tasks performed by unskilled workers with advanced machinery. As a result, the demand for skilled labor rises while the demand for unskilled labor contracts. That change in the pattern of demand for labor is responsible for exacerbating labor earnings inequality.[1]

The chapter then examines the effect of capital market imperfections on the allocation of investments in education and the supply of skills, using a stylized model.[2] When capital markets are less than perfect, investments in education, health, and nutrition usually are constrained by wealth and wealth inequality creates unequal opportunities in the accumulation of human capital. Hence, the supply of skills becomes a function of the distribution of wealth, and wealth inequality often leads to inefficient economic outcomes due to underinvestment in human capital. Moreover, unequal opportunities in the accumulation of human capital tend to reproduce the initial pattern of inequality over time. For example, children of wealthy parents usually are better nourished, receive more and better education, and are healthier than children born in poor families. As a result, children born in poor families usually earn less throughout their lives, reproducing the initial pattern of economic inequality. The chapter concludes with a discussion of the potential effects on the supply of skills of other factors, such as population growth and discrimination.

Technological Change and the Demand for Skills

Interest in the redistributive properties of new technologies was reignited in the 1990s by the trends in wage and employment structures of developed countries since the 1970s. Many member countries of the Organization for Economic Cooperation and Development (OECD) experienced an increase in wage inequality during the 1970s and 1980s.[3] At the same time, the share of college graduates in total employment increased in most countries while the college premium showed no tendency to decrease. Moreover, increased demand for highly educated workers was predominantly a within-industry phenomenon, while labor reallocation from low-skill to high-skill industries was relatively small. Several studies argue that those trends point to strong demand shifts favoring highly edu-

1. The demand for labor by skills can be affected by other factors, of course. For example, Kuznetzian shifts in the composition of output as the development process takes hold and Engel effects that link inequality with the pattern of demand for goods will affect the pattern of demand for different types of labor; see, for instance, Mani (2001). However, skill-biased technological change seems to play a preeminent role in explaining changes in the overall pattern of demand for different types of labor.

2. Ideally, one would like to model skill-biased technological change and capital market imperfections jointly. However, the predictive capacity of such a model is severely limited by its mathematical complexity.

3. Wage inequality rose sharply in the United Kingdom and the United States while countries like Australia, Austria, Belgium, Canada, Japan, New Zealand, and Sweden experienced a more moderate rise. By contrast, wage inequality remained relatively stable in Finland and France and declined in Germany and Italy (Aghion, Caroli, and García-Peñalosa 1999).

cated workers that reflect skill-biased technological change.[4] The main premise is that wage inequality was relatively stable before the 1970s because the rate of technological progress was relatively stable. The increase in wage inequality in the latter part of the twentieth century was a consequence of the acceleration of the rate of skill-biased technological change, which led to an increase in the demand for skills.[5] The explanation most frequently given for the acceleration of the rate of skill-biased technological change is the widespread use of computers in the workplace in an era of rapid advances in information technology.[6]

Skill-Biased Technological Change

Several theories have been proposed to explain the link between technological change and labor earnings inequality. For instance, Greenwood and Yorukoglu (1997) argues that technological change increases total factor productivity and therefore has little effect on the relative demand for skilled labor. However, the adoption of new technologies involves a substantial learning cost, and skilled labor has an advantage over unskilled labor at learning. Thus, the demand for skilled labor increases during the initial phases of adoption and implementation of new technologies. Once the learning phase is over and workers become fully efficient at using the new technology, firms substitute relatively expensive skilled labor with more economical unskilled labor. As a result, earnings inequality increases during the initial phases of adoption and implementation of new technologies and falls as new technologies become established.

By contrast, Galor and Tsiddon (1997) examines the effect of technological change on the allocation of high-ability workers between new and old technologies. The authors suggest that individual labor earnings depend on ability and sector-specific human capital inherited from parents. Consequently, individual decisions to acquire the skills necessary to operate new technologies depend on the relative strength of the ability and parental effects on labor earnings. New technologies require a more educated labor force than previous technologies but yield a higher return on ability. Hence, during periods of rapid technological progress in which new technologies are invented the ability effect becomes the dominant factor and intergenerational mobility increases. That leads to a concentration of individuals with high levels of ability and education in technologically advanced sectors, exacerbating earnings inequality between high-skill and low-skill workers. As

4. See, for example, Berman, Bound, and Griliches (1994), Autor, Katz, and Krueger (1998), Berman, Bound, and Machin (1998), Machin and Van Reenen (1998), Aghion, Caroli, and García-Peñalosa (1999), and Acemoglu (2002).

5. Not everybody agrees, however. Goldin and Katz (2008) suggests that the increase in the gap between skilled and unskilled wages in the United States in the latter part of the twentieth century was caused by a decline in the rate of growth of the supply of college graduates after the 1970s.

6. See, among others, Krueger (1993), Greenwood and Yorukoglu (1997), Autor, Katz, and Krueger (1998), and Caselli (1999).

the pace of technological progress slows down and innovations make existing technologies more accessible, the return on ability decreases. As a result, the parental effect becomes the dominant factor, intergenerational mobility is attenuated, and earnings inequality declines because the ability dispersion increases for high-skill and low-skill workers.

Caselli (1999) focuses instead on the effect of technological change on the allocation of capital between new and old technologies. Caselli argues that if capital markets are perfectly competitive, then, in equilibrium, the return on capital investments must be the same across all technologies. Since technological change increases total factor productivity, that can be achieved only by increasing the capital-labor ratio of high-skill workers. Thus, technological change increases earnings inequality because high-skill workers use a more productive technology and have a higher capital-labor ratio than low-skill workers. If the earnings differential between high-skill and low-skill workers increases sufficiently quickly as the economy approaches its steady state, then all individuals eventually acquire the skills to operate the new technology and earnings inequality vanishes in the long run. Otherwise, the labor market remains split into high-skill and low-skill workers and inequality persists in the long run.

One limitation of the previous theories is that the direction of technological progress—that is, the skill content of new technologies—is exogenously determined. Acemoglu (1998) and Krusell and others (2000) provide alternative theories in which the skill content of new technologies is endogenously determined. Acemoglu suggests that the direction of technological change depends on the relative profitability of developing different types of technologies. When the relative supply of skilled labor increases, the market for skill-biased technologies expands, making the development of such technologies more profitable. By contrast, new technologies are skill-replacing when the relative supply of unskilled labor increases.

According to this theory, technological change in the United States has been skill-biased since the 1970s because the supply of skilled labor increased sharply in the late 1960s due to the large supply of college graduates from the baby-boom generation. The acceleration of the rate of growth of demand for skilled labor in the 1970s is then explained by a change in the direction of technological progress. On the other hand, Krusell and others (2000) argues that the increase in the stock of physical equipment resulting from the decline in the relative price of that equipment in the post–World War II period led to an increase in the demand for skilled labor. Their premise is that physical equipment is more complementary to skilled than to unskilled labor. The acceleration in the rate of growth of demand for skilled labor during the 1970s is then explained by the accelerated decline in the relative price of physical equipment since the early 1970s, which led to an acceleration in the accumulation of physical equipment. Both theories provide compelling explanations of the trends discussed at the beginning of this section.

However, it is difficult to distinguish between the predictions of these two theories and the predictions of the theories in Greenwood and Yorukoglu (1997), Galor and Tsiddon (1997), and Caselli (1999) based on the evidence of the last decades.

Trade-Induced Skill-Biased Technological Change

An interesting empirical regularity in many developing countries is that changes in labor markets similar to those experienced in developed countries seem to coincide with episodes of trade liberalization. For example, the evidence for Latin American countries during the 1980s and 1990s suggests a pattern of changes in labor markets that resembles the changes experienced in developed countries during the 1970s and 1980s. Wage inequality increased in most Latin American countries during the 1980s and 1990s. There also is strong evidence of an increase in the share of skilled workers in total employment and in wage costs in several countries in the region. Most of the skill upgrading took place within industries; there is little evidence of labor reallocation between industries. Moreover, the college premium increased in all countries for which data are available.[7]

In most Latin American countries those changes in labor market conditions took place during periods of trade liberalization. The coincidence in the timing of trade reforms and changes in wage and employment structures often is interpreted as evidence in favor of trade-induced skill-biased technological change. For example, Goldberg and Pavcnik (2007) argues that "the most credible explanations for the distributional changes witnessed [in developing countries] in the past few decades would most likely involve interactions of trade openness with skilled-biased technological change."[8]

One of the earliest studies to link trade liberalization and skill-biased technological change is Wood (1994), which argued that increased competition from abroad could lead to defensive skill-biased innovations. This idea is formalized by Thoenig and Verdier (2003), which suggests that trade openness increases the threat of imitation of a firm's production process by outside competitors. Imitation, in turn, reduces the competitive advantage of a firm. Since simple unskilled labor–intensive technologies are easy to imitate, firms undertake defensive skill-biased innovations to lessen the increased threat of imitation after trade liberalization. According to this theory, skill-biased technological change should be more pronounced in industries that liberalized more. Acemoglu (2003) provides an alternative link between trade liberalization and skill-biased technological change. The author argues that the extent of skill bias in technologies used in less developed countries after trade reforms depends on the relative supply of skilled

7. See, for example, Cragg and Epelbaum (1996), Robbins (1996), Attanasio and Székely (2000), Berman and Machin (2000), Sanchez-Paramo and Schady (2003), and Goldberg and Pavcnik (2007).

8. Goldberg and Pavcnik (2007, p. 63). In chapter 5 of this volume, Gasparini and Cruces suggest a similar argument to explain the rise in labor earnings inequality in Argentina during the 1990s.

labor in those countries. Although trade opening may reduce the cost of skill-biased technologies in developing countries, it will lead to an increase in imports of those technologies only in countries in which a relatively large supply of skilled labor makes the use of skill-biased technologies profitable.[9]

Capital Market Imperfections and the Supply of Skills

When capital markets are perfect, economic agents can always borrow what they need to finance their investments. Hence, intergenerational transfers do not create unequal opportunities in access to education and the distribution of wealth does not affect the supply of skills or the relative wages in the economy. Markets, however, are not perfect, and intergenerational transfers do play a significant role in the transmission of inequality and in the investment decisions of economic agents.[10] When capital markets are less than perfect and investment decisions are credit constrained, the distribution of wealth will influence the allocation of investments in education and, as a result, the supply of skills. Consequently, relative wages and labor earnings inequality become a function of the inequality in the distribution of wealth.[11]

A simple model may be useful to illustrate the effect of capital market imperfections on the supply of skills. Consider a small open economy in a one-good world. The good can be produced by two technologies: one, the unskilled labor technology, can be operated by workers with any level of education; the other, the skilled labor technology, requires workers with more than $\underline{h}$ efficiency units of labor. Production in the unskilled sector is described by $Y_t^u = A^u f(L_t^u)$ while production in the skilled sector is described by $Y_t^s = A^s f(L_t^s)$, where Y_t^j is output at time t in sector $j = u, s$; L_t^j is efficiency units of the labor input in sector j; $A^s > A^u > 0$; and the production function $f(\cdot)$ is strictly concave and satisfies the usual endpoint conditions. The labor market is competitive and the equilibrium wages per efficiency unit of labor for skilled and unskilled workers equal their respective marginal products—that is, $w_t^j = A^j f'(L_t^j)$.

In each generation there is a continuum of individuals of size 1 who live for one period and have a single offspring. Individuals start their lives with initial wealth ω_i, inherited from their parents, which they allocate between investments

9. Although both theories make persuasive arguments in favor of the hypothesis that skill-biased technological change has been an endogenous outcome of trade liberalization policies in Latin American countries, there is no conclusive empirical evidence to support these theories. See, for example, the discussion in Goldberg and Pavcnik (2007).

10. World Bank (2006, chapter 5) reviews the empirical evidence on the extent of market imperfections in developing countries and its effect on investment decisions.

11. There is an extensive literature studying the effects of the interaction between capital market imperfections and wealth inequality on economic outcomes and the evolution of earnings inequality. See, for example, Loury (1981), Banerjee and Newman (1993), Galor and Zeira (1993), Ljungqvist (1993), Aghion and Bolton (1997), Piketty (1997), and Mookherjee and Ray (2006). The model developed in this section synthesizes some of the main insights derived from this literature.

in education and savings in order to maximize their end-of-period wealth. At the end of their lives they consume a fraction, $1 - \beta$, of their end-of-period wealth and bequeath the rest to their children. The efficiency units of labor and the labor earnings of an individual in sector j who invests e in education are given by $h = g(e)$ and $w_t^j g(e)$, respectively, where $g(\cdot)$ is a strictly concave function satisfying the usual endpoint conditions. Hence, education increases the earnings potential of both unskilled and skilled workers.

Capital is assumed to be perfectly mobile across countries so that individuals have free access to the international capital markets. The world interest rate is equal to $r > 0$ and is assumed to be constant over time. Individuals can save any amount at that interest rate. However, following Aghion, Banerjee, and Piketty (1999), I assume that capital markets are imperfect and individuals can borrow only up to γ times their initial wealth at the world interest rate r.[12] Hence, only those individuals with inherited wealth $\omega_i > \underline{\omega}$, where $\underline{\omega}$ satisfies $g((\gamma + 1)\underline{\omega}) = \underline{h}$, have access to the skilled labor sector of the economy. Given an equilibrium wage at time t in sector j, the optimal investment in education in sector j, e_t^j, is then given by the equality of the marginal return to education and the world interest rate—that is, $w_t^j g'(e_t^j) = r$. Therefore, those individuals in sector j for whom $\omega_i \geq \omega_i / e_t^j (\gamma + 1)$ will invest e_t^j in education while the rest will invest all that they can—that is, $(\gamma + 1)\omega_i$. Their end-of-period wealth will equal $\omega_t^j = w_t^j g(e_t^j) + r(\omega_i - e_t^j)$ if $\omega_i \geq e_t^j / (\gamma + 1)$; it will equal $\omega_t^j = w_t^j g((\gamma + 1)\omega_i) - r\gamma\omega_i$ otherwise.[13] Therefore, an individual will choose to work in the skilled sector only if $\omega_t^s \geq \omega_t^u$.

A steady state for this economy is fully characterized by the ratio of skilled workers in the population. Let λ be the ratio of skilled workers and let $e^u(\lambda)$ and $e^s(\lambda)$ be the steady state investments in education for unskilled and skilled workers.[14] The steady state wages per efficiency unit of labor for unskilled and skilled workers are then given by $w^u(\lambda) = A^u f'((1 - \lambda)g(e^u(\lambda)))$ and $w^s(\lambda) = A^s f'(\lambda g(e^s(\lambda)))$, and the end-of-period wealth of an individual in sector j is given by $\omega^j(\lambda) = w^j(\lambda)g(e^j(\lambda)) + r(\omega_i - e^j(\lambda))$. This economy has, at least, one steady state, $\bar{\lambda}$, defined by $w^s(\bar{\lambda})g(e^s(\bar{\lambda})) - w^u(\bar{\lambda})g(e^u(\bar{\lambda})) = r(e^s(\bar{\lambda}) - e^u(\bar{\lambda}))$. That is the steady state with the largest ratio of skilled workers. Note that when $\lambda = \bar{\lambda}$ the returns to education exactly compensate for the opportunity cost of education. Thus, there is labor earnings inequality but not wealth inequality—that is, $\omega^s(\bar{\lambda}) = \omega^u(\bar{\lambda})$—and individuals are indifferent between working in the skilled and unskilled sectors of the economy. Moreover, note that when $\lambda = \bar{\lambda}$, credit constraints are not binding and the allocation of investments in education is efficient.

---

12. This specification of capital market imperfections provides a simple framework to study the effect of financial development on labor earnings inequality.

13. A fraction β of that end-of-period wealth will be left to their children, giving us the inherited wealth of the next generation.

14. Hence, $e^u(\lambda)$ satisfies $A^u f'((1 - \lambda)g(e^u(\lambda)))g'(e^u(\lambda)) = r$ while $e^s(\lambda)$ satisfies $A^s f'(\lambda g(e^s(\lambda)))g'(e^s(\lambda)) = r$ and $g(e^s(\lambda)) = \underline{h}$.

Are there other steady states in this economy? Multiple steady states arise if the following condition, which can be called the "poverty trap condition," holds: $g((\gamma + 1)\beta\omega''(0)) \leq \underline{h}$. The poverty trap condition states that if everyone works in the unskilled sector—that is, $\lambda = 0$—then the labor earnings of unskilled workers will be sufficiently low that their children will not inherit enough wealth to become skilled workers.[15] If the poverty trap condition holds, then there exists $\widetilde{\lambda} \leq \overline{\lambda}$ such that any $\lambda \in [0,\widetilde{\lambda}]$ is a steady state. These steady states can be ranked in terms of overall inequality and aggregate output. Steady states with higher ratios of skilled workers are associated with lower degrees of inequality and higher levels of income per capita. Intuitively, as λ increases, the wage premium decreases because the wage for skilled labor decreases while the wage for unskilled labor increases. Consequently, the level of education of unskilled workers increases while the level of education of skilled workers decreases. Hence, steady states with higher ratios of skilled workers exhibit lower levels of labor earnings inequality because both the returns to education and the inequality in educational attainment decrease. Moreover, whenever $\lambda \leq \overline{\lambda}$ we have $w^s(\lambda)g(e^s(\lambda)) - w^u(\lambda)g(e^u)\lambda)) > r(e^s(\lambda) - e^u(\lambda))$—that is, the returns to education overcompensate for the opportunity cost of education.[16] Therefore, with the exception of the steady state in which $\lambda = \overline{\lambda}$, all steady states exhibit wealth inequality in addition to labor earnings inequality. Accordingly, when $\lambda < \overline{\lambda}$, individuals strictly prefer working in the skilled sector to working in the unskilled sector. However, credit constraints are binding for unskilled workers; as a result, the allocation of investments is inefficient. These inefficiencies are lessened as the ratio of unskilled workers increases, leading to a higher output per capita. Finally, note that the existence of a continuum of steady states implies an extreme form of history dependence. In middle-income countries like those in Latin America, economies with more egalitarian distributions of wealth are more likely to converge to steady states with lower levels of inequality and higher levels of income per capita. Moreover, even small redistributions of wealth or small improvements in access to education may increase λ and move the economy to a different steady state, reducing inequality and increasing income per capita permanently.[17]

15. Note that the poverty trap condition is a restriction on the parameters of the model but not on the initial conditions of the economy, namely, the initial average wealth and the way wealth is distributed. Whether the economy converges to the steady state $\lambda = 0$ or not depends on the initial conditions.

16. This result partly explains why the returns to education appear to be convex in Latin American countries; see, for instance, Bouillón, Legovini, and Lustig (2005) and Binelli (2008). Imperfections in capital markets emphasize the role of wealth inequality on investment decisions. In turn, the high levels of wealth inequality in Latin American countries lead to wage premiums that substantially overcompensate for educational expenditures, resulting in convex returns to education.

17. This extreme form of history dependence is not robust to idiosyncratic shocks to the income of individuals; see Mookherjee and Napel (2007). When heterogeneity is introduced to generate steady state mobility, the continuum of steady states may be replaced by locally isolated steady states with large basins of attraction. Therefore, long-run economic performance becomes less history dependent and the effect of

While there is no empirical evidence on the effect of capital market imperfections on the supply of skills in Latin America, these theoretical results may explain why public policies aimed at improving access to education in countries like Brazil, Mexico, and Peru might have been successful at reducing labor earnings inequality in those countries.[18] A substantial expansion in educational access (through both supply- and demand-side interventions) would lead to a substantial increase in the supply of skills, reducing the wage for skilled labor while increasing the wage for unskilled labor. In turn, the higher wage for unskilled labor would provide greater incentives for unskilled workers to invest in education. Consequently, both the wage premium and the inequality in educational attainment would fall, reducing labor earnings inequality. Thus, improvements in the quality of education, educational subsidies, or conditional cash transfer programs (such as Bolsa Família in Brazil or Progresa/Oportunidades in Mexico), by enhancing equality of opportunities in the present, may allow a larger fraction of the population to accumulate enough wealth to undertake productive investments in the future. That process may generate a virtuous circle, leading to greater equity and growth in the long run.[19] Note that improvements in the health and nutrition of the unskilled would have an effect on the supply of skills and on inequality similar to that of improvements in access to education. In other words, both would increase the earnings capacity of unskilled workers and would likely lead to an increase in the supply of skills, reducing earnings inequality.

What is the effect of financial development on labor earnings inequality? In the previous model, the development of financial institutions that reduce the severity of capital market imperfections is captured by increases in γ. As γ increases and access to credit improves, family wealth becomes less important in the decision to acquire skills because individuals can finance a larger fraction of their investments in education through borrowing. Hence, only those steady states with a sufficiently low ratio of skilled workers—that is, a sufficiently low λ, implying sufficiently low labor earnings for unskilled workers—could be self-sustaining. That implies that, as financial institutions develop, economies with sufficiently low levels of wealth inequality are less likely to be trapped in an inefficient steady state and more likely to converge to the efficient steady state $\lambda = \bar{\lambda}$. Indeed, as γ becomes sufficiently large and credit constraints cease to be binding,

temporary policy interventions on long-run macroeconomic outcomes is lessened. See Banerjee and Newman (1993) for a more general discussion of the dynamic behavior of this class of models.

18. See, for example, Barros and others (chapter 6), Esquivel, Lustig, and Scott (chapter 7), and Jaramillo and Saavedra (chapter 8) in this volume.

19. Interestingly, Goldin and Katz (2008) suggests that the increase in the gap between skilled and unskilled wages in the United States in the latter part of the twentieth century was caused by a decline in the rate of growth of the supply of college graduates after the 1970s. That decline, in turn, is associated with problems in the quality of secondary education (a rising share of high school graduates are not "college ready") and imperfections in the market for student loans.

the poverty trap condition, $g((\gamma + 1)\beta\omega''(0)) \leq \underline{b}$, ceases to hold and all inefficient steady states vanish. Therefore, labor earnings inequality should eventually fall as financial institutions develop and capital market imperfections become less severe. Note, however, that the most inefficient and most unequal steady states are the last to vanish as financial institutions develop. Thus, in countries with high levels of wealth and earnings inequality, financial development alone may take too long to effectively reduce inequality and policy interventions aimed at improving access to education may be essential.

Before concluding this discussion, it is worth exploring the impact of macro-economic shocks on the supply of skills. When capital markets are less than perfect, economic booms and crises influence the allocation of investments in education by tightening or loosening credit constraints. During an economic crisis, some individuals who would have pursued a college education otherwise find that they can no longer afford the cost of doing so simply because they were hit especially hard by the crisis. Consequently, the relative supply of unskilled labor would tend to increase, leading to an increase in earnings inequality. Similarly, during economic booms individuals who would not have been able to pursue a college education otherwise may find it possible to do so. As a result, the relative supply of skilled labor increases, reducing earnings inequality.

Other Determinants of the Supply of Skills

There are factors in addition to capital market imperfections that could influence the supply of skills. The most obvious one has to do with changes in population growth. Two types of changes in population growth may affect the supply of skills: changes in cohort sizes and changes in relative rates of growth of different segments of the population. If, on average, younger generations are more educated than older generations, then changes in cohort size will affect the composition of the labor force, influencing earnings inequality. For example, a substantial increase in the size of a new cohort will increase the relative supply of skills, reducing earnings inequality. Alternatively, changes in relative rates of growth of different segments of the population may influence the relative supply of skilled labor. If the rate of growth of the poorest members of society falls (either because of a fall in fertility rates or outmigration), then the relative supply of unskilled labor falls. Consequently, the wages of unskilled workers should rise, increasing their incentives to acquire education and reducing earnings inequality.

Another factor that can influence the relative supply of skills is discrimination and social norms. For example, unequal access to education or credit due to discrimination or social norms may reduce the relative supply of skilled labor. In the case of unequal access to credit, members of groups that suffer discrimination will be less likely to become skilled workers because they have to finance a larger share of educational expenses with their own wealth. Consequently, the supply of skilled labor decreases while the supply of unskilled labor increases, leading to higher labor earnings inequality because both the returns to education and the inequality in educational attainment between skilled and unskilled workers increase. Unequal access to education will have the same result.

The supply of skills can also be affected if discrimination takes the form of unequal access to high-skilled jobs. Suppose that one group of the population is less likely to have access to jobs in the skilled sector. To be more precise, suppose that those suffering discrimination have a probability $\alpha < 1$ of finding a job in the skilled sector while the rest of the population can find a job with certainty, assuming that they have acquired the necessary skills. What is the effect of unequal access to the skilled sector on the investments in education of those being discriminated against? Since in this example discrimination is assumed to apply only to the skilled sector of the economy, investments in education for unskilled workers would not change regardless of whether the workers belong to the group being discriminated against. Thus, discrimination will affect only investments in education in the skilled sector.

Let e_d^s be the optimal investment in education in sector s for a member of the group being discriminated against, and let e^s be the corresponding investment for an individual not being discriminated against—that is, e^s satisfies $w^s g'(e^s) = r$. A member of the group being discriminated against who plans to acquire the skills to work in the skilled sector knows that with probability α, he or she will find a job as a skilled worker and with probability $1 - \alpha$, he or she will end up as an unskilled worker. Thus, the optimal investment in education satisfies $\alpha w^s g'(e_d^s) + (1 - \alpha)w^u g'(e_d^s) = r$. Since $w^s > w^u$ in equilibrium, we have $e^s > e_d^s$—that is, those suffering from discrimination will invest less in education. Consequently, unequal access to skilled professions will increase labor earnings inequality within the group of skilled workers. What is the effect on labor earnings inequality between skilled and unskilled workers? Since a smaller fraction of the population has access to the skilled sector, unequal access to skilled professions leads to a lower ratio of skilled workers in the population and, as a result, to higher labor earnings inequality between skilled and unskilled workers. Hence, overall earnings inequality increases because both within- and between-groups earnings inequality increase.

Finally, the supply of skills also can be affected if discrimination takes the form of unequal pay for the same job. Suppose that all workers have equal access to all occupations in the economy but that one group receives lower pay in both the skilled and the unskilled sectors of the economy. Let w^j be the equilibrium wage in sector j, and let $w_d^j < w^j$ be the wage offered to those who are being discriminated against. In this case, both unskilled and skilled members of the group suffering discrimination will invest less in education than the rest of the population.[20] Hence, there will be labor earnings inequality within the groups of skilled and unskilled workers because workers suffering discrimination receive a lower wage rate and have a lower level of education than the rest of the population. What will be the effect on labor earnings inequality between skilled and unskilled workers? The answer in this case is not clear because average labor earnings decrease for both skilled and unskilled workers. However, overall earnings inequality increases because within-group earnings inequality increases.

Concluding Remarks

This chapter surveys the theoretical literature on the effect of technological progress on the demand of skills, including possible interactions between trade openness and skill-biased technological change. It also examines the possible effects of the interaction between capital market imperfections and wealth inequality on the allocation of investments in education and the supply of skills. As the country studies included in this volume suggest, skill-biased technological change and educational upgrading appear to have played a significant role in the evolution of earnings inequality in Latin American countries during recent decades. According to these studies, skill-biased technological change may account for a substantial part of the increase in earnings inequality in the region in the 1990s. Although the evidence is not conclusive, in some Latin American countries skill-biased technological change during that period appears to be an endogenous outcome of trade liberalization policies. Technological progress, however, seems to account for only half of the story. The other half, the fall in earnings inequality experienced by some Latin American countries in the 2000s, appears to be driven mostly by improvements in educational attainment. In most cases, those improvements were the result of public policies aimed at improving access to education. A possible explanation for these findings is that governments' push for expanding access to education loosened the credit constraints faced by some low-income families, allowing them to invest more in education. The resulting increase in the supply of skills lowered the skill premium. Consequently, earnings inequality fell because both the wage premium and the inequality in educational attainment decreased.

References

Acemoglu, Daron. 1998. "Why Do New Technologies Complement Skills? Directed Technical Change and Wage Inequality." *Quarterly Journal of Economics* 113, no. 4: 1055–89.

20. The optimal investment in education in sector j for those suffering discrimination e_d^j is given by $w_d^j g'(e^j) = r$ while the optimal investment for the rest of the population e^j is given by $w^j g'(e^j) = r$. Since $w_d^j < w^j$, we have $e_d^j < e^j$.

————. 2002. "Technical Change, Inequality, and the Labor Market." *Journal of Economic Literature* 40, no. 1: 7–72.

————. 2003. "Patterns of Skill Premia." *Review of Economic Studies* 70, no. 2: 199–230.

Aghion, Philippe, Abhijit V. Banerjee, and Thomas Piketty. 1999. "Dualism and Macro-Economic Stability." *Quarterly Journal of Economics* 109, no. 2: 1359–97.

Aghion, Philippe, and Patrick Bolton. 1997. "A Trickle-Down Theory of Growth and Development with Debt Overhang." *Review of Economic Studies* 64, no. 2: 151–72.

Aghion, Philippe, Eve Caroli, and Cecilia García-Peñalosa. 1999. "Inequality and Economic Growth: The Perspective of the New Growth Theories." *Journal of Economic Literature* 37, no. 4: 1615–60.

Attanasio, Orazio, and Miguel Székely. 2000. "Household Saving in East Asia and Latin America: Inequality Demographics and All That." In *Annual World Bank Conference on Development Economics*, edited by B. Pleskovic and N. Stern. Washington: World Bank.

Autor, David H., Lawrence F. Katz, and Alan B. Krueger. 1998. "Computing Inequality: Have Computers Changed the Labor Market?" *Quarterly Journal of Economics* 113, no. 4: 1169–213.

Banerjee, Abhijit V., and Andrew F. Newman. 1993. "Occupational Choice and the Process of Development." *Journal of Political Economy* 101, no. 2: 274–98.

Berman, Ely, John Bound, and Zvi Griliches. 1994. "Changes in the Demand for Skilled Labor within U.S. Manufacturing Industries: Evidence from the Annual Survey of Manufacturers." *Quarterly Journal of Economics* 109, no. 2: 365–67.

Berman, Ely, John Bound, and Stephen Machin. 1998. "Implications of Skill-Biased Technological Change: International Evidence." *Quarterly Journal of Economics* 113, no. 4: 1245–280.

Berman, Ely, and Stephen Machin. 2000. "Skill-Biased Technology Transfer: Evidence of Factor-Biased Technological Change in Developing Countries." Unpublished paper. Department of Economics, Boston University.

Binelli, Chiara. 2008. "Returns to Education and Increasing Wage Inequality in Latin America." Working Paper. Rimini, Italy: Rimini Centre for Economic Analysis.

Bouillón, C., A. Legovini, and N. Lustig. 2005. "Can Education Explain Changes in Income Inequality in Mexico?" In *The Microeconomics of Income Distribution Dynamics in East Asia and Latin America*, edited by F. Bourguignon, F. Ferreira, and N. Lustig. Washington: World Bank.

Caselli, Francesco. 1999. "Technological Revolutions." *American Economic Review* 89, no. 1: 78–102.

Cragg, Michael Ian, and Mario Epelbaum. 1996. "Why Has Wage Dispersion Grown in Mexico? Is It the Incidence of Reforms or the Growing Demand for Skills?" *Journal of Development Economics* 51, no.1: 96–116.

Galor, Oded, and Daniel Tsiddon. 1997. "Technological Progress, Mobility, and Economic Growth." *American Economic Review* 87, no. 3: 363–82.

Galor, Oded, and Joseph Zeira. 1993. "Income Distribution and Macroeconomics." *Review of Economic Studies* 60, no. 1: 35–52.

Goldberg, Pinelopi K., and Nina Pavcnik. 2007. "Distributional Effects of Globalization in Developing Countries." *Journal of Economic Literature* 45, no. 1: 39–82.

Goldin, Claudia, and Lawrence F. Katz. 2008. *The Race between Education and Technology.* Belknap Press of Harvard University Press.

Greenwood, Jeremy, and Mehmet Yorukoglu. 1997. "1974." Carnegie-Rochester Conference Series on Public Policy 46, pp. 49–95.

Krueger, Alan B. 1993. "How Computers Have Changed the Wage Structure: Evidence from Microdata, 1984–1989." *Quarterly Journal of Economics* 108, no. 1: 33–60.

Krusell, Per, Lee E. Ohanian, Jose-Victor Rios-Rull, and Giovanni L. Violante. 2000. "Capital-Skill Complementarity and Inequality: A Macroeconomic Analysis." *Econometrica* 68, no. 5: 1029–53.

Ljungqvist, Lars. 1993. "Economic Underdevelopment: The Case of a Missing Market for Human Capital." *Journal of Development Economics* 40, no. 2: 219–39.

Loury, Glenn. 1981. "Intergenerational Transfers and the Distribution of Earnings." *Econometrica* 49, no. 4: 843–67.

Machin, Stephen, and John Van Reenen. 1998. "Technology and Changes in Skill Structure: Evidence from Seven OECD Countries." *Quarterly Journal of Economics* 113, no. 4: 1215–44.

Mani, Anandi. 2001. "Income Distribution and the Demand Constraint." *Journal of Economic Growth* 6, no. 2: 107–33.

Mookherjee, Dilip, and Stefan Napel. 2007. "Intergenerational Mobility and Macroeconomic History Dependence." *Journal of Economic Theory* 137, no. 1: 49–78.

Mookherjee, Dilip, and Debraj Ray. 2006. "Occupational Diversity and Endogenous Inequality." Unpublished paper. Department of Economics, Boston University.

Piketty, Thomas. 1997. "The Dynamics of the Wealth Distribution and the Interest Rate with Credit Rationing." *Review of Economic Studies* 64, no. 2: 173–89.

Robbins, Donald J. 1996. "Evidence on Trade and Wages in the Developing World." Technical Paper 119. Organization for Economic Cooperation and Development.

Sanchez-Paramo, Carolina, and Norbert Schady. 2003. "Off and Running? Technology, Trade, and the Rising Demand for Skilled Workers in Latin America." Policy Research Working Paper 3015. Washington: World Bank (http://go.worldbank.org/BWBRP91A50).

Tinbergen, Jan. 1975. *Income Distribution: Analysis and Policies.* Amsterdam: North Holland.

Thoenig, Mathias, and Thierry Verdier. 2003. "A Theory of Defensive Skill-Biased Innovation and Globalization." *American Economic Review* 93, no. 3: 709–28.

Wood, Adrian. 1994. *North-South Trade, Employment, and Inequality: Changing Fortunes in a Skill-Driven World.* Oxford: Clarendon Press.

World Bank. 2006. *World Development Report 2006: Equity and Development.* Oxford University Press.

3

The Political Economy of Redistributive Policies

JAMES A. ROBINSON

Many factors influence the distribution of assets and income that a market economy generates, including the distribution of innate abilities, the nature of technology, and the types of market imperfections that determine investment opportunities and the distribution of human and physical capital.

But any market system is embedded in a larger political system that, independently of the influence of the market, may either create or reduce inequalities of assets or incomes. The impact of the political system on distribution depends on the laws, institutions, and policies of that system. What institutions or policies a political system generates depends on the distribution of power in society and how political institutions and mobilized interests aggregate preferences. The political system tends to generate inegalitarian forces if political power is concentrated in narrow elites or oligarchies, but it may produce more egalitarian outcomes if political power is distributed widely or if many rather than a few interests are mobilized.

In fact, it is not possible to talk about "the market distribution of income" as if that were somehow free of politics. It is the political system, after all, that determines the nature of property rights and how free the market is. The outcomes that

This chapter was written as a background paper for the UNDP project "Markets, the State, and the Dynamics of Inequality: How to Advance Inclusive Growth," coordinated by Luis Felipe López-Calva and Nora Lustig. I am grateful to Nora Lustig for her detailed comments on a previous draft and for the suggestions of an anonymous referee.

the market itself generates are heavily determined by policies and regulations passed by the state. Consider, for example, the impact of fiscal redistribution on inequality. As Lustig (2007) points out, the post-fisc distribution of income in Scandinavia is much lower than the pre-fisc distribution. But the pre-fisc distribution is already much lower than it might be because of the policy interventions of the state, such as its support for centralized wage bargaining, which move the income distribution in a direction that is much more egalitarian than it would be if wages were set in a more decentralized wage process (Wallerstein 1999; Golden and Londregan 2006). To consider another extreme, in apartheid South Africa prior to 1994, government regulations on the occupation and residential choices of Africans acted to change the wage structure and redistribute income from blacks to whites. They did so by reducing competition for white labor, thus increasing white wages, and forcing blacks into unskilled occupation, thus pushing down their wages and simultaneously raising the profits of those, such as white farmers and mine owners, who hired unskilled labor. Thus government regulations, such as the Homelands policy or the Colour Bar, led to a much more inegalitarian distribution of income than would have resulted had wages been set in a "free" labor market (Lundahl 1982). The cross-national facts are clearly inconsistent with a view of inequality as stemming only from "market forces." The role of institutions, particularly labor market institutions, and the policies of the state are critical (Freeman 2007).

It is impossible to say a priori how political forces will move the distribution of income relative to the distribution generated solely by "market" outcomes and what sort of market outcomes will be generated in the first place. But if one wants to think about the cross-country stylized facts about the distribution of assets and incomes, the right place to start is comparative politics. For instance, the fact that rich countries tend to be much more egalitarian than middle-income countries stems from their different political economies in addition to purely economic factors such as the technologies that they use or the extent to which they are globalized.

In thinking about inequality, it is interesting to begin with the observation that the general world trend over the last 100 years has been toward a much more equal distribution of political rights and power, which can be attributed to the spread of democracy. Though the forces unleashed by democracy are complex, a simple expectation is that the move from nondemocratic political systems, such as those that ruled all of the world prior to the late nineteenth century, to more democratic systems ought to have the effect of broadening the base of political power. In most cases power was monopolized by the richer segments of society before the onset of democracy,[1] and one would naturally conjecture that the move toward democracy would have led to pressure for polities and regulations that

---

1. Nondemocracy would tend to be dominated by the rich either because the rich wield sufficient power to create such a regime or because those who wield power for other reasons subsequently use their power to become rich.

would be relatively favorable to the newly enfranchised and would thus involve some redistribution of income toward the relatively poor. In short, one would expect democracy to reduce inequality relative to the levels experienced under nondemocratic regimes.

To a large extent that expectation is fulfilled in the developed world. Though inequality has risen quite steeply in the United States and Britain in the last 20 years, available evidence suggests that in the developed world, including these countries, it is quite substantially lower than it was 100 years ago. There is, of course, controversy over why that is. For example, work by Piketty and colleagues (see Piketty and Saez 2006 for an overview of their findings) has emphasized the importance of big shocks, such as World War I and II, in driving down inequality in Western Europe and the United States. Yet Piketty and Saez (2006) finds that the persistence of those shocks can be explained by institutional changes wrought by democracy. Similarly, though Stasavage and Sheve (2009) argues that long-run trends of inequality are not consistent with the large effect that centralized wage bargaining appears to have in cross-sectional regressions, the authors' data also are consistent with the onset of democracy as being the main force behind falling inequality in the OECD countries.

It is very plausible that the decline in inequality in OECD countries played an important role in generating the acceleration of economic growth that they experienced after World War II. Eichengreen (2006) characterizes that period as one of "coordinated capitalism"—coordination that almost certainly was facilitated by the much more egalitarian distribution of assets and income.

Many poor and middle-income countries have yet to go through that process, and that probably is the main reason why their levels of inequality are so much higher. Democracy is a much more recent phenomenon in those countries, and indeed it has yet to come to many, at least in a fully consolidated form (to use the terminology of Acemoglu and Robinson 2001b and 2006). So it is possible that those countries are on the brink of the path followed by the OECD countries, albeit with a 150-year lag. However, there also is evidence that that is not the case. We already know that democracy may be qualitatively different in, for example, Latin America, Africa, and Southeast Asia, and therefore it may not have the same effects. In South Africa, though growth has resumed since the political transition to democracy in 1994, inequality has actually risen quite sharply. In Argentina, as Gasparini and Cruces show in chapter 5 of this volume, inequality rose dramatically under military governments in the 1970s but even more dramatically under democratic governments in the 1990s. Moreover, the recent empirical work on the relationship between economic growth and democracy (Acemoglu and others, 2008) suggests that there probably is nothing inevitable about the path that democracy took in Western European and North American countries over the past century and that there is no reason why it would be replicated mechanically elsewhere.

If democratization does not lead to falling inequality and increased growth and if there is no other natural tendency for inequality to fall,[2] then the great inequality of assets and income in many middle-income countries may present a significant barrier to growth and achievement of the Millennium Development Goals. That suggests that to reduce poverty and inequality in poor and middle-income countries and to achieve those goals is going to require important changes in public policies to ensure that more assets and income are redistributed to the poor. Understanding what policies are effective and politically feasible requires an understanding of the political economy of redistribution in those countries. It also necessitates delving into the issues of why such policy changes have not already occurred, given that many of the countries have such high levels of inequality.

In this chapter I therefore survey our current understanding of the political economy of income redistribution, for the most part in democracies. I focus on a key set of questions: who benefits from redistribution? What determines the extent of income redistribution in a society? When will redistribution promote equality? Why has the Western European pattern of income redistribution and falling inequality apparently not been so pronounced elsewhere in the world? What could be done to promote redistribution in highly unequal countries?

It is convenient to distinguish between the supply of policies by politicians and the demand for policies by citizens. I break each of those categories into the target of redistribution, extent of redistribution, and form of redistribution. After summarizing what is known about the forces that drive those aspects of the supply and demand for redistribution, I talk about comparative statics and how socioeconomic structure or political institutions would tend to influence the answers given to the questions raised above. Because a lot of ideas and mechanisms are at play here, I then make a stab at putting together a stylized characterization of the political economy of redistribution in an unequal middle-income country, focusing on what forces stop redistribution from eradicating inequality. I then discuss policy interventions. I begin with the supply side of redistribution.

The Supply of Income Redistribution

Though simple median voter models of income redistribution in the spirit of Meltzer and Richard (1981) are powerful tools and generate some important comparative static results, we almost certainly need a richer model of the forces

2. That would certainly seem to be the case in Latin America. For example, Reynolds (1971) showed that though inequality may have fallen as a consequence of the Mexican Revolution, it then stayed persistently high decade after decade despite quite strong economic growth (see Scott 2008, on the impact of revolutionary land reforms on land distribution). Even more striking, Kelley and Klein (1981) found that the reduction in inequality triggered by the reforms of the Bolivian Revolution in 1952 was unwound within 15 years.

that determine the equilibrium amount of income redistribution in a society on both the demand and supply sides.

I start by considering the supply of policies by politicians and examine the circumstances under which that supply leads to the redistribution of income to the poor and therefore to more egalitarian outcomes. An important issue is that politicians may not have the correct incentives to implement redistributive policies or, if they do, they may not be interested in offering redistribution to the poor. That issue has two aspects, an ex ante and an ex post aspect. In ex ante terms, equilibrium policies chosen by politicians favor individuals or groups with desirable political characteristics. Even if the poor are enfranchised, if they do not have the right political characteristics then, ex ante, politicians will not have the right incentives to design policies that benefit them, even in a democracy. In ex post terms, politicians may not find it optimal to implement the policies that they promised to introduce. That problem can be solved only if mechanisms of accountability are established. If the poor do not have access to such mechanisms, then policy promises to them will not be honored.

Most of the academic literature tends to focus on general "redistribution." Redistribution may involve pure transfers with no implications for efficiency, or it may take the form of public goods, either general ones such a defense or perhaps a clean environment, or "local" public goods.

Ex Ante

What political characteristics drive ex ante policy?

REDISTRIBUTION TO WHOM? One of the key issues is who benefits from redistribution. In simple models like that in Meltzer and Richard (1981), this issue does not arise because everyone benefits in the same way from redistribution. Moreover, if politicians propose any policies other than those preferred by the median voter, they have no chance of winning, so the only issue is how much redistribution the median voter demands. Supply is irrelevant. Nevertheless, richer models, such as those that feature probabilistic voting or uninformed voters, give politicians both greater leeway in making choices and far richer policy instruments. Those models suggest that in a democracy it will not necessarily be the poor who benefit from income redistribution. Indeed, the famous "Directors Law" of income redistribution claims that it is the middle class that benefits (Persson and Tabellini 2000, chapter 3). The formal political economy literature finds that redistribution in democracies targets groups that

—are relatively numerous.

—are able to solve the collective action problem when others are not (Bates 1981; Persson and Tabellini 2000, section 3.5; Grossman and Helpman 2001).

—manage to form political parties while others do not (Wittman 1983; Acemoglu and Robinson 2006).

—are un-ideological, "swing" or "floating" voters (Lindbeck and Weibull 1987; Dixit and Londregan 1996).

—are relatively well-informed (Strömberg 2004; Besley and Burgess 2002).

—turn out to vote in high numbers.

—are relatively poor (Dixit and Londregan 1996).

—are in the same social network as politicians (Dixit and Londregan 1996; Robinson and Verdier 2002; Stokes 2005; Kasara 2007).

To the extent that a group does not have those characteristics, they can be expected to lose out in determining policy.

Two characteristics in the list above are almost certainly highly relevant—the ability of groups to solve the collective action problem and to form political parties. The political situation in Bolivia after 2005 is a telling instance. The political system generated few benefits for indigenous people even after democracy arrived in 1982 until the indigenous people, with the help of the trade union of coca growers, managed to solve the collective action problem and form a political party—Movimiento al Socialismo (MAS).

The social basis of the political parties may be very important in determining who receives benefits. Jaramillo and Saavedra (2009) notes the large extent of urban bias in the provision of public services in Peru, which is perhaps unsurprising given that even the Alianza Popular Revolucionaria Americana (APRA), the most pro-poor party, has a strong base in urban unions. In contrast, MAS formed in the rural areas of Bolivia and Partido dos Trabalhadores (PT) has strong links with rural movements in Brazil, such as that for landless workers. Such factors are important in determining where political parties look for support.

The mechanisms discussed above regarding who gains from public policies and income redistribution are derived from formal political economy models of voting and political influence. In contrast to that approach, the political science literature has focused on simple dichotomies to answer the "to whom" question. Scholars make a distinction between "clientelistic" and "programmatic" approaches, which are conceived of as two polar political strategies that parties or groups contesting power might adopt. On one hand, political parties can compete for support by offering different types of public goods that affect the entire population. Their policies might concern ideological issues, such as human rights, or they may deal with more economic issues, such as law and order (for example, property rights), trade and macroeconomic policy, or regulatory regimes. On the other hand, instead of focusing on such collective or public goods, parties can concentrate on offering particularistic benefits or private goods to groups of supporters.

One of the problems facing the adoption of policies to eliminate poverty in middle-income countries is precisely the fact that clientelism is highly prevalent in those countries. The pertinent question then becomes under what circumstances the poor might be expected to be the clients of politicians? Clientelistic politics is worse than programmatic politics, but if one is in a clientelistic regime, it is better to be a client than to be completely excluded from patronage. Unfortunately, there are few generalizations in the political science literature on who clients are, and it is difficult to draw any conclusions about the circumstances under which clients are poor. The general idea is that there is some extrapolitical relationship, possibly economic, possibly social, that matches patrons with clients.

How Much Redistribution? Theoretically, how much redistribution politicians offer depends on its costs and benefits. Benefits are conceived of as the extra support that redistribution generates. If swing voters are very sensitive to redistribution, they may get a lot of transfers; if they are not, they may get little. How much also depends on how costly it is to raise taxes and redistribute resources—a cost that may depend on the extent of tax evasion and the structure of the economy, which help determine the elasticity of the tax base.

The question of how much has been addressed empirically in a large literature, reevaluated and extended in Persson and Tabellini (2003). The authors show by using cross-sectional data that the size of government (government spending as a percent of GDP) is greater when old people are a greater proportion of the population (a variable also emphasized in Perotti 1996), the more democratic a country is, and the more open the economy is (a result initially emphasized in Rodrik 1998). They find that federal nations have lower spending, all other things being equal. Many other candidate covariates—such as ethno-linguistic fragmentation, per capita income, and income inequality—are not robustly significant, although they appear to be statistically significant in some specifications. The authors also consider a panel data set, thus exploiting time-series variation, and find that in addition to the above results, per capita income has a positive and significant coefficient (Wagner's Law).

It is worth noting, however, that what is equally important from the point of view of impact on inequality are things like the progressivity of spending, not just total spending. However, there are few investigations of the cross-country determinants of the progressivity of spending.

What Form of Redistribution? A key issue, in addition to how much redistribution and who gets it, is what form redistribution takes. One of the major problems in designing redistributive policies to reduce inequality is that even in circumstances in which the poor have the right political characteristics to make them attractive recipients of redistribution, political incentives may dictate that they get redistribution in something other than the optimal form.

Research on the form of redistribution has tried to elucidate political mechanisms that might lead inefficient forms of redistribution to be politically attractive. Recent literature suggests that inefficiencies in the form of redistribution may be based on politicians' desire

—to conceal that they are really redistributing (Coate and Morris 1995).

—to reduce the total amount of redistribution that they have to undertake (Rodrik 1986; Wilson 1990; Becker and Mulligan 2003).

—to create incentives for voters to support them (Bates 1981; Persson and Tabellini 1999; Lizzeri and Persico 2001; Robinson and Verdier 2002; Robinson and Torvik 2005).

—to take credit for policy and influence the beliefs of voters about politicians' preferences.

Inefficiencies also may arise when interest groups

—seek to maintain their political power (Acemoglu and Robinson 2001a).

—seek to influence the type of game (and therefore the terms of trade) between them and politicians (Dixit, Grossman, and Helpman 1997).

—use redistribution to help them solve the collective action problem.

A key finding in the literature is that even when the poor get redistribution, the form of redistribution is biased against public goods provision because of political incentives. The main reason for that was brilliantly illustrated by Robert Bates in his seminal study of the political economy of agricultural policy in Africa (Bates 1981): clientelistic redistribution must target specific people or groups. That idea has been elegantly formalized by Persson and Tabellini (1999) and Lizzeri and Persico (2001). Clientelistic redistribution leads to underprovision of public goods because such goods, by definition, benefit all people.

Robinson and Verdier (2002) extends those ideas, emphasizing not only that public goods cannot target specific groups but also that they provide nonexcludable benefits—a politically unattractive proposition when politicians want to reward their clients only and exclude others. Moreover, if politicians want to punish citizens who did not support them, then they will tend to underprovide such goods.

All of these ideas about the form of redistribution are of course deeply related to the issue of clientelism. Probably the main problem with clientelism as a form of politics is that patrons have an incentive to redistribute to clients in socially undesirable forms. That creates a lot of problems even when the government to a large extent is pro-poor, as can be seen in the recent Venezuelan experience.

In addition to clientelism, another style of redistributive politics, populism, has received a lot of attention in the political science literature. Though Dornbusch and Edwards (1991) defined populism simply as bad economic policies, in fact populism is a political strategy (see Conniff 1999). Its essence is that it involves redistribution using very inefficient, typically unsustainable instruments, usually macroeconomic and wage policy. It is, however, distinct from clientelism. Colombia, for example, never had populism in the twentieth century, but it certainly had clientelism, though as Robinson (2007) points out, one can think of populism as clientelism with macro policy instruments.

Ex Post

The problem of moral hazard is endemic in politics. Regardless of what politicians may promise before an election, they may have incentives to renege on their promises after they are elected. Given the nature of politics, it is not possible to enforce promises using third parties, such as judges, since it is the government itself that is supposed to enforce contracts and that controls the judiciary. Politicians may deviate from promises because they themselves prefer other policies, or simply because they want to steal for themselves money that they promised to spend on providing public goods for citizens. The main issue here is whether citizens have mechanisms of accountability to make sure that politicians carry through with their promises and do not engage in venal activities.

Though the ex post literature is much less developed than the ex ante literature, it has some implications that are interesting for the current discussion. Barro (1973), Ferejohn (1986), and Persson, Roland, and Tabellini (1997) examined the conditions under which voters could use punishment strategies to discipline politicians who renege on commitments or engage in corruption. To be effective in disciplining politicians, citizens have to coordinate their voting strategies; so, again, the ability of groups to solve the collective action problem is crucial for ensuring accountability. Groups that cannot do that will not be able to sanction politicians effectively.

Many of the mechanisms mentioned in the ex ante discussion apply also in this context. If people are poorly informed they may not understand that the policies that they had been promised have not been implemented properly—or at all— and again there will be a failure of accountability. However, un-ideological "swing voters" will be effective at punishing miscreant incumbents because such voters are relatively willing to switch and support an alternative political party. The flip side of that, pointed out in Padró-i-Miquel (2007), is that when citizens have strong ideological (in his model, ethnic) allegiances to politicians, that may considerably loosen the bonds of accountability on politicians. Citizens from the same ethnic group as the politician in power may fear that if they try to replace that person, another ethnic group may take over, which may result in a very bad outcome for them.

Recent empirical work from Brazil in Ferraz and Finan (2008) illustrates how important the media are in facilitating accountability, and McMillan and Zoido (2004) presents the same lesson. They found that it was cheaper for Vladimiro Montesinos to bribe a majority of the Supreme Court than to bribe one television station, suggesting that the latter was a greater constraint on the policies of President Alberto Fujimori.

The Demand for Redistribution

The questions that can be raised regarding supply and demand for redistribution are very similar. However, I drop the question of redistribution for whom to focus on only the two most important questions—how much redistribution, in what form?

How Much?

How much redistribution voters want is the basis of simple models of income redistribution such as in Meltzer and Richard (1981). There the median voter rationally trades off the costs and benefits of redistribution, with the costs coming from the deadweight losses caused by levying taxes on income and changing labor supply decisions.

One can think of many factors that influence those costs and benefits. I focus on a few on which there has been recent research and that are possibly of first-order importance for the issues at hand.

One key determinant of preferences for redistribution may be social mobility. An old idea about income redistribution in the United States is that it is relatively low because of high social mobility. If rates of taxation are inertial, those who are poor today may reduce their demand for redistribution because they anticipate that they may be rich tomorrow. That argument was formalized in Wright (1996) and Benabou and Ok (2001). However, the calibration undertaken in the latter study shows quite convincingly that observed differences in rates of social mobility across countries are nowhere near large enough to account for the differences in the equilibrium amount of redistribution. Recent evidence presented in Alesina and La Ferrara (2005) about people's beliefs about social mobility is more consistent with the idea that their beliefs have a first-order effect on preferences for redistribution in the United States. Moreover, using data from the Latinbarometer, Carter (2007) and Carter and Morrow (2007) show that expectations about upward social mobility do influence strongly people's preferences for redistribution. The authors argue that it is in precisely those Latin American countries with very polarized views about upward social mobility that left-wing parties have come to power.

A related seminal study, Piketty (1995), argued that a society's beliefs about the returns on personal effort could be self-fulfilling. Specifically, the author argued that Europeans may believe that effort is not rewarded and thus that taxing income is not distortionary, while citizens of the United States may believe the opposite. That study has been greatly extended in Benabou and Tirole (2006) and Benabou (2008), which also introduce behavioral components; these studies suggest that redistribution is greater in Sweden than in, say, Colombia, because the two societies are in different equilibria, both of which generate self-fulfilling expectations. Colombians do not demand high taxes because they think that effort pays in society and thus that such taxation would be very costly, while Swedes have very different beliefs. The introduction of behavioral elements is one approach to reconciling the divergence between the findings in Benabou and Ok (2001), based on observed rates of social mobility, and those in Alesina and La Ferrara (2005) or Carter (2007), based on beliefs about social mobility.

Another important explanation of the demand for redistribution relates demand to the extent of heterogeneity of a community. Alesina, Baqir, and Easterly (1999) showed that within the United States, redistribution in cities decreased with higher ethno-linguistic fragmentation, and Alesina and Glaeser (2004) argued that that can explain why relatively homogeneous European countries redistribute more than the United States.

Another important argument is that one of the problems with simple models of income redistribution is that the set of policy dimensions used is not rich enough. When we allow for more policy dimensions, there may be cross-cutting cleavages that reduce the demand for redistribution. A famous statement of this argument is in Frank (2005), where the author claims that poor people in the United States vote against their economic interests because they have been fooled into voting on the basis of ideological or symbolic issues such as gay marriage (see Ansolabehere, Rodden, and Snyder 2006; Bartels 2008; and Gelman and others 2008 for discussion of whether the data support that idea in the United States). Roemer (1998) provided a formalization of this argument showing that if people had preferences over the religious affiliation of parties, it could break a coalition in favor of redistribution.

In What Form?

Above we discussed the rationality of different forms of redistribution from the point of view of politicians. One of the issues with political strategies like clientelism and populism is that their appeal may have something to do with citizens themselves. It may well be that people demand clientelistic favors and do not have individual incentives to demand public goods. Indeed, though this issue has been little studied, there may be a collective action problem among voters in demanding public goods. In particular, no individual client would have an incentive to demand public instead of private goods from a politician unless the citizen placed enormous value on the public good.

Determinants of Equilibrium Political Strategies

I now focus on the comparative statics of the mechanisms already discussed to some extent above. It is impossible to exhaust this topic here, so I focus on some of the effects that seem to be more important and most relevant to policymaking, such as the impact of political institutions. I am interested in issues such as what determines the extent of clientelism in a society and the factors that lead politics to be clientelistic rather than programmatic. What factors might influence the intensity of clientelism? What is known about the conditions under which some political characteristics dominate others? What determines the form of income redistribution or government policies? What makes populist political strategies likely, and what can be done to make them less attractive?

Evidence on any of those questions is highly tentative. There are quite a few ideas in both the formal and qualitative literatures, but as yet few conclusive results. For example, though the theoretical models that follow Lindbeck and

Weibull (1987) emphasize the idea that swing voters are important, there is not much evidence that swing voters are important in determining actual redistributive outcomes. Ansolabehere and Snyder (2002), using a panel of U.S. states, finds no evidence that swing voters are important; the authors find instead that government spending is concentrated in the districts that tend to support the incumbent party. Their empirical work is interesting because it tends to support a view of the world related to the "citizen-candidate" model of Besley and Coate (1997) and Osborne and Slivinski (1996). In that model, politicians have preferences regarding the policies that they adopt and are unable to commit to any other type of policy. Anticipating that, voters vote for politicians whose preferences are relatively like their own. That echoes the theme of the importance of political party objectives and suggests that the poor will benefit from policies only when they organize their own political parties (such as the PT in Brazil and MAS in Bolivia) and poor people themselves manage to run for office.

Democracy versus Dictatorship

The first and most obvious factor in policymaking is the nature of political institutions. I begin by considering the extent of democracy. To get at that, we need to reflect a little more on what we would expect to happen in a nondemocracy. The factors discussed above are derived from formal models nearly all of which place voting and elections at the heart of policy determination. What about nondemocracies? There have been few attempts to construct a theory of dictatorship at the same level as the theory of democracy, so it is quite hard to draw as many implications. Most (see Acemoglu and Robinson 2006, chapter 5) start from the idea that in a dictatorship some group chooses policy to maximize its own welfare subject to the constraint that it stays in power. To stay in power a dictatorship needs support, and that support must be bought with policies, transfers, favors, and so forth. The support base may be very narrow, however, and certainly narrower than the base of support needed to sustain a democratic regime. For example, many scholars argue that the regime of Jerry Rawlings in Ghana, West Africa, was able to stay in power almost without a social base and therefore without the need to engage in patrimonialism (see, for example, Herbst 1993).

Though dictatorships clearly use repression to stay in power much more than democracies do, the analytics of support may be related to the analytics of democratic support. If that is right, then there are some important lessons in the above results. Nevertheless, despite the fact that some of the qualitative forces driving redistribution in dictatorships are quite similar to forces that one might expect to apply in a democracy, it seems reasonable to expect that a shift from dictatorship to democracy would lead to a change in policies more favorable to the relatively poor. As suggested in the introduction, that conjecture is in fact consistent with quite a bit of evidence, particularly from Western Europe (see Aidt, Dutta, and Loukoianova 2006). Acemoglu and Robinson (2000) pointed out that the peak of the Kuznets curve for many European countries coincided with moves toward mass enfranchisement, and the authors argued that the forces unleashed by democratization were responsible for subsequent declines in inequality.

That there are forces in democracy that may promote a more egalitarian distribution of assets is evident not only in the experience of Western Europe. In the experience of Latin America, however, those forces have been much less clear because they often have been so powerful as to lead ultimately to the overthrow of a democratically elected government (Acemoglu and Robinson 2001b, 2006). The introduction of uncorrupt universal suffrage in many countries—such as Venezuela and Guatemala in 1945, Bolivia in 1952, and Chile after the secret ballot reforms of 1958 (Baland and Robinson 2008)—led to radical demands for the redistribution of land, which often quickly led those threatened by it to sponsor coups (Lapp 2004). Moreover, the observed rapid increases in inequality in dictatorships, such as those in Chile after 1973 and Argentina after 1976, fit very well with the ideas developed above. Acemoglu and Robinson (2006) point out that the dynamics of income distribution in Argentina over the entire twentieth century are closely related to movements backward and forward between authoritarian and democratic regimes. There also is cross-national evidence, notably Rodrik (1999), that suggests that democracy leads to more egalitarian outcomes, at least in terms of the share of wages in national income.

Chapter 6 in this volume, by Barros, Carvalho, Franco, and Mendonça, speaks directly to these issues. The authors show that the rapid fall in inequality in Brazil over the past decade is a consequence of massive expansion of education and income redistribution targeting the poor. The origins of those policy changes in Brazil are certainly related to the democratization that began in 1985. Significantly, redistribution targeting the poor really came only after the PT won the presidential election in 2002. Eberhard and Engel (2008) shows that the reestablishment of democracy in Chile in 1990 led to a change in the dynamics of wage inequality: by 2006 most of the large increase in wage inequality that took place during the dictatorship had been unwound. The authors attribute that to massive educational expansion, much of which occurred prior to 1990. In fact, their data suggest that even prior to the coup in 1973 a structural expansion of education was taking place, which the repression and terror of the military regime did not alter. Bruni, Fuentes, and Rosada (2008), a study of inequality in Guatemala, also is revealing. The authors find little change in inequality over the last decade, despite the fact that peace and democracy arrived after 1996, except for a brief period between 1945 and 1954. That there has been little impact on social policy or inequality is probably not surprising. Unlike the poor in Brazil or Bolivia, the poor in Guatemala are not politically organized, and just how consolidated democracy is in Guatemala could be questioned. For instance, former dictator Efraín Ríos Montt, who was responsible for massive human rights abuses estimated by some to have resulted in as many as 200,000 deaths, ran for president in 2003. In the nineteenth century, Guatemala probably had the most repressive labor market institutions in Latin America, and it remains a society with a great deal of ingrained discrimination. Solving that problem will require a political revolution along the lines of the one that has taken place in Bolivia. The main issue is whether it can be achieved in a way that really reduces inequality or whether one type of inegalitarian society will be abolished only to create a new one (as, for instance, happened in Bolivia after 1952; see Kelley and Klein 1981). The situation in Peru, discussed in Jaramillo and Saavedra (chapter 8 of this volume), may be similar. Though Peru returned to democracy in 1980, democracy in Peru has been very unstable, and during the 1990s the Fujimori regime was able to essentially suspend the constitution and all checks and balances on its power (McMillan and Zoido 2004), suggesting that consolidated democracy may be still quite far off.

Nonetheless, there are some quite severe empirical puzzles regarding the impact of democracy. For instance, despite the evidence discussed here, Gil, Mulligan, and Sala-i-Martin (2004) provocatively claimed that democracies and dictatorships have the same policies, at least in some dimensions (see also Cheibub 1998). For example, the authors find that the ratio of government expenditures to GDP or spending on pensions relative to national income does not vary between dictatorships and democracies. However, there are quite a few problems with their research. First, they exploit only the cross-sectional variation in the data, and they treat whether or not a country is democratic as exogenous. Thus, they cannot make any real claim that they have identified the causal effect of democracy on those policy variables. Second, dictatorships certainly also redistribute income and raises taxes, but the burden of such policies tends to fall on those without political power. Most important, one would expect democracies to raise different taxes and spend the revenues gained differently.

That implies that one might not expect government expenditures as a percent of GDP to vary much between dictatorships and democracy, but one might expect things such as whether or not taxation is progressive or regressive to differ (Lee 2003).[3] Finally, the empirical work may focus too much on income redistribution and after-tax income. In reality, interventions in the labor market and other regulations that influence wage structure and market returns to different assets may be more important in determining the consequences of democracy and dictatorship for inequality.

The types of puzzles discussed here also arise in other chapters of this volume. For instance, Jaramillo and Saavedra (chapter 8) demonstrate that in Peru there was a quite large decline in inequality from early 1971 to 1996, with the Gini coefficient falling from 0.55 to 0.38. One cause was the redistributive policies, such as radical land reform, introduced by the left-wing military government of

---

3. A pioneering study by Aidt and Jensen (2007) examines the forces that led to the introduction of income taxes in OECD countries. Somewhat counterintuitively, they find that democracy reduces the probability that a country will introduce the income tax.

General Juan Velasco, which took power in 1968. Dictatorships are not invariably anti-poor and pro-elite. Gasparini and Cruces (chapter 5) also generate some puzzles since, as I noted, while inequality rose significantly under the military in the late 1970s, it rose even more under democracy in the 1990s.

Leaving these caveats aside, it is certainly surprising that there is no conditional correlation in the data between a measure of democracy, such as the polity score for a country, and at least some readily available measures of social spending. Even if there are left-wing dictatorships, there are not many of them. One extreme interpretation of such a finding would be that political institutions are irrelevant for public policy, as argued in Mulligan and Tsui (2006). Such a view would be hard to accept even if one believed that a political version of the Coase theorem held, so that public policy, whether in a dictatorship or a democracy, is always Pareto efficient. That is because even if the equilibrium of a society was Pareto efficient, different distributions of political power would have implications for where on the Pareto frontier a society would be and hence for observable policies and inequality (Acemoglu 2003).

The claim that in general there are no public policy implications of transitions between dictatorship and democracy is not consistent with either the historical evidence discussed above or with a great deal of empirical work. For example, Besley and Kudamatsu (2006) showed that life expectancy is systematically higher in democracies, and Kudamatsu (2006) showed, in the contexts of democratic transitions in Africa, that health outcomes had improved in countries that democratized compared with those that did not, at least if there was a change of leader. Returning to Latin America, the adoption and spread of programs such as Progresa in Mexico is clearly related to the democratization that took place under the PRI, which shifted political power away from corporatist groups like labor unions toward rural voters (Scott 2008). One can see the same forces in action in Brazil with the Bolsa Família program under the PT, which was galvanized by the election of President Luiz Inácio Lula da Silva.

In short, there are many pieces of evidence that are consistent with the view that democracy promotes equality and that a primary reason why OECD countries tend to be more equal than middle-income countries is that they are more democratic. Nevertheless, it also is clear that the Western European experience may not be completely representative. To see why, it is useful to delve into another apparent empirical puzzle in the literature on redistributive politics—the relationship between inequality and income redistribution. Meltzer and Richard (1981) proposed a simple positive model of income redistribution that suggested that, other things being equal, in a democracy greater inequality would be associated with greater income redistribution. That model also suffers from some empirical problems. As Perotti (1996) pointed out, there is no simple correlation across countries between inequality and income redistribution. Obviously the model does not predict a simple positive relationship between inequality and redistribution across countries because there are many differences between countries that may be correlated with either the demand or the supply of redistribution at a particular level of inequality.

For example, countries with bad institutions may tend to have high inequality, but in such countries any income that is taxed away is likely to be wasted by corrupt officials or diverted by elites, reducing the demand for redistribution by poor people at any level of inequality. Without being able to control for omitted variables properly, it is difficult to infer from cross-national data that there is no partial relationship between inequality and redistribution.

Nevertheless, both the empirical findings in Gil, Mulligan, and Sala-i-Martin (2004) and the failure of a simple cross-country correlation between inequality and redistribution can be given a different interpretation. In particular, it is likely that simple models of democratic politics, such as the median voter model used by Meltzer and Richard (1981) and Acemoglu and Robinson (2006), do not adequately capture the political forces that generate redistribution in the real world. Acemoglu and Robinson (2006) notes that and develops a more general model of redistributive politics in which the "political power" of different groups is parameterized by the weight that their preferences get in determining the equilibrium level of redistribution. In Meltzer and Richard (1981), it is only the preferences of the median voter that matter; in a more general model of democracy, however, the preferences of other groups will matter too. That means that nondemocratic elites may influence policy in a democracy in a way that reduces the difference between democratic and nondemocratic outcomes. Indeed, Acemoglu and Robinson (2008) presents a model in which the elite can solve the collective action problem, thereby influencing the equilibrium policy, and shows that a transition from dictatorship, in which the elite control policy, to democracy, in which ordinary citizens have more power, may have zero impact on the policies chosen. That is because the elite are able to use lobbying to completely offset the implications of the change in political institutions. Though that is an extreme and somewhat special result, it drives home that the elite has the incentive—and may have the ability—to capture democracy. Acemoglu and Robinson (2007) further argues that the reason that inequality has risen in South Africa since 1994 is that the existing white economic elite have managed to co-opt the new black political elite in a way that gives the black elite a vested interest in the current distribution of assets and income. The authors argue that the situation is unlikely to change unless greater political competition or a new political party emerges.

Such a "conservation result" may hold with respect to the comparative statics of democracy. For instance, in Meltzer and Richard (1981), greater inequality increases the demand for redistribution by the median voter, but it simultaneously makes redistribution worse for the elite. As the desire of the median voter to redistribute increases with increasing inequality, the desire of the rich to avoid it increases at the same time, and the net effect may well be ambiguous if the elite have instruments to try to offset the power of the median voter. The latter type of model was proposed in Barenboím and Karabarbounis (2007) (anticipated in many ways by Benabou 1996), an important study that tests its implications by regressing income redistribution on two measures of inequality. The first is the ratio of the median income to the mean income; the second is the ratio of the proportion of income that accrues to the top decile to the proportion that goes to the bottom decline. The first ratio is meant to capture the incentive of the median voter to demand more redistribution, the second the incentive of the rich to avoid it. The authors find, other things being equal, that the lower median income is relative to mean income, the greater the redistribution demanded. However, they also find that the greater the ratio of the top to the bottom decile, the smaller the redistribution demanded.[4]

It is natural to believe that democracy tends to change the identity of the recipients of redistribution and that it also tends to increase the extent of redistribution. Democracy also may influence the form of redistribution. That happens because those newly enfranchised by democracy, such as the poor, naturally have different preferences for things like public goods and because they demand different policies. Will politicians supply them? Lizzeri and Persico (2004) argues yes, because when politicians have to gain a larger number of votes to win power, offering voters public goods will become a more attractive political strategy and vote buying will be less feasible. Indeed Cox (1987) also argued that democratization in Britain in the nineteenth century led to a switch from clientelism to programmatic appeals because clientelism is simply infeasible in large electorates. In that case we might expect, other things equal, less clientelism under democracy than under dictatorship. There is not much evidence relevant to that question.

Also relevant is the literature on the connection between democracy and educational expenditures. Though examples such as India are often used to suggest that democracy does not help to promote education, there is both cross-country (Baum and Lake 2003) and historical work suggesting that, others things equal, democracy does promote education. Acemoglu and Robinson (2000) first pointed out that within Western Europe educational expansion historically followed democratization, and that point has been firmly supported by Lindert (2001, 2004). Engerman and Sokoloff (2005) shows that a similar relationship holds within the Americas. Though that shows only correlation, not causation, case studies suggest that the relationship is indeed causal—that greater democracy leads to public demand for education and that that demand actually becomes policy.

---

4. Moene and Wallerstein (2001) takes as a fact that there is no relationship between inequality and the size of government or tax revenues and argues that the reason is that most government spending programs are about social insurance, not redistribution. The authors develop a model wherein the demand for social insurance can decrease as inequality increases. They do not explain, however, why the poor would not still prefer to introduce redistributive policies.

In conclusion, the evidence from the OECD suggests that democratization had large effects on labor market institutions and redistributive policies and played a key role in reducing inequality over the last 150 years. It is very easy to understand these facts in theoretical terms. For the rest of the world, however, the relationship is less evident. Though there are instances in which it is clear that democracy induced the same mechanisms, there also seems to be less redistribution in highly unequal middle-income countries than one might expect and democracy seems to have had a much less radical impact on the distribution of power in society. That generates the possibility that unlike Western Europe, current middle-income countries will be able to democratize without setting in motion a virtuous dynamic of falling inequality and rapid growth. Instead, they may stay unequal and relatively poor.

The Constitution and Electoral System

Another obvious source of variation in equilibrium political strategies is differences in political institutions within democracies and dictatorships. Though taxonomies of different types of authoritarian regimes have been proposed, I focus on institutional variation within democratic regimes.

The most important work linking democratic institutions to redistribution is Persson, Roland, and Tabellini (2000), a study of the effects of constitutions. The authors examine the different incentives with respect to public policy that stem from different forms of constitutions. For example, they argue that presidential systems tend to provide fewer public goods than parliamentary systems but that more government revenues are extracted by politicians in parliamentary systems. Persson and Tabellini (2000) developed some simple models of how the form of electoral system influences the form and extent of redistribution, arguing that systems of proportional representation were more likely to induce politicians to appeal to broad electorates and therefore to offer more public goods than politicians operating in majoritarian systems. The authors also argue, however, that majoritarian systems may promote accountability since there is a clear connection between voters and their representatives, who can be disciplined by voters.

Leaving aside the specifics of particular models, one overriding fact seems to be that clientelism is associated with presidentialism and the personal style of politics that goes along with it. Though in the United States presidentialism is associated with checks and balances and the separation of powers, presidentialism in the rest of the world is a rather different animal (see Huntington 1968, on the uniqueness of U.S. presidentialism). For instance in Argentina, Chile, and Taiwan, only the president can introduce a budget and congress cannot increase expenditures (Shugart and Haggard 2001), and it is quite common for presidents to have agenda-setting power with respect to budgets (Carey and Shugart 1992, table 8.2). In Argentina, Brazil, Colombia, and Russia, presidents can decree new legislation without authorization from the legislature (see Carey, Neto, and Shugart 1997 for a comprehensive discussion of the powers of Latin American

presidents). In Africa the situation is even clearer and more extreme, with scholars referring to the "imperial presidency" (Carlson 1999; Nwabueze 1975). Moreover, as Robinson and Torvik (2008) points out, with the exception of Botswana,
Mauritius, and South Africa, every African country that began at independence
as a parliamentary regime switched to presidentialism. Though that switch makes
it difficult to establish the causal effect of presidentialism as an institution, presidentialism obviously facilitates clientelism and probably also reduces rather than
increases checks and balances.

An important political science literature has examined the impact of electoral
institutions on political strategies, particularly the incentives of politicians to
engage in clientelism. Carey and Shugart (1995) provided an analysis of the types
of features of electoral systems that lend themselves to clientelism, or what the
authors call "personalism." They argue that clientelism tends to arise when political parties are weak and have little influence on candidate selection and when
votes are cast for individuals rather than parties. Also important is whether or not
votes pool across electoral lists and whether lists are open or closed. Also important is the size of electoral districts and the number of votes that a politician needs
to win. This literature qualifies the claims of Cox (1987) about Britain, stressing
that the infeasibility of clientelism in Britain after the 1870s may have been due
to the form of electoral institutions. In other countries, such as Italy and Colombia, clientelism seems to be consistent with large electorates. The literature also
qualifies the claims of Persson and Tabellini (2000) that proportional representation leads to greater provision of public goods; that may depend a lot on the form
that proportional representation takes.

More recent empirical work—Persson and Tabellini (2003) and Milesi-
Ferretti, Perotti, and Rostagno (2002)—has examined the effect of institutional
variation on the level of spending. Persson, Tabellini, and Trebbi (2003) examines
the implications of institutional variation for corruption. The authors find that
larger voting districts—and thus lower barriers to entry—are associated with less
corruption, whereas larger shares of candidates elected from party lists—and thus
less individual accountability—are associated with more corruption. Individual
accountability appears to be most strongly tied to personal ballots in plurality-
rule elections, even though open party lists also seem to have some effect. Because
different elements roughly offset each other, a switch from strictly proportional
to strictly majoritarian elections has only a small negative effect on corruption.

Unfortunately, it is quite hard to draw strong conclusions from the literature on
the form of the constitution and electoral systems as it stands. First, many of the
empirical implications seem quite unrobust to small changes in the model and
many aspects of the models can be questioned for not capturing well the basic
structure of different constitutional arrangements (Robinson and Torvik 2008).
Second, it is not clear what causes what. For example, following Carey and Shugart
(1995), to describe an institutional environment in which political parties are weak

and have little influence on candidate selection and in which votes are cast for individuals rather than parties as an environment that leads to clientelism seems to confuse a description of a phenomenon with its explanation. Moreover, the notion that electoral institutions have large independent effects on the level and composition of government expenditures takes as axiomatic the exogeneity of the electoral institutions, something which is clearly problematic.

State Capacity

Apart from the extent of democracy or the form of the constitution, the "strength" of state institutions clearly is an important determinant of the equilibrium amount and form of redistribution. Above I emphasize that the cost of redistribution influences both the demand and supply of redistribution, and cost surely depends on the development of state institutions such as the tax system and bureaucracy. One of the major problems with redistributing income in middle-income countries probably is that the state does not have effective ways to monitor people's income and thereby prevent tax evasion (a horrendous problem in countries like Argentina) and then redistribute income. Indeed, Menaldo (2007) shows that historically democratization in Latin American countries led to increases in taxation only in countries with sufficiently developed banking industries. It is quite likely that strategies such as populism owe at least part of their attractiveness to the fact that state incapacity means that other instruments of redistribution are not available (see also Soifer 2008).

There are many sweeping theories of the origins of state capacity, though most of them are quite far removed from any likely policy conclusions. The academic literature—Tilly (1990), Ertman (1997), Herbst (2000), Bates (2001), Centeno (2002), and Mazzuca (2007), for instance—tends to emphasize deep historical causes for the failure of some parts of the world to develop effective states. For example, intensive interstate warfare is argued to be a potent source of fiscal capacity in Western Europe. Leaving deep history aside, a more relevant question probably is why governments do not have incentives to create state capacity. This is a political issue. Bolivia does not have an income tax, and when President Gonzalo Sánchez de Losada tried to introduce one, poor people rioted in La Paz and he withdrew the proposal. But poor people are exactly the ones who ought to benefit from the introduction of the income tax. This is a puzzle.

Though it is again difficult to disentangle cause from effect, the poor state capacity of middle-income countries seems to play a potentially important role in explaining the lack of redistribution. That is because state capacity influences the cost of redistribution but also because it determines how level the playing field is and whether or not the interests of poor people get represented in the political system. Perhaps this argument should not be overemphasized. It was not the sudden development of state capacity that led to a huge decline in inequality and poverty in Brazil after 2002; it was the election of the Partido dos Trabalhadores and a radical change in policy. It turned out that even the Brazilian state had the capacity required to give cash transfers to poor people—and, also important, the state had enough capacity to make sure that PT candidates were not murdered, something that the Colombian state could not guarantee the candidates of the left-wing Unión Patriótica in the 1980s.

Modernization

Could development itself and the structural changes that it brings change the equilibrium amount of redistribution? On a general level there are many potential mechanisms for change. For example, increased education may make voters more sensitive to economic policies and less prone to vote on the basis of ascriptive characteristics such as ethnicity, a shift that would tend to lead to more redistribution. Several of the chapters in this volume—for instance, Barros, Carvalho, Franco, and Mendonça (chapter 6), Esquivel, Lustig, and Scott (chapter 7), and Jaramillo and Saavedra (chapter 8)—emphasize the key role of the distribution of education in driving the dynamics of inequality.

Modernization has featured heavily in the political science literature that discusses the conditions under which a society tends to have clientelistic politics. The basic idea in political science is that clientelism characterizes "unmodernized" polities (see, for example, Lemarchand and Legg 1972). Indeed, clientelism is seen as an extension of premodern politics. In some models the attractiveness of clientelism may depend on the level of per capita income. For example, in Robinson and Verdier (2002), the higher per capita income is, other things being equal, the greater the opportunity cost of inefficient clientelistic redistribution and the less attractive it is. In that model, income growth can lead to the abandonment of clientelism, and that certainly formalizes some of the ideas in the political science literature.

A central characteristic of modernization, conceptualized by Lipset (1959), was the emergence of a strong middle class. A large group of theories in political science connect the middle class to institutional change (for example, Moore 1966, on democracy), and the rise of the middle class has also been seen as a driving force behind the Progressive Movement in the United States, which significantly reduced corruption and clientelism. Thus the development of a strong middle class ought to promote better policy outcomes.

The cross-country evidence that exists is roughly consistent with that expectation. Apart from the evidence cited above on the cross-country determinants of transfer income, very little work has been done on how to measure or account for clientelism. I know of no good work that tries to explain the composition of government expenditures across countries in order to test some of the ideas discussed here. One idea is to look at corruption. Empirical studies that use cross-sectional variation find that the level of per capita income has a robust negative effect, other things being equal, on corruption (see, for example, Treisman 2000; Persson,

Tabellini, and Trebbi 2003; and Persson and Tabellini 2003). Nevertheless, examples such as the persistence of endemic clientelism in Italy at least into the 1990s and the widespread clientelism argued to exist currently in middle-income countries such as Argentina and Colombia suggest that simply waiting for growth to end clientelism is not a very attractive option.

Finally, the evidence of Acemoglu and others (2008) strongly suggests that one ought to be careful in assigning strong properties to modernization. Once one examines "within variation," many institutional developments are much less connected to economic growth than they appear to be from "between variation."

Factor Endowments and Natural Resources

Natural resource endowments also may be an important source of policy variation. Countries whose economies are centered on the extraction of natural resources such as oil or precious minerals like gold and diamonds are seen to be especially prone to clientelism, for example, because such endowments give the government a solid resource base to use for patronage. Even if the rest of the economy collapses due to state incapacity or failure to provide necessary public goods, the income from the resources keeps flowing. In addition, since natural resource rents can easily be taxed in poor countries with inadequate fiscal systems, the greater the share of such resources in income, the greater the benefits of holding power. Since clientelism is a strategy aimed at staying in power, the greater the benefits of being in power, the more endemic clientelism will be (see Robinson, Torvik and Verdier 2006 for a formalization of that argument).

The relevant empirical evidence on this, in Treisman (2000), looks at the connection between natural resource exports and corruption. The study offers some evidence suggesting that countries in which natural resources are a high fraction of income tend to be more corrupt, other things being equal. Persson and Tabellini (2003) also shows that the size of government is larger in such economies. There also are many arguments in the literature linking natural resources to political institutions, such as democracy (Dunning 2008) and the development of state capacity.

Political Competition

The extent to which any of these mechanisms come into play plausibly depends on the amount of political competition. For example, even that a group cannot solve the collective action problem may not matter if its members are numerous enough that politicians need their support. An interesting example of that comes from Bates (1997). Bates (1981) showed that because cocoa farmers in Ghana were smallholders, they had been unable to solve the collective action problem; they also were politically disadvantaged because they were primarily Ashanti and the early post-independence governments in Ghana, particularly under Nkrumah, were based on a non-Ashanti coalition of ethnic groups. As a result, cocoa farmers were heavily penalized. Compare that to the situation in Colombia, where the majority of coffee growers also are smallholders. Bates (1997) argued that coffee growers had been favored by policy because of the intense political competition between the Liberal and Conservative parties. Thus Bates provided a very interesting example of a situation in which political entrepreneurs had solved the collective action problem for producers because they had seen that it was in their direct electoral interests (unfortunately, as Bautista 2009 has recently shown, historical data do not support Bates's hypothesis).

The question of the impact of political competition on pro-poor policy is especially interesting because despite the Chicago School-style intuition that political competition, like market competition, must be good, many of the recent theoretical models suggest that in fact it is bad. That is true of the model in Lizzeri and Persico (2005), which is highly relevant for this chapter. The authors allow the number of political parties to vary exogenously in a model wherein parties can compete by offering broad public goods that benefit all citizens or transfers that can target individuals. They show that when there are more parties, a situation that they call more competitive, the smaller the expected vote share of any particular political party, and that the smaller the vote share, the less attractive the provision of public goods (since they benefit all agents, even those who are not expected to support a particular vote seeker) and the less efficient in expectation is the equilibrium.

One might complain about the definition of political competition here; moreover, it seems somewhat unrealistic to imagine that political competition is always and everywhere bad. There is as yet very little hard empirical evidence about the impact of political competition. Besley and Preston (2007) finds that increased political competition within Britain leads to more political accountability. In their analysis and interpretation of the evidence, greater competition means that politicians have to work harder to improve their reputations and that that is socially efficient. Besley, Persson, and Sturm (2005) uses the enfranchisement of African Americans in the U.S. South after the 1965 Voting Rights Act as a natural experiment in political competition and argues that it played an important role in the economic catch-up of the South. Unfortunately, there are issues of identification here, since the Voting Rights Act went along with many other social and political changes; indeed non-Southern states also had poll taxes, which were abolished at the same time. Moreover, the mechanisms seem quite surprising. For instance, the authors find that enfranchisement led to lower corporate taxes, not at all what one would have expected from giving voting rights to relatively poor people.

While political competition seems potentially important, it is hard not to see it as a consequence of deeper cleavages and forces in society that it may be more enlightening to investigate.

The Political Equilibrium in Unequal Middle-Income Countries

Let us now try to pull the threads of this discussion together. The typical highly unequal middle-income country will be one that has only quite recently become a democracy. Chile, for example, returned to democracy only in 1990, and Brazil did so in 1985—and even then in an initially restricted form with a constitution crafted by the military. Bolivia redemocratized in 1982 and Argentina in 1983; Colombia and Venezuela did so earlier, in 1958, although democracy there took a very uncompetitive and oligarchic form. Democratization in South Africa and Mexico is even more recent, and neither Egypt nor Tunisia are democracies. The British and Western European evidence suggests that even after democracy is created, it takes quite some time, probably at least 20 years, for the change in political power to be manifested in different parties and policies that favor the poorer segments of society. That means that it may be too early to expect a lot of redistribution in newly democratized Latin American countries. Seen from that angle, the signs are good in Brazil and Chile, for instance, and the signs in Guatemala and Peru are not very surprising.

Nevertheless, one should not take for granted that the experiences of Latin American or other middle-income countries will follow those of Western Europe, with socialist or other parties in favor of reducing inequality naturally emerging after some lag. Many Latin American countries did experience quite long spells of democracy in the twentieth century, but that did not seem to generate the same forces that came into play in Western Europe. As Coatsworth (2008) has so persuasively argued, the political equilibrium in Latin America has been path dependent for 200 years. I see no reason for that to stop now. Populist parties have been more common in Latin America than the socialist parties that were highly associated with mobilizing resistance to inequality in Europe. The return to democracy in Latin America has also led to the resurgence of populism, particularly in Argentina and Venezuela. Even if it is left-wing populism, it seems highly clientelistic in form (on Venezuela, see Hsieh and others 2007).[5] It is also likely that elites who disfavor redistribution will continue to wield far more power than the poor under democracy in those countries. It is not a coincidence that they democratized much later than the countries of Western Europe and that they have grown much more slowly in the last 150 years—that was the outcome of policies favored by the elite, who had a large incentive to avoid mass democracy and, when it came, a large incentive to capture it (Acemoglu and Robinson 2008).

The typical country under consideration will have a presidential system and a proportional representation electoral system. It will probably experience quite

---

5. The political science literature emphasizes that the fact that many Latin American countries adopted Washington Consensus–style reforms in the 1990s does not imply that populism vanished; it survived using different instruments. See Gibson (1997); Roberts (1995, 2008); Roberts and Arce (1998); and Weyland (2002).

volatile fiscal policy with a pronounced electoral cycle. Indeed, Drazen and Brender (2005) finds that among developing countries it is only in new democracies that an electoral cycle exists. The authors explain that as stemming from politicians' desire to convince skeptical citizens that democracy "works." Such a country probably does not have a very effective state apparatus and probably does have a long history of politically driven appointments in the bureaucracy, though some institutions, maybe the central bank, may have a history of greater meritocracy. Finally, such a country will probably have very clientelistic policies and experience an endemic undersupply of public goods.

Policy Implications

What are the policy implications of this analysis? If high levels of inequality in middle-income countries are an obstacle to their growth and if neither natural market nor political dynamics will remove that inequality, what policies can the international community propose that will help?

The political economy view, of course, is that policy advice as such is irrelevant. Policy and institutional outcomes in a particular country are the result of political actors and groups acting rationally given the constraints and incentives that they face—they know that they could have done different things, but they did what was optimal for them. Indeed, it was not policy advice from those concerned about inequality that led to changes in social policies in Brazil and Bolivia, it was the rise of the PT and MAS. Poor people got organized and influenced the political equilibria in a direction that was favorable to their interests and probably conducive to the interests of society in some more general sense. These are hopeful examples, although as the Venezuelan experience emphasizes, there is a distinct concern that what is required is not simply mobilization of the poor and the emergence of pro-poor clientelism but a transition from clientelistic to non-clientelistic politics. It is possible that Brazil has managed to make that transition and maybe Chile as well.[6] It is much less clear that that is the case in Bolivia.

Though policy advice may not be powerful, incentives and constraints are. The international community can provide both. How should it attempt to promote equity in middle-income countries? It should not stress the impact of policies such as Bolsa Família. If that had played an important part in getting President Lula reelected, Latin American politicians would have understood that much faster than the UN Development Programme. Rather, international institutions should focus on influencing the institutional environment in which particular policies get chosen in order to nudge the political equilibrium in the direction of greater equity. I have emphasized that even if democracy in Bolivia or Guatemala may not be qualitatively similar to democracy in Sweden or Belgium, it is nevertheless a movement

---

6. Personal correspondence with Susan Stokes about her ongoing research in Chile.

in the right direction. It is crucial for international institutions to support the institutions of democracy and their consolidation.

But democracy is not enough. Institutional reform is required to make democracy work well and to make it really representative of most people's preferences. The most powerful examples in this chapter illustrate how important political parties are in this respect. Income redistribution did not begin in earnest in Britain until the Labour Party became an important political force, and that example is powerfully echoed in the Brazilian and Bolivian cases. The most powerful ideas in political science about the demise of clientelism link it also to the rise of new political parties (Shefter 1977). Because the arrival of parties with non-clientelistic redistributive agendas probably cannot be expected to be a natural outcome of democracy, international institutions have an important role to play in helping civil society to mobilize and act collectively. Much more research is needed in that area to achieve a deeper understanding of when collective action is successful and why it fails.

Another factor that appears to be critical in deepening democracy is the independence of the media, something vividly shown by the Peruvian experience. Formal political institutions are crucial as well. An obvious factor is the nature of the executive. Presidents in Latin America and Africa have too much power. In the past that has been a potent source of political instability and democratic collapse (Linz and Valenzuela 1994), and it is almost certainly connected to clientelism and populism. Both styles of politics have a personalist flavor that complements clientelism and patronage-driven politics. Often presidentialism is also connected to the weakness of political parties, which again seems to mitigate against reforms that promote equality. An important agenda for institutional reform in Latin America would emphasize the strengthening of legislatures and the restriction of presidential powers.

Unfortunately, the countries that need institutional reform are precisely the ones where improving institutions will be difficult. Acemoglu, Robinson, and Torvik (2008) raises the question of why, when the normative political economy literature emphasizes the desirability of checks and balances to executive power, voters in Venezuela, Peru, Colombia, and Argentina are prepared to vote to strengthen the powers of presidents and remove checks and balances. The authors argue that it is because the institutions that generate checks and balances and thereby reduce the rents to politicians also reduce the probability that policies that directly serve the interests of the median voter get on the political agenda. That may be because when politicians extract few rents, they are easy for elites to co-opt. In societies with great inequalities, the median voter may be prepared to concede rents to politicians and even risk being saddled with politicians whose preferences do not align with the national interest in order to increase the chance that they will get their preferred policy.

Conclusion

In this chapter I have provided a survey of the political economy of income redistribution. My main argument is that it is impossible to think about the distribution and redistribution of assets and income without thinking about politics, and I summarize some of the factors that seem to be important in determining the distribution of political power in society and thus in determining inequality.

I put these ideas together to provide a stylized picture of the political economy of middle- income countries and the barriers that they are likely to face to moving toward greater equality. Political economy emphasizes that equality and growth cannot be improved just by suggesting good policies; political actors must have the right incentives to adopt them and people must have the incentive to demand them. Even if foreign aid might potentially be used to create incentives, middle-income countries are not going to be big recipients of such aid. That means that international institutions, such as the UNDP, have to use their influence and clout to promote adoption of political institutions, such as democracy, that are likely to move the political equilibria of these countries in a direction that is more likely to trigger the virtuous circle of falling inequality and increasing growth that OECD countries experienced for much of the twentieth century.

References

Acemoglu, Daron. 2003. "Why Not a Political Coase Theorem?" *Journal of Comparative Economics* 31, no. 4: 620–52.

Acemoglu, Daron, and James A. Robinson. 2000. "Why Did the West Extend the Franchise?" *Quarterly Journal of Economics* 115, no. 4: 1167–199.

———. 2001a. "Inefficient Redistribution." *American Political Science Review* 95, no. 3: 649–62.

———. 2001b. "A Theory of Political Transitions." *American Economic Review* 9, no. 4: 938–63.

———. 2006. *Economic Origins of Dictatorship and Democracy.* Cambridge University Press.

———. 2007. "A Model of the Iron Law of Oligarchy." Unpublished paper.

———. 2008. "Persistence of Power, Elites, and Institutions." *American Economic Review* 98, no. 1: 267–91.

Acemoglu, Daron, James A. Robinson, and Ragnar Torvik. 2008. "Endogenous Checks and Balances." Unpublished paper.

Acemoglu, Daron, and others. 2008. "Income and Democracy." *American Economic Review* 98, no. 3: 808–42.

Aidt, Toke S., J. Jaysri Dutta, and Elena Loukoianova. 2006. "Democracy Comes to Europe: Franchise Expansion and Fiscal Outcomes, 1830–1938." *European Economic Review* 50, no. 2: 249–83.

Aidt, Toke S., and Peter S. Jensen. 2007. "The Taxman Tools Up: An Event History Study of the Introduction of the Personal Income Tax in Western Europe, 1815–1941." Cambridge Working Papers in Economics 0766.

Alesina, Alberto, Reza Baqir, and William Easterly. 1999. "Public Goods and Ethnic Divisions." *Quarterly Journal of Economics* 114, no. 4: 1243–284.

Alesina, Alberto, and Edward L. Glaeser. 2004. *Fighting Poverty in the U.S. and Europe: A World of Difference*. Oxford University Press.

Alesina, Alberto, and Eliana La Ferrara. 2005. "Preferences for Redistribution in the Land of Opportunities." *Journal of Public Economics* 89, no. 5–6: 897–931

Ansolabehere, Stephen, Jonathan Rodden, and James M. Snyder. 2006. "Purple America." *Journal of Economic Perspectives* 20, no. 2: 97–118.

Ansolabehere, Stephen, and James M. Snyder. 2002. "Party Control of State Government and the Distribution of Government Expenditures." Unpublished paper. Department of Political Science, Massachusetts Institute of Technology.

Baland, Jean-Marie, and James A. Robinson. 2008. "Land and Power: Theory and Evidence from Chile." *American Economic Review* 98, no. 5: 1737–765.

Barenboím, Igor, and Loukas Karabarbounis. 2007. "Redistribution and the Two Faces of Inequality." Unpublished paper. Department of Economics, Harvard University.

Barro, Robert J. 1973. "The Control of Politicians: An Economic Model." *Public Choice* 14, no. 1: 19–42.

Barros, Ricardo Paes de, and others. 2009. "Markets, the State, and the Dynamics of Inequality: Brazil's Case Study." Paper prepared for the UNDP project "Markets, the State, and the Dynamics of Inequality: How to Advance Inclusive Growth," coordinated by Luis Felipe López-Calva and Nora Lustig (http://undp.economiccluster-lac.org/).

Bartels, Larry M. 2008. *Unequal America*. Princeton University Press.

Bates, Robert H. 1981. *Markets and States in Tropical Africa*. University of California Press.

———. 1997. *Open Economy Politics*. Princeton University Press.

———. 2001. *Prosperity and Violence: The Political Economy of Development*. New York: W. W. Norton.

Baum, Matthew A., and David A. Lake. 2003. "The Political Economy of Growth: Democracy and Human Capital." *American Journal of Political Science* 47, no. 2: 333–47.

Bautista, María Angélica. 2009. "Does Coffee Stimulate Political Competition?" Unpublished paper. Department of Political Science, Brown University.

Becker, Gary S., and Casey Mulligan. 2003. "Deadweight Costs and the Size of Government." *Journal of Law and Economics* 46, no. 2: 293–340.

Benabou, Roland. 1996. "Inequality and Growth." In *NBER Macroeconomic Annual 1996*, edited by Benjamin Bernanke and Julio Rotemberg. MIT Press.

———. 2008. "Ideology." *Journal of the European Economic Association* 6, no. 2–3: 321–52.

Benabou, Roland, and Efe Ok. 2001. "Social Mobility and the Demand for Redistribution: The POUM Hypothesis." *Quarterly Journal of Economics* 116, no. 2: 447–87.

Benabou, Roland, and Jean Tirole. 2006. "Belief in a Just World and Redistributive Politics." *Quarterly Journal of Economics* 121, no. 2: 699–746.

Besley, Timothy F., and Robin Burgess. 2002. "The Political Economy of Government Responsiveness: Theory and Evidence from India." *Quarterly Journal of Economics* 117, no. 4: 1415–452.

Besley, Timothy F., and Steven T. Coate. 1997. "An Economic Model of Representative Democracy." *Quarterly Journal of Economics* 112, no. 1: 85–114.

Besley, Timothy F., and Masa Kudamatsu. 2006. "Health and Democracy." *American Economic Review* 96, no. 1: 313–18.

Besley, Timothy J., Torsten Persson, and Daniel M. Sturm. 2005. "Political Competition and Economic Performance: Theory and Evidence from the United States." Working Paper W11484. Cambridge, Mass.: National Bureau of Economic Research (July).

Besley, Timothy F., and Ian Preston. 2007. "Electoral Bias and Policy Choice: Theory and Evidence." *Quarterly Journal of Economics* 122, no. 4: 1473–510.

Bruni, Lucilla, Alberto Fuentes, and Tomás Rosada. 2008. "Dynamics of Inequality in Guatemala: Breaking with History or Perpetuating Trends?" Paper prepared for the UNDP project "Markets, the State, and the Dynamics of Inequality: How to Advance Inclusive Growth," coordinated by Luis Felipe López-Calva and Nora Lustig (http://undp.economic cluster-lac.org/).

Carey, John M., Octávio A. Neto, and Matthew S. Shugart. 1997. "Appendix: Outlines of Constitutional Powers in Latin America." In *Presidentialism and Democracy in Latin America,* edited by Scott Mainwaring and Mathew S. Shugart. Cambridge University Press.

Carey, John M., and Matthew S. Shugart. 1992. *Presidents and Assemblies: Constitutional Design and Electoral Dynamics.* Cambridge University Press.

———.1995. "Incentives to Cultivate a Personal Vote: A Rank-Ordering of Electoral Formulas." *Electoral Studies* 14, no. 4: 417–39.

Carlson, Rolf. 1999. "Presidentialism in Africa: Explaining Institutional Choice." Ph.D. dissertation, Department of Political Science, University of Chicago.

Carter, Michael R. 2007. "The Economics of Polarization and the Design of Public Policy to Mitigate Inequality." Unpublished paper. Department of Agricultural and Resource Economics, University of Wisconsin–Madison.

Carter, Michael R., and John Morrow. 2007. "Zero Upward Mobility and Redistribution." Unpublished paper. Department of Agricultural and Resource Economics, University of Wisconsin–Madison.

Centeno, Miguel. 2002. *Blood and Debt: War and the Nation-State in Latin America.* Penn State University Press.

Cheibub, José Antonio. 1998. "Political Regimes and the Extractive Capacity of Governments: Taxation in Democracies and Dictatorships." *World Politics* 50, no. 3: 349–76.

Coate, Steven T., and Stephen E. Morris. 1995. "On the Form of Transfers to Special Interests." *Journal of Political Economy* 103, no. 6: 1210–235.

Coatsworth, John H. 2008. "Inequality, Institutions, and Economic Growth in Latin America." *Journal of Latin American Studies* 40, no. 3: 545–69.

Conniff, Michael L. 1999. *Populism in Latin America.* University of Alabama Press.

Cox, Gary W. 1987. *The Efficient Secret.* Cambridge University Press.

Dixit, Avinash K., Gene Grossman, and Elhanan Helpman. 1997. "Common Agency and Coordination." *Journal of Political Economy* 105, no. 4: 752–69.

Dixit, Avinash K., and John B. Londregan. 1996. "The Determinants of Success of Special Interests in Redistributive Politics." *Journal of Politics* 58, no. 4: 1132–155.

Dornbusch, Rudiger, and Sebastian Edwards. 1991. *The Macroeconomics of Populism in Latin America.* University of Chicago Press.

Drazen, Allan M., and Adi Brender. 2005. "Political Budget Cycles in New versus Established Democracies." *Journal of Monetary Economics* 52, no. 7: 1271–295.

Dunning, Thad. 2008. *Crude Democracy.* Cambridge University Press.

Eberhard, Juan, and Eduardo Engel. 2008. "Decreasing Inequality in Chile." Paper prepared for the UNDP project "Markets, the State, and the Dynamics of Inequality: How to Advance Inclusive Growth," coordinated by Luis Felipe López-Calva and Nora Lustig (http://undp. economiccluster-lac.org/).

Eichengreen, Barry. 2006. *The European Economy since 1945: Coordinated Capitalism and Beyond.* Princeton University Press.

Engerman, Stanley L., and Kenneth L. Sokoloff. 2005. "The Evolution of Suffrage Institutions in the New World." *Journal of Economic History* 65, no. 4: 891–921.

Ertman, Thomas. 1997. *Birth of the Leviathan: Building States and Regimes in Medieval and Early Modern Europe.* Cambridge University Press.

Ferejohn, John A. 1986. "Incumbent Performance and Electoral Control." *Public Choice* 50: 5–26.

Ferraz, Claudio, and Frederico Finan. 2008. "Exposing Corrupt Politicians: The Effects of Brazil's Publicly Released Audits on Electoral Outcomes." *Quarterly Journal of Economics* 123, no. 2: 703–45.

Frank, Thomas. 2005. *What's the Matter with Kansas? How Conservatives Won the Heart of America.* New York: Holt.

Freeman, Richard B. 2007. "Labor Market Institutions around the World." Working Paper 13242. Cambridge, Mass.: National Bureau of Economic Research.

Gasparini, Leonardo, and Guillermo Cruces. 2009. "A Distribution in Motion: The Case of Argentina." Paper prepared for the UNDP project "Markets, the State, and the Dynamics of Inequality: How to Advance Inclusive Growth," coordinated by Luis Felipe López-Calva and Nora Lustig (http://undp.economiccluster-lac.org/).

Gelman, Andrew, and others. 2008. *Red State, Blue State, Rich State, Poor State: Why Americans Vote the Way They Do.* Princeton University Press.

Gibson, Edward L. 1997. "The Populist Road to Market Reform: Policy and Electoral Coalitions in Mexico and Argentina." *World Politics* 49 (April): 339–70.

Gil, Ricard, Casey B. Mulligan, and Xavier Sala-i-Martin. 2004. "Do Democracies Have Different Public Policies than Nondemocracies?" *Journal of Economic Perspectives* 18, no. 1: 51–74.

Golden, Miriam, and John B. Londregan. 2006. "Centralization of Wage Bargaining and Inequality: A Correction of Wallerstein." *American Journal of Political Science* 50, no. 1: 208–13.

Grossman, Gene M., and Elhana Helpman. 2001. *Special Interest Politics.* MIT Press.

Herbst, Jeffrey I. 1993. *The Politics of Reform in Ghana, 1982–1991.* University of California Press.

———. 2000. *States and Power in Africa: Comparative Studies in Authority and Control.* Princeton University Press.

Hsieh, Chang-Tai, and others. 2007. "The Price of Political Opposition: Evidence from Venezuela's Maisanta." University of California–Berkeley (http://elsa.berkeley.edu/~emiguel/research2.shtml).

Huntington, Samuel P. 1968. *Political Order in Changing Societies.* Yale University Press.

Jaramillo, Miguel, and Jaime Saavedra. 2009. "Inequality in Post–Structural Reform Peru: The Role of Market and Policy Forces." Paper prepared for the UNDP project "Markets, the State, and the Dynamics of Inequality: How to Advance Inclusive Growth," coordinated by Luis Felipe López-Calva and Nora Lustig (http://undp.economiccluster-lac.org/).

Kasara, Kimuli. 2007. "Tax Me If You Can: Ethnic Geography, Democracy, and the Taxation of Agriculture in Africa." *American Political Science Review* 101, no. 1: 159–72.

Kelley, Jonathan, and Herbert S. Klein. 1981. *Revolution and the Rebirth of Inequality.* University of California Press.

Kudamatsu, Masa. 2006. "Has Democratization Reduced Infant Mortality in Sub-Saharan Africa? Evidence from Micro Data." Unpublished paper. Institute for International Economics, University of Stockholm.

Lapp, Nancy D. 2004. *Landing Votes: Representation and Land Reform in Latin America.* New York: Palgrave Macmillan.

Lee, Woojin. 2003. "Is Democracy More Expropriative Than Dictatorship? Tocquevillian Wisdom Revisited." *Journal of Development Economics* 71, no. 1: 155–98.

Lemarchand, Renéand, and Keith Legg. 1972. "Political Clientelism and Development: A Preliminary Analysis." *Comparative Politics* 4, no. 2: 149–78.

Lindbeck, Assar, and Jörgen Weibull. 1987. "Balanced-Budget Redistribution as the Outcome of Political Competition." *Public Choice* 52: 272–97.

Lindert, Peter H. 2001. "Democracy, Decentralization, and Mass Schooling before 1914." Unpublished paper. Department of Economics, University of California at Davis.

———. 2004. *Growing Public: Social Spending and Economic Growth since the Eighteenth Century.* Cambridge University Press.

Linz, Juan J., and Arturo Valenzuela. 1994. *The Failure of Presidential Democracy.* Johns Hopkins University Press.

Lipset, Seymour M. 1959. "Some Social Prerequisites for Democracy: Economic Development and Political Legitimacy." *American Political Science Review* 53 (March): 69–105.

Lizzeri, Alessandro, and Nicola Persico. 2001. "The Provision of Public Goods under Alternative Electoral Incentives." *American Economic Review* 91, no. 1: 225–45.

———. 2004. "Why Did the Elites Extend the Suffrage? Democracy and the Scope of Government, with an Application to Britain's 'Age of Reform.'" *Quarterly Journal of Economics* 119, no. 2: 707–65.

———. 2005. "A Drawback of Electoral Competition." *Journal of the European Economics Association* 3: 1318–348.

Lundahl, Mats. 1982. "The Rationale for Apartheid." *American Economic Review* 72, no. 5: 1169–179.

Lustig, Nora. 2007. "A Note on Markets, the State, and the Dynamics of Inequality." Concept note for the UNDP project "Markets, the State, and the Dynamics of Inequality in Latin America," coordinated by Luis Felipe López-Calva and Nora Lustig (http://undp.economic cluster-lac.org/).

Mazzuca, Sebastián. 2007. "Southern Cone Leviathans." Ph.D. dissertation, Department of Political Science, University of California–Berkeley.

McMillan, John, and Pablo Zoido. 2004. "How to Subvert Democracy: Montesinos in Peru." *Journal of Economic Perspectives* 18, no. 4: 69–92.

Meltzer, Allan M., and Scott F. Richard. 1981. "A Rational Theory of the Size of Government." *Journal of Political Economy* 89, no. 5: 914–27.

Menaldo, Victor. 2007. "Banking on Redistribution: Financial Institutions and Fiscal Redistribution in Latin American Democracies." Unpublished paper. Department of Political Science, Stanford University.

Milesi-Ferretti, Gian Maria, Roberto Perotti, and Massimo Rostagno. 2002. "Electoral Systems and Public Spending." *Quarterly Journal of Economics* 117, no. 2: 609–57.

Moene, Karl Ove, and Michael Wallerstein. 2001. "Inequality, Social Insurance, and Redistribution." *American Political Science Review* 95, no. 4: 859–74.

Moore, Barrington. 1966. *The Social Origins of Dictatorship and Democracy: Lord and Peasant in the Making of the Modern World.* Boston: Beacon Press.

Mulligan, Casey B., and Kevin K. Tsui. 2006. "Political Competitiveness." Working Paper 12653. Cambridge, Mass.: National Bureau of Economic Research.

Nwabueze, Benjamin O. 1975. *Presidentialism in Commonwealth Africa.* London: C. Hurst.

Osborne, Martin J., and Al Slivinski. 1996. "A Model of Political Competition with Citizen Candidates." *Quarterly Journal of Economics* 111, no. 1: 65–96.

Padró-i-Miquel, Gerard. 2007. "The Control of Politicians in Divided Societies: The Politics of Fear." *Review of Economic Studies* 74, no. 4: 1259–274.

Perotti, Roberto. 1996. "Growth, Income Distribution, and Democracy: What the Data Say." *Journal of Economic Growth* 1, no. 2: 149–87.

Persson, Torsten, and Guido Tabellini. 1999. "The Size and Scope of Government: Comparative Politics with Rational Politicians." *European Economic Review* 43, no. 4–6: 699–735.

———. 2000. *Political Economics: Explaining Economic Policy*. MIT Press.

———. 2003. *The Economic Effects of Constitutions: What Do the Data Say?* MIT Press.

Persson, Torsten, Guido Tabellini and Francesco Trebbi. 2003. "Electoral Rules and Corruption." *Journal of the European Economic Association* 1, no. 4: 958–89.

Persson, Torsten, Gérard Roland, and Guido Tabellini. 1997. "Separation of Powers and Political Accountability." *Quarterly Journal of Economics* 112, no. 4: 1163–202.

———. 2000. "Comparative Politics and Public Finance." *Journal of Political Economy* 108, no. 6: 1121–161.

Piketty, Thomas. 1995. "Social Mobility and Redistributive Politics." *Quarterly Journal of Economics* 110, no. 3: 551–84.

Piketty, Thomas, and Emmanuel Saez. 2006. "The Evolution of Top Incomes: A Historical and International Perspective." *American Economic Review* 96, no. 1: 200–05.

Reynolds, Clark W. 1971. *The Mexican Economy: Twentieth-Century Structure and Growth*. Yale University Press.

Roberts, Kenneth M. 1995. "Neoliberalism and the Transformation of Populism in Latin America." *World Politics* 48, no. 1: 82–116.

———. 2008. *Changing Course: Parties, Populism, and Political Representation in Latin America's Neoliberal Era*. Cambridge University Press.

Roberts, Kenneth M., and Moisés Arce. 1998. "Neoliberalism and Lower-Class Voting Behavior in Peru." *Comparative Political Studies* 31, no. 2: 217–46.

Robinson, James A. 2007. "Un País Típico de America Latina." In *Economía Colombiana del Siglo XX,* edited by Miguel Urrutia and James A. Robinson. Bogotá: Fondo de Cultura Económica.

Robinson, James A., and Ragnar Torvik. 2005. "White Elephants." *Journal of Public Economics* 89, no. 2–3: 197–210.

———. 2008. "Endogenous Presidentialism." Working Paper 14603. Cambridge, Mass.: National Bureau of Economic Research.

Robinson, James A., Ragnar Torvik, and Theirry Verdier. 2006. "The Political Economy of the Resource Curse." *Journal of Development Economics* 79, no. 2: 447–68.

Robinson, James A., and Thierry Verdier. 2002. "The Political Economy of Clientelism." CEPR Discussion Paper 3205. London: Centre for Economic Policy Research.

Rodrik, Dani. 1986. "Tariffs, Subsidies, and Welfare with Endogenous Policy." *Journal of International Economics* 21, no. 3–4: 285–99.

———. 1998. "Why Do More Open Economies Have Bigger Governments?" *Journal of Political Economy* 106, no. 5: 997–1032.

———. 1999. "Democracies Pay Higher Wages." *Quarterly Journal of Economics* 114, no. 3: 707–38.

Roemer, John E. 1998. "Why the Poor Do Not Expropriate the Rich: An Old Argument in New Garb." *Journal of Public Economics* 70, no. 3: 399–424.

Scott, John. 2008. "The Political Economy of Inequality in Mexico." Paper prepared for the UNDP project "Markets, the State, and the Dynamics of Inequality: How to Advance Inclusive Growth," coordinated by Luis Felipe López-Calva and Nora Lustig (http://undp. economiccluster-lac.org/).

Shefter, Martin. 1977. "Party and Patronage: Germany, England, and Italy." *Politics and Society* 7, no. 4: 403–51.

Shugart, Matthew S., and Stephan Haggard. 2001. "Institutions and Public Policy in Presidential Systems." In *Presidents, Parliaments, and Policy,* edited by Stephan Haggard and Mathew D. McCubbins. Cambridge University Press.

Soifer, Hillel. 2008. "The Redistributive Threat: State Power and the Effect of Inequality on Democracy." Unpublished paper. Department of Political Science, Bates College.

Stasavage, David, and Kenneth Sheve. 2009. "Institutions, Partisanship, and Inequality in the Long Run." *World Politics* 61, no. 2: 215–53.

Stokes, Susan. 2005. "Peverse Accountability: A Formal Model of Machine Politics with Evidence from Argentina." *American Political Science Review* 99, no. 3: 315–25.

Strömberg, David. 2004. "Radio's Impact on Public Spending." *Quarterly Journal of Economics* 119, no. 1: 189–221.

Tilly, Charles. 1990. *Coercion, Capital, and European States AD 990–1990*. New York: Basil Blackwell.

Treisman, Daniel. 2000. "The Causes of Corruption: A Cross-National Study." *Journal of Public Economics* 76, no. 3: 399–457.

Wallerstein, Michael. 1999. "Wage-Setting Institutions and Pay Inequality in Advanced Industrial Countries." *American Journal of Political Science* 43, no. 3: 649–80.

Weyland, Kurt. 2002. *The Politics of Market Reform in Fragile Democracies: Argentina, Brazil, Peru, and Venezuela*. Princeton University Press.

Wilson, John D. 1990. "Are Efficiency Improvements in Government Transfer Policies Self-Defeating in Political Equilibrium?" *Economics and Politics* 2, no. 3: 241–58.

Wittman, Donald. 1983. "Candidate Motivation: A Synthesis of Alternative Motivations." *American Political Science Review* 77 (March): 142–57.

Wright, Randall D. 1996. "Taxes, Redistribution, and Growth." *Journal of Public Economics* 62, no. 3: 327–38.

4

The Dynamics of Income Concentration in Developed and Developing Countries: A View from the Top

FACUNDO ALVAREDO AND THOMAS PIKETTY

The primary objective of this chapter is to summarize the trends in income concentration during the twentieth century for four groups of countries: Western English-speaking countries (United Kingdom, Ireland, United States, Canada, New Zealand, and Australia); continental European countries (France, Germany, Netherlands, and Switzerland) and Japan; Nordic and Southern European countries (Norway, Sweden, Finland, Spain, Italy, and Portugal); and developing countries (Argentina, China, India, Singapore, and Indonesia).[1] Did income distribution become more unequal or more equal over the course of the years? When did income inequality increase, and when did it decrease? What income fractiles were most affected? What differences and similarities exist among countries?

The second objective is to understand those trends. What are the economic mechanisms and processes that allow us to understand the way that income con-

---

1. We rely on the results of a series of studies that, beginning with research by Piketty on the long-run distribution of top incomes in France (Piketty 2001 and 2003), has constructed top income share series for more than twenty countries: Atkinson (2005 and 2007b); Atkinson and Leigh (2007a and b); Dell (2007); Dell, Piketty, and Saez (2007); Nolan (2007); Piketty and Saez (2003); Saez and Veall (2005); Salverda and Atkinson (2007); Aarberge and Atkinson (2010); Alvaredo (2009 and 2010a); Alvaredo and Pisano (2010); Alvaredo and Saez (2009); Atkinson (2010); Banerjee and Piketty (2005); Leigh and van der Eng (2010); Moriguchi and Saez (2008); Piketty and Qian (2009); Jäntti and others (2010); and Roine and Waldenström (2008). Other works on income and wealth concentration in the same countries include Atkinson and Harrison (1978); Atkinson and Leigh (2008); Guilera (2008); Kopczuk and Saez (2004); Landais (2007); and Piketty, Postel-Vinay, and Rosenthal (2006).

centration evolved? What impact have market forces, state policies, and other historical and sociopolitical factors had on inequality? What lessons can developing countries, such as the four Latin American nations examined in this book, learn from the experiences of advanced countries?

The chapter refers briefly to methodological issues and describes the dynamics of top income shares in the United States and France, which best exemplify two different patterns in the evolution of inequality. It summarizes the findings for developed countries and then focuses on developing economies. The chapter makes explicit reference to market forces, state policies, history, and institutions in order to understand the observed facts.

Motivation, Methodological Issues, and Warnings

This analysis relies on income tax statistics, the only source of income data that are consistently available on a long-term basis. Progressive income tax systems were established in most Western countries at the beginning of the twentieth century (in 1913 in the United States, 1914 in France, and 1932 in Argentina and Spain), and in all countries the tax administration has compiled and published tabulations based on its exhaustive set of income tax returns. Those tabulations generally report, for a large number of income brackets, the corresponding number of taxpayers, as well as their total income and tax liability. The tabulations are usually broken down by income source: capital income, wage income, business income, rents, and so forth. We can then use standard Pareto interpolation techniques to compute top fractile thresholds and average incomes.[2] We can also construct a top fractile income share series from the data by using aggregate income sources (national accounts) to compute total income.

Although tax statistics are superior in a number of ways to data from household surveys, they are not free of shortcomings.[3] The definitions of taxable income and tax unit tend to change over time according to the tax laws, and tax codes vary across countries. There is a tendency to underreport certain types of

2. Assuming that the distribution is Pareto in form has been the standard practice; see Feenberg and Poterba (1993) and Piketty (2001). An alternative approach is based on the mean-split histogram, as described in Atkinson (2005).

3. Household income surveys are a relatively recent venture: they were virtually nonexistent prior to 1950, and in most countries they were not available in a homogenous, machine-readable format until the 1970s or 1980s. Consequently, survey-based inequality data sets suffer from serious shortcomings: they display little homogeneity across countries and over time, they are not long run, and they offer hardly any reliable decomposition of income between capital income and labor income sources. In addition, household surveys generally are not representative at the top of the income distribution, where non-sampling errors (underreporting in particular) may play an important role. That is especially relevant in the case of developing countries, where household surveys often are the only data source available for analyzing income inequality in spite of the fact that high incomes and even moderately high incomes generally are not reported at all.

income, and taxpayers adopt a variety of ways to avoid paying taxes, including planning, renaming, and retiming activities to legally reduce their tax liability. Nonetheless, no other source of information allows for the study of the distribution of top incomes over virtually the entire twentieth century.

The same cannot be said of the rest of the income distribution. Before World War II, the proportion of individuals subject to progressive income taxation in most countries rarely exceeded 10 percent, so we can only estimate the upper part of the Lorenz curve. Long-run series are confined to top income shares (and wealth shares, when available) and contain little information about bottom segments of the distribution. Nonetheless, the concentration of income at the top is economically and politically significant. Even when the number of well-off individuals is small, changes in their income can have a significant impact on the overall distribution. As advanced in Atkinson (2007a), when the richest group, infinitesimal in number, owns a finite share f of total income, the Gini coefficient G turns out to be close to $\phi + (1 - \phi) G^*$, where G^* is the Gini for the rest of the population (excluding the richest).[4] In a case in which G^* is 0.40, an increase of 8 percentage points in the share of the rich results, ceteris paribus, in an increase of 4.8 percentage points in the Gini for the whole economy,[5] which is roughly equal to the increase in the overall Gini recorded in the United States between the 1970s and the 1990s.[6] In addition, income concentration at the top can have an important impact on public policy by enabling the rich to opt out of communal provision of services and thus reducing their willingness to finance public goods through redistribution, taxation, and other public policies. The separation of the general population and the elites—whose members use private schools, health care providers, and police services and live in gated communities—has been a standard feature of Latin American society.

Top Incomes in Advanced Countries: The Cases of France and the United States

The four panels in figure 4-1 display the top 1 percent income share for all the countries for which estimates have been produced, grouped according to the classification mentioned at the beginning of this chapter. In the advanced countries (panels A, B, and C), top capital incomes declined abruptly during the 1914–45 period and fell more slowly thereafter until the 1970s, when top wages rose suddenly in Anglo-Saxon economies while remaining relatively stable in continental

---

4. For a simple formal proof, see Alvaredo (2010b).

5. This simply says that $\Delta G \approx \Delta\phi (1 - G^*)$. For an initial situation of $G^* = 0.40$ and $\phi = 0.1$, then G $\approx 0.1 + (1 - 0.1) 0.40 = 0.46$. After an increase in ϕ from 0.1 to 0.18, then G $\approx 0.18 + (1 - 0.18) 0.40$ = 0.508. The difference between the two Gini coefficients is 4.8 percentage points.

6. Atkinson (2007a).

Europe and Japan. We briefly describe the cases of the United States and France as representative examples of each of the two groups: the *U-shaped* and the *L-shaped*.[7]

Figure 4-2 presents the income shares of the top deciles in the United States and France over the twentieth century. In the United States, the overall pattern of the top decile share is U-shaped. It fluctuated around 40 to 45 percent during the interwar period, declined substantially to just above 30 percent during World War I, and stayed more or less flat, at 31 to 32 percent, until the 1970s. After decades of stability in the postwar period, the top decile share has increased dramatically over the last 25 years and is now close to the pre-war level. That timing is difficult to reconcile with a Kuznets-type model, which explains the decline in income inequality as the result of a continuous process of reallocating activities from low productivity to high productivity sectors (for example, from rural to urban activities as in Kuznets's original model).

The decline in top income shares witnessed by Kuznets for the United States and confirmed by Piketty and Saez also took place in France between 1914 and 1945, coming to an end right after World War II.[8] As figure 4-2 shows, the share of total household income received by the top 10 percent in France dropped from about 45 percent in the 1920s to about 32 percent in the 1990s. In other words, the average income of the top 10 percent was 4.5 times larger than the average income of the entire population at the beginning of the century and it was 3.2 to 3.3 times larger in the 1990s. The decline was far from steady. The top decile income share dropped during World War I and recovered during the 1920s and the first half of the 1930s.

It is instructive to decompose the top decile into the top percentile (top 1 percent), the next 4 percent (top 5 to 1 percent) and the bottom half of the top decile (top 10 to 5 percent). Figure 4-3 presents the results for the United States (panel A) and France (panel B). Panel A shows that most fluctuations of the top decile in the United States were due to fluctuations within the top percentile. The drop in the top 5 to 1 percent and top 10 to 5 percent shares during World War II was far less dramatic and partially reversed relatively quickly. In contrast, the top percentile in the United States experienced larger fluctuations through the course of the twentieth century. The top percentile share declined during World War I, recovered during the 1920s, and declined again during the Great Depression and World War II.

Similarly, panel B of figure 4-3 shows that in France the income share of top 10 to 5 percent group was essentially stable: between 1900 and 1998, that share fluctuated around a mean value of 11 to 11.5 percent of total household income (which means that the income of the top 10 to 5 percent of households was always about 2.2 to 2.3 times the average). The income share of the top 5 to

7. This characterization may be changing. Several economies in Europe have experienced recent rises in top shares, although much more limited than the one exhibited by Anglo-Saxon countries.

8. Kuznets (1953); Piketty and Saez (2003).

Figure 4-1. *The Top 1 Percent Income Share in Twenty-Two Countries*

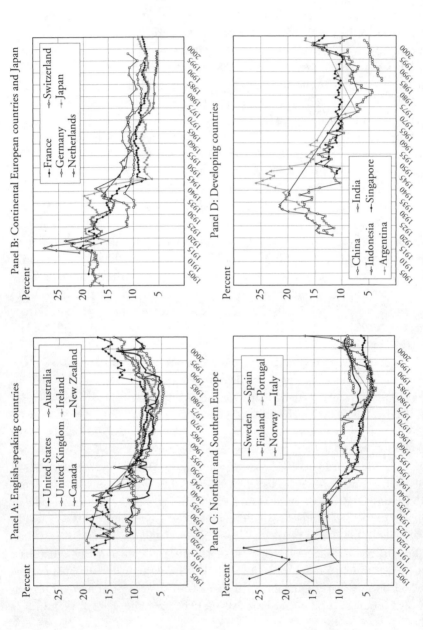

Sources: Aaberge and Atkinson (2010), Alvaredo (2009), Alvaredo (2010), Atkinson (2007b), Atkinson and Leigh (2007a and b), Nolan (2007), Piketty and Saez (2003), Alvaredo and Pisano (2010), Alvaredo and Saez (2009), Dell (2007), Dell, Piketty and Saez (2007), Moriguchi and Saez (2008), Piketty (2001), Roine and Walderström (2008), Saez and Veall (2005), Salverda and Atkinson (2007), Banerjee and Piketty (2005), Piketty and Qian (2009), Atkinson (2010), and Leigh and van der Eng (2010).

Figure 4-2. *Top 10 Percent Income Share, United States and France*

Percent income share

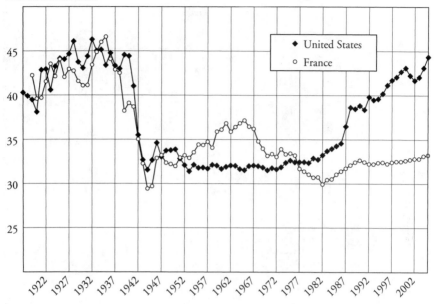

Sources: United States:Piketty and Saez (2003); France: Piketty (2001).

1 percent experienced a modest secular decline, from about 15 percent of total household income at the beginning of the twentieth century to about 13 percent during the 1990s, a drop of about 10 percent. In contrast, the top percentile income share dropped by more than 50 percent. The share of total income received by the top 1 percent was about 20 percent at the beginning of the twentieth century, but it was only about 7 to 8 percent during the 1990s. In other words, the average income of the top 1 percent was about 20 times larger than the average income of the entire population at the beginning of the century, but it was only 7 to 8 times larger at the end. Results show that the higher we go within the top percentile of the income distribution, the larger the secular decline. The most extreme case is that of the top 0.01 percent: their income share has dropped from about 3 percent to about 0.5 to 0.6 percent since 1945. The average real income of the top 0.01 percent has not increased at all during the twentieth century, while the average real income of the entire population has been multiplied by 4.5. Almost 90 percent of the secular decline of the top 10 percent income share is due to the top 1 percent, and more than half of the top 1 percent drop is due to the top 0.1 percent.

The timing of the fall of very top incomes is also striking in France. Between 1945 and 1998, the income share of the top 1 percent was fairly stable. The secular fall took place exclusively during the 1914–45 period, in particular between the Great

Figure 4-3. *Decomposing the Top 10 Percent Income Share,*
United States and France

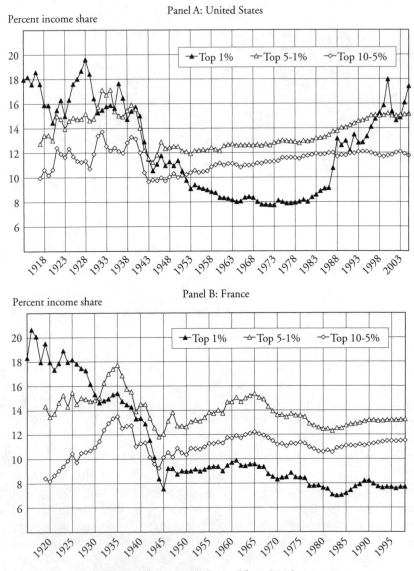

Sources: United States:Piketty and Saez (2003); France: Piketty (2001).

Depression and World War II. It is interesting to note than the deflationary years of the Great Depression had a very different impact on moderately high incomes and on very top incomes. While the income shares of the top 10 to 5 percent and the top 5 to 1 percent (the "upper middle class") increased sharply during the early 1930s, the income shares of the top 1 percent and above (the "rich") fell.

Figure 4-4. *The Top 0.01 Percent Income Share and Composition, United States*[a]

Percent income share

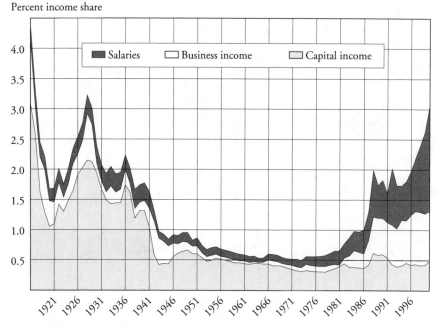

Source: Piketty and Saez (2003).
a. The figure displays the top 0.01 percent income share (top curve) and its composition (excluding capital gains).

Figure 4-4 displays the share and composition of income in the United States from 1916 to 2000 for the top 0.01 percent. Until the 1970s, very top incomes were composed primarily of capital income (mostly dividend income) and to a smaller extent business income; the wage income share was very modest. Figure 4-4 confirms that the large decline of top incomes observed during the 1914–45 period was predominantly a capital income phenomenon. It also shows that the income composition pattern at the very top changed remarkably between 1960 and 2000. Wage income has been driving up top incomes and has now become the main source of income at the very top.[9] National accounts data show that the share of capital income in aggregate personal income has been stable in the long run. Therefore, the secular decline of top capital incomes is the consequence of a decreased concentration of capital income and not a decline in the share of capital income in the economy as a whole.

In France the 1914–45 drop in top income shares was also due entirely to the fall of top capital incomes. Figure 4-5 plots the top 1 percent income share and

9. As capital incomes are a result of a process of accumulation, the rise in top wages may lead to the revival of the rentiers.

Figure 4-5. *Fall of the Top Capital Incomes, France*

Percent share

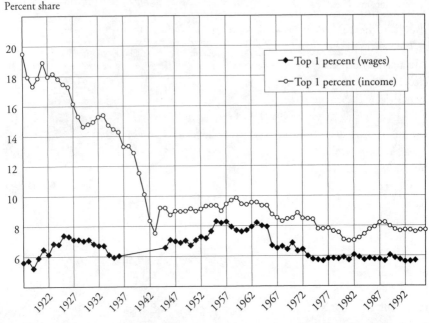

Source: Piketty (2001).

the top 1 percent wage share (wage distribution). Top wage shares did not decline at all. The same picture is derived from using other inequality measures or by looking at the top decile share rather than the top percentile share.

Top Incomes in Advanced Countries: The Contrast between English-Speaking Countries and Continental, Northern, and Southern Europe and Japan

The experience of other English-speaking Western economies generally mirrors that of the United States, and much of Europe and Japan show patterns similar to those identified in France. However, there are differences by country.

Among the six English-speaking countries,[10] the income share of the top 1 percent forms a U shape over time, but the timing of the fall in inequality differs from case to case. In all cases, there was a fall during World War II, but in both Australia and New Zealand there was an immediate postwar recovery, influenced by the improvement of international prices for raw materials. In Canada and the United States, there was limited change in the period 1955–75, whereas Australia, New Zealand, and the United Kingdom all exhibited significant peacetime

10. In considering the results, the reader should bear in mind the warnings about comparability mentioned in Atkinson and Piketty (2007b) and in Atkinson, Piketty, and Saez (2009).

declines. The six English-speaking countries display a remarkable convergence up the to 1970s; subsequently there was some divergence, with the top 1 percent share starting to rise in the United States but continuing to fall in the other countries. But there is considerable commonality in the rise from the 1980s.

The share of the top 1 percent for four Continental Europe countries (France, Germany, the Netherlands, and Switzerland) and Japan follows a path that is closer to an L shape. The difference between the periods before and after World War II is again marked. After 1945 the picture is one of stability, with only the Netherlands showing a pronounced reduction in inequality from 1960 to 1975. Most countries exhibit either small changes or a limited recent rise in top shares. There was a period of falling shares in the 1960s and 1970s, except in Germany, but over the past twenty years there has been broad stability.

Closer analysis shows interesting details. In Switzerland, top shares have been basically flat over the long run. Countries like Ireland, Australia, and New Zealand, which were less affected by the wars, also witnessed a limited decline in inequality during the 1914–45 period, although less limited than in Switzerland, for reasons that probably have to do with differences in trade structure. The case of Germany reveals another pattern: top German capital incomes were strongly hit by World War II, but they seemed to have recovered quickly and to be structurally higher than in other Western countries, probably due to the limited tax progressivity of the German fiscal system in the immediate postwar years. Sweden experienced an important reduction in concentration during the 1970s and 1980s, while the surge in top shares in Norway since the late 1990s appears to be connected with behavioral responses to changes in the tax code (in particular, in the rules for taxing dividends). As analyzed in Moriguchi and Saez (2008), in Japan "the dramatic fall in income concentration at the top was primarily due to the collapse of capital income during the Second World War." The relative stability of top income shares in this country between 1945 and 1995 is remarkable. According to the authors, "the defining event for the evolution of income concentration in Japan was a historical accident, namely the Second World War."

Due to the historical and cultural links that Italy, Spain, and Portugal have with Latin America, it is pertinent to make an explicit reference to their experiences (figure 4-1, panel C). Estimates for Italy for the period 1974–2004 show a persistent increase in the share of top incomes since the mid-1980s, driven mainly by top wages and self-employment income.[11]

In Spain, which was isolated from the two world wars but hit by a ravaging civil war, income concentration was much higher during the 1930s than it is today; it dropped during the 1940s and remained fairly stable throughout the fast-growth period from the 1950s to the 1970s. Although Spain had to wait until the return of democracy in 1975–77 to start implementing a modern welfare state

---

11. Alvaredo and Pisano (2010).

and redistributive tax policies, income concentration in Spain had been quite low since the early 1950s, which possibly played a role in the stability and longevity of Franco's dictatorship.[12] The fact that top shares declined since the 1950s in Spain in the absence of a clear progressive taxation policy may point to the forces affecting the elites in a global environment. During the period from 1980 to 2005, income concentration increased significantly, especially in the top fractiles within the top 1 percent. A large fraction of the increase is due to the surge in realized capital gains following the stock market boom of the late 1990s and since 2002.

In Portugal, the level of concentration between 1950 and 1970 remained relatively high compared with that in countries such as Spain, France, the United Kingdom, and the United States.[13] The decrease in top shares, which started very moderately at the end of the 1960s and accelerated after the left-wing revolution of 1974, began to be reversed during the first half of the 1980s, as soon as Portugal launched a set of reforms to join the European Union. During the last fifteen years top income shares have increased steadily. The rise in wage concentration has contributed to this process in a significant way. Notwithstanding these trends, the increase in income concentration in Mediterranean Europe has been very small relative to the surge experienced by top incomes in the Anglo-Saxon world.

Top Incomes in Developing Countries

Panel D of figure 4-1 displays the top 1 percent income share in Argentina, China, India, Indonesia, and Singapore. Observations for Argentina cover 39 years (1932–54, 1956, 1958–59, 1961, 1970–73, and 1997–2004). In the case of China, there is information for 18 years (1986–2003), but it is based on household income surveys.[14] Tax data in India permitted estimating top income shares for 71 years (1922–88). For Indonesia, tax statistics cover 34 years (1920–39 and 1990–2003), and they have been complemented by and compared with information from household surveys between 1982 and 2003. Data covering 54 years have been analyzed in Singapore (1947–2005). These countries also display a U- or an L-shaped pattern, although there is substantial heterogeneity in this group.[15]

---

12. Alvaredo and Saez (2009).

13. Alvaredo (2009).

14. It is worth making an explicit reference to the case of China even if the estimates for 1983–2003 are not based on tax statistics but on household income surveys. The fact that top income share estimates are lower than in the most egalitarian developed countries shows that they are likely to be underestimated, but the rising trend is robust and can be taken as an indicator of the true dynamics of concentration at the top. Piketty and Qian (2009) shows that income inequality increased at a very high rate during the period. The top decile share rose from about 17 percent in 1986 to almost 28 percent in 2003—that is, by more than 60 percent. The top 1 percent income share more than doubled between 1986 and 2001, from slightly more than 2.6 percent in 1986 to 5.9 percent in 2003.

15. As Atkinson, Piketty, and Saez (2009) argues, "The different pieces of evidence indicate that tax evasion and tax avoidance need to be taken seriously and can quantitatively affect the conclusions drawn.

—*Argentina*. The results for Argentina suggest that income concentration was higher during the 1930s and the first half of the 1940s than it is today (Alvaredo 2010). The recovery of the economy after the Great Depression and the policies implemented during the Perón years between 1946 and 1955 generated an inverted U-shape in the dynamics of top shares. The top percentile share increased from 17 percent in 1933 to 25 percent in 1943 but dropped to 15.3 percent in 1953.[16] Any interpretation of that performance in terms of Kuznets's hypothesis would be at best difficult to accept in light of the inequality trends in the following years.

Two facts can be seen. First, the level of top shares in Argentina in 1942 is not very far from that observed in the United States in 1916. Second, the dynamics in Argentina between 1932 and 1951 seem to reproduce the shape of U.S. top income shares between 1922 and 1940 (concentration in Argentina being always higher), as if the Argentine cycle lagged about 10 to 13 years with respect to the U.S. cycle. Consequently, while top shares began a sustained decrease by the beginning of World War II in the advanced economies, they kept growing in Argentina, favored by export demand from Europe.

The Perón years (1946–55) coincide with a clear decline in the share of the top percentile. However, the limits of the Peronist redistributive policy are marked by the fact that although the top shares were lower in 1956 than in 1945, they were still above those observed in the developed world—they were higher than in the United States, France, and even Spain. A striking contrast exists between Argentina and Australia, two countries that are the subject of constant comparison among scholars. As Atkinson and Leigh (2007a) has described, the effect of the commodity price boom after World War II directly affected top shares in Australia, generating a clear spike in 1950 that was due mainly to the peak wool prices that sheep farmers received that year. On the contrary, state management of exports in Argentina during Perón's presidency seems to have been a powerful tool in extracting a fraction of the surplus from exporters.

Since then top shares seem to have followed a U-shaped pattern, although several gaps in the data limit the interpretation of their movements. Interestingly, the share of the top 1 percent in 1954 (16.5 percent) was very similar to that found in 2004 (16.7 percent), although they reflect two very different moments in history. The first corresponds to a period when the country was working toward improving social conditions, while the general belief is that the second was characterized by a clear regression in that area.

Data from Argentina also illustrate the limitations of household surveys, as opposed to tax tabulations, as a source of information on the incomes of the top

---

They need to be borne in mind when considering the results, but they are not so large as to mean that the tax data should be rejected out of hand."

16. Due in part to immigration but also to the presence of large foreign companies in the country, there was a substantial presence of foreign citizens among the top income earners. On average, 40 to 45 percent of individuals and reported income corresponded to foreigners between 1932 and 1946.

Table 4-1. *Top Income Shares and Gini Coefficient in Argentina, 1997–2004*[a]

	Argentina				
	Top 1 percent income share (1)	Top 0.1 percent income share (2)	Gini coefficient G* (3)	Gini coefficient G¹ (4)	Gini coefficient G² (5)
1997	12.39	4.27	0.469	0.492	0.535
1998	12.57	4.37	0.485	0.508	0.550
1999	13.53	5.22	0.470	0.497	0.541
2000	14.34	5.68	0.486	0.516	0.560
2001	12.91	5.22	0.511	0.536	0.574
2002	15.53	6.92	0.519	0.552	0.594
2003	16.85	7.40	0.509	0.546	0.592
2004	16.75	7.02	0.488	0.524	0.573

a. Top shares in columns 1 and 2 are taken from Alvaredo, 2010.

G* denotes the Gini coefficient of individual income based on the Greater Buenos Aires household survey, (authors' calculations). All results correspond to October surveys, except for 2003 (May). Only income earners with positive income were considered, and no further adjustments were applied. $G^1 \approx \phi + (1 - \phi)G^*$, where ϕ is the estimate of the top 0.1 percent income share. $G^2 \approx \phi + (1 - \phi)G^*$, where ϕ is the estimate of the top 1 percent income share.

The Greater Buenos Aires household survey is taken as representative of Argentina as a whole (see chapter 5 in this volume).

0.1 percent individuals or even the top 1 percent.[17] Recall the formula mentioned earlier, $G \approx \phi + (1 - \phi) G^*$, where G is the Gini coefficient of the whole population, ϕ is the income share of a top group, and G* is the Gini of the rest of the population (excluding the richest). We can compute G by using the estimates of top income shares from Alvaredo (2010) and the survey-based Gini coefficient.[18] Results are presented in table 4-1 and figure 4-6, where G¹ and G² are the Gini coefficient G under the assumption that the top 0.1 percent and the top 1 percent, respectively, are not represented in the surveys. Two facts are notable. First, G can be several percentage points above G*. For instance, in 2004 (the most recent year for which the comparison can be done) G* was 0.487, while G¹ was 0.523 and G² was 0.573.

Second, not only can levels be different, but also the trends of G and G* can diverge. According to survey results, for example, G* displays almost no change when 2001 and 2003 are compared, going from 0.511 to 0.509 in those years. However, G² was 0.574 in 2001 and 0.592 in 2003.[19] That means that even when

17. See Alvaredo (2010) for Argentina and Székeley and Hilgert (1999) for Latin America. Burkhauser and others (2009) shows, for the United States, that the top 1 percent share measured by the internal Current Population Survey (CPS) is consistently lower than the top 1 percent share measured by tax data, mainly because the CPS does not record important income sources at the top (capital gains, stock option gains) and because the CPS records top incomes by means of codes instead of actual income figures.

18. The Greater Buenos Aires household survey is taken as representative of Argentina as a whole (see chapter 5 in this volume).

19. Determining whether those estimates of the Gini coefficient are statistically different or identical is beyond the scope of this analysis.

Figure 4-6. *Gini Coefficient in Argentina, 1980–2004*[a]

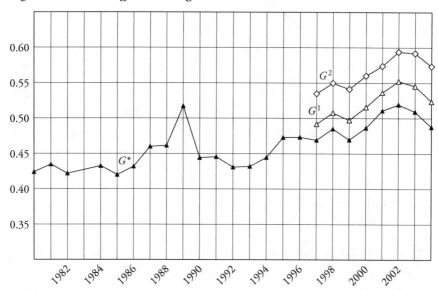

a. The black triangle denotes the Gini coefficient G* of individual income based on the Greater Buenos Aires household survey (authors' calculations). Database for 1983 is missing. All results correspond to October surveys, except for 2003 (May). Only income earners with positive income were considered, and no further adjustments were applied. The white triangle denotes the Gini coefficient $G^1 \approx \phi + (1 - \phi)G^*$, where ϕ is the estimate of the top 0.1 percent income share from Alvaredo (2010). The white diamond denotes the Gini coefficient $G^2 \approx \phi + (1 - \phi)G^*$, where ϕ is the estimate of the top 1 percent income share from Alvaredo, 2010. The Greater Buenos Aires household survey is taken as representative of Argentina (see chapter 5 in this volume).

survey-based results seem to indicate that inequality between those years was stable, overall inequality might have risen because the share of top incomes not captured by surveys increased substantially.[20]

This type of outcome has important implications for developing countries in which a decline in inequality has been documented over the last years, such as the ones analyzed in this book. If the top incomes ignored by surveys experience a large enough relative increase, then the true dynamics of overall inequality may display a rising trend even when survey-based estimates show the opposite result. As long as surveys do not properly record what is happening at the top of the distribution, survey-based estimates showing a decline in inequality can *at most* indicate that such a reduction is happening among *non-top individuals.*

—*India.* Results for India show that income concentration followed a U-shaped pattern over the 1922–2000 period. From 1922 to 1939, top shares increased. After a partial recovery, they shrank substantially from the 1950s to the mid-1980s but then rose again, so that today they are only slightly below what

20. As another example, figure 4-6 shows that G* declines when 2001 and 2004 are compared, while G2 remains virtually at the same level.

they were in the 1920s and 1930s. As Banerjee and Piketty (2005) explains, this U shape is broadly consistent with the evolution of economic policy in the country: although from the 1950s to the early to mid-1980s there was a period of "socialist" policies, the subsequent period, starting with the rise of Rajiv Gandhi, saw a gradual shift toward more pro-business policies. Although the initial share of the top income group was small, the fact that the rich were getting richer had a nontrivial impact on the overall income distribution. The authors argue that the gradual liberalization of the Indian economy since the 1980s did make it possible for the rich to substantially increase their share of total income. However, although in the 1980s the gains were shared by everyone in the top 1 percent, in the 1990s the big gains went only to those in the top 0.1 percent. The 1990s were also the period when the economy opened up. That suggests the possibility that the ultra-rich were able to amass most of the income gains in the 1990s because they alone were in a position to sell what world markets wanted.

That the decline in India occurred mostly during the 1950s to 1970s rather than during the interwar and World War II periods seems consistent with the interpretation posited by Piketty (2003) and Piketty and Saez (2003): the shocks induced by the Great Depression of the 1930s and World War II were less severe in India, whereas tax progressivity was extremely high during the 1950s through the 1970s. Available data do seem to indicate that the fall in top shares was due primarily to a fall in top capital incomes. The rise in top Indian incomes during the recent period was not due to the revival in top capital incomes, but top wages did play a key role.

—*Indonesia*. The results for Indonesia are based on Leigh and van der Eng (2010). There was an increase in the top 1 percent income share between 1921 and 1933, possibly caused by adverse changes in markets for agricultural commodities (such as copra and rubber) that affected farm incomes. The data subsequently display a four-decade break until the early 1980s. For the years 1982–2004, a period of high economic growth, the authors find that the income share of the top 5 percent was lower than in the early 1930s. While the top 10 percent increased only slightly over the 1982–2004 period, a more marked increase can be observed in the top 1 percent share. Notably, the sharp economic contraction during 1997–98 was associated with a rise in the share of the very richest groups (top 1 percent and above) but with little change in the top 10 to 1 percent share. The rise in the top 1 percent share in the late 1990s coincided with a fall in average per capita GDP, suggesting that part of the explanation may have been that the top 1 percent was better able to withstand the 1997–98 economic downturn and its aftermath than the bottom 99 percent. During 1996–2001, rapid inflation and currency depreciation eroded wage incomes in different sectors. Until the consequences of the crisis subsided after 2001, wages in private enterprises that were not heavily affected by the crisis (for example, export sectors that used domestic inputs, such as agricultural exports) may have experienced a faster upward adjustment than wages in the public sector and in private enterprises that were affected by the crisis (particularly the manufacturing export sector, which depended on imported inputs).

—*Singapore.* The results for Singapore cover the end of the colonial period and the subsequent political upheaval. Atkinson (2010) finds that no political transitions appear to be associated with changes in top shares. Interestingly, the evolution of the upper part of the income distribution cannot be linked very directly to the rapid structural changes in the economy, to the shifts in development policy, or to the different phases of real wage growth. Over a 30-year period there was broad stability of the very top income shares. Atkinson (2010) finds that "it is indeed remarkable that an economy whose labor market flexibility has been widely commended should have exhibited distributional stability from the 1960s to the late 1980s." After the Asian financial crisis of 1997–98, top income shares rose substantially, around 50 percent. By 2005, top shares were comparable with those in the commodities boom at the start of the 1950s.

The Drop in Income Concentration until 1945: Market Forces and Historical Factors

The fact that before 1945 the drop in income inequality is due solely to the fall in top capital incomes and that it took place mostly during wartime, the stock market crash, and the Great Depression suggests an obvious explanation: for the most part, income inequality dropped because capital owners were hurt by major shocks to their capital holdings (destruction, inflation, bankruptcy, the way that war debts were financed). That is confirmed by the very peculiar timing of the fall: top capital incomes and inequality at large did not start falling until World War I. The labor market and the rural-urban migration process played no role: low-wage rural workers slowly disappeared, but they were replaced by low-wage urban workers at the bottom of the distribution, so that overall wage inequality hardly changed. The idea that capital owners incurred large shocks and that those shocks had a big impact on income distribution is not new; Kuznets (1955) mentions that factor. What is new is that there is not much else going on. The decline in income inequality that took place during the first half of the century was mostly accidental.

Kuznets did stress in his 1955 article the key role played by wars, inflation, recessions, and the rise of progressive taxation, though that is not the part of the explanation that most economists chose to remember. It was only at the end of his presidential address to the 1954 annual meeting of the American Economic Association that he suggested that an additional process (based on the two-sector model) might also have played a role. Kuznets was fully aware that he had no empirical support favoring that interpretation: "This is perhaps 5 percent empirical information and 95 percent speculation, some of it tainted by wishful thinking."[21] As he himself put

---

21. Kuznets (1955, p. 26).

it quite bluntly, what was at the stake in the 1950s was nothing but "the future prospect of the underdeveloped countries within the orbit of the free world."[22] To a large extent, the optimistic theory of the inverse-U curve is the product of the cold war.

It is interesting to note that the structural decline of capital concentration that took place between 1914 and 1945 in developed countries does not seem to have had a negative impact on their growth. On the contrary, per capita growth rates have been substantially higher in the postwar period than during the nineteenth century and all the more so in countries such as France and Germany. That is consistent with the theory of capital market imperfections: in the presence of credit constraints, excessive wealth inequality entails negative consequences for social mobility and growth. There are good reasons to believe that the 1914–45 shocks allowed new generations of entrepreneurs to replace old-style capitalist dynasties at a faster pace than would have otherwise been the case. High capital concentration was not a prerequisite for growth.

State Action: The Role of Progressive Taxation in the Post–World War II Period

A greater challenge is explaining the nonrecovery of top capital incomes during the period after 1945. Here the proposed explanation is that the 1914–45 shocks had a permanent impact because the introduction of high income and estate tax progressivity (there was virtually no tax progressivity prior to 1914, and top rates increased enormously between 1914 and 1945) made it impossible for top capital holders to fully recover. Simple simulations suggest that the long-run impact of tax progressivity on wealth concentration is indeed large enough to explain the observed changes.[23]

In all countries for which we have data, the secular decline in income inequality took place for the most part during the 1914–45 period and most of the decline was due to the fall of top capital incomes. The 1914–45 drop was larger in countries that were hard hit by the war (France and Germany) than in the United States, and there was no drop at all in neutral countries (such as Switzerland), which is consistent with the proposed explanation based on capital shocks. Moreover, wealth concentration seems to have recovered better during the postwar period in countries with less tax progressivity (especially estate tax progressivity), such as Germany, which again seems broadly consistent with the tax explanation. How can we account for the fact that large fortunes never recovered from

22. Kuznets (1955, p. 24).

23. Piketty (2003). The progressive taxation system as the explanation for observed changes in income and wealth concentration was already mentioned by Lampman (1962) and Kuznets (1955). For the United States, DeLong (1998) also stresses the potential of the antitrust law, more loosely enforced before 1929 and after 1980.

the 1914–45 shocks, while smaller fortunes recovered perfectly well? The large fortunes that generated the top capital incomes observed at the beginning of the twentieth century were accumulated during the nineteenth century, at a time when progressive taxation did not exist and capitalists could use almost the totality of their pre-tax income to consume and accumulate. Most of the analyzed countries started to adopt very progressive income and inheritance tax structures during the interwar years, with top marginal rates often in excess of 75 percent. During the decades following World War II, those rates remained extremely high. In the United States, the top marginal rate was 91 percent up to 1963. The high marginal rates affected only a small fraction of individuals, but the point is that to a large extent they were designed to hit the top 1 percent of the income distribution and even more so the top 0.1 percent and 0.01 percent—that is, the incomes that relied primarily on capital income and capital accumulation.[24]

Before the creation of a progressive income tax in 1914, personal taxation in France relied on individual characteristics such as housing rents, the number of doors and windows in a structure, and so forth. Effective tax rates were roughly proportional and never exceeded 3 to 4 percent.[25] An inheritance tax did exist during the nineteenth century, but it was purely proportional and the rate was very low: 1 percent. In France the top marginal rate of the income tax was set to only 2 percent in 1915, but it quickly reached very high levels (above 60 percent) during the interwar period, and it stabilized around 60 to 70 percent after 1945. Effective average tax rates have always been fairly moderate, at the level of the P90-95 fractile: less than 1 percent during the interwar period and between 5 percent and 10 percent since World War II. In contrast, effective average tax rates borne by fractile P99.99-100 reached 30 percent during the interwar period and have stabilized at around 40 to 50 percent since World War II, as shown in figure 4-7.[26] It therefore would not be surprising if progressive taxation had a substantial impact on capital accumulation at the very top and a negligible impact for smaller fortunes.

24. In Latin America the establishment of the income tax was generally a policy response to negative outcomes in the state budget. It was enforced during the 1920s in Mexico, Chile, and Brazil and in the 1930s in Argentina, when public revenues (mainly based on tariffs) were severely hit by the world crisis. Nevertheless, historically the number of individuals filing for the income tax has been rather low. Latin American countries show a clear preference for nonpersonal taxation. For example, in 1932 in Argentina, international trade–based taxes accounted for 41 percent of total tax revenues while the income tax represented 6 percent; in 2000 the income tax from personal files represented 4 percent and the sales tax, 52 percent. In Spain in 2000, the income tax and the VAT (value-added tax) each accounted for 35 percent of total taxes collected. It is worth recalling the negative effect that high inflation (pervasive in Latin America during several decades) has had on income tax collections through the Olivera-Tanzi effect. See Olivera (1967) and Tanzi (1978).

25. Piketty (2001).

26. Estimates of marginal tax rates for some of the countries under study can be found in Atkinson and Piketty (2007a and 2010). The large year-to-year variations of tax rates displayed in figure 4-7, especially for top incomes, show how chaotic the history of the income tax can be. For instance, the 1968 and 1981 spikes correspond to the large increases in taxes on the rich that occurred in the aftermath of the 1968 general strike and the 1981 socialist victory. A detailed historical account can be found in Piketty (2001). As

Figure 4-7. Effective Average Income Tax Rates in France, 1915–1998

Percent

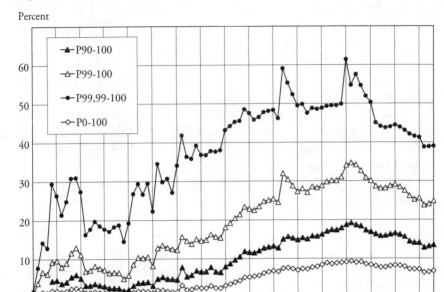

Source: Piketty (2001).

In the United States, top tax rates were very high from the end of World War I to the early 1920s and continuously from 1932 to the mid-1980s. Moreover, the United States imposed a sharply progressive estate tax after 1916 and a substantial corporate income tax after World War II. Those very high marginal tax rates applied only to a very small fraction of taxpayers but created a substantial burden on the very top income groups, whose wealth was composed primarily of capital income. In contrast to progressive labor income taxation, which simply produces a level effect on earnings through labor supply responses, progressive taxation of capital income has cumulative or dynamic effects because it reduces the net return on wealth, which generates tomorrow's wealth.

The case of Switzerland, which did not experienced the shocks of the two world wars and never established a very progressive tax structure, offers a test of this hypothesis and provides some credence to the tax progressivity explanation. In Switzerland, the majority of income taxes are levied at the local level. Probably due to fiscal competition and mobility across counties, taxes have a relatively flat

---

another example, the Second Republic established the first personal income tax in Spain in 1932 with the explicit aim of targeting high incomes. However, the marginal rates were initially rather low, although they increased during the Franco years. The number of taxpayers was extremely limited. Only after its return to democracy did Spain succeed in enforcing a modern income tax, which it has had since 1978.

rate structure with low marginal rates. The federal income and wealth tax rate has been only modestly progressive, with very low top rates. Thus, over the twentieth century, the average tax rate on the capital income of the wealthy has been much lower in Switzerland than in the other developed countries. Dell, Piketty, and Saez (2007) shows that top wealth and income shares fell during the Great Depression and the world wars—when Switzerland did increase taxes to build up defense and discourage attack—but less than in other countries. Most important, top wealth and income shares fully recovered from those shocks in the post–World War II period. Consequently, Switzerland is the only case among developed economies to display the same concentration of wealth and income in the decades following World War II as in the early part of the twentieth century.

Needless to say, that is not sufficient to prove in a rigorous way that the dynamic effects of progressive taxation on capital accumulation and pre-tax income inequality are of the "right" quantitative magnitude to account for the observed facts. We would need to know more about the saving rate of capitalists, how their accumulation strategies have changed since 1945, and so forth. Note, however, that it is not unreasonable to assume that the owners of large fortunes, whose pre-tax incomes and lifestyles were already severely hit by the 1914–45 shocks, were not willing to reduce their consumption down to very low levels and to increase their savings in order to counteract the rise in tax rates.[27]

In fact, in most standard economic models of capital accumulation, the behavioral response tends to amplify, not to counteract, the rise in tax rates. That is, a rise in tax rates imposed on very top incomes leads wealthy taxpayers to increase their consumption and to reduce their savings. In the Barro-Becker dynastic model of capital accumulation, that behavioral response is so significant that large fortunes completely disappear in the long run. Progressive taxation leads to truncated wealth distribution in the long run, in the sense that there is nobody above the top marginal rate threshold. In less extreme and more realistic models of capital accumulation, the impact of progressive taxation is smaller and large fortunes remain, but the impact is still substantial. For instance, simple computations show that a capitalist will deplete her wealth at a very high rate if she maintains the same pattern of consumption after progressive taxation is introduced. In the absence of taxation (say, before World War I), the capital stock of a capitalist consuming each year the full return to her capital stock (say 5 percent) is stationary. But if an effective tax rate of 30 percent is suddenly introduced (say, in the interwar period) and this capitalist keeps consuming the full before-tax return, then she will need to consume some of her capital stock each year. In that case, 18 percent of the initial capital stock is destroyed after ten years, 42 percent after twenty years, and so on—until, after 35 years, there is no capital left. The mechanism is

27. Existing evidence shows that the negative shocks incurred between 1914 and 1945 and the rise in progressive taxation induced French wealthy families to reduce drastically their savings rate between 1873–1913 and 1946–1953, according to Perrot (1961).

Table 4-2. *Impact of Progressive Taxation on Capital Accumulation*[a]

Percent

	$r = 5$ $t = 0$	$r = 5$ $t = 30$	$r = 5$ $t = 50$	$r = 10$ $t = 0$	$r = 10$ $t = 30$	$r = 10$ $t = 50$
$c = 100$	1.0	0.0	0.0	1.0	0.0	0.0
$c = 80$	3.1	0.3	0.0	24.3	0.0	0.0
$c = 60$	5.2	1.7	0.5	47.6	5.1	0.0
$c = 40$	7.3	3.0	1.5	70.8	13.2	3.1
$c = 20$	9.4	4.3	2.5	94.1	21.3	7.3
$c = 0$	11.5	5.6	3.4	117.4	29.5	11.5

Source: Authors' calculations.

a. The table reads as follows. Assume that a capitalist's consumption level is equal to a fixed fraction c (say $c = 20$ percent) of the full return r (say $r = 5$ percent) to his capital stock; in the absence of taxation ($t = 0$ percent) his capital stock will be multiplied by 9.4 after 50 years. Under a tax rate of $t = 50$ percent, his capital stock will be multiplied by 2.5 in 50 years. We assume that the capitalist keeps the same absolute consumption level over the 50 years. The formula is given by $x(n) = c/(1-t)+[1 + (1-t)r]^n \times [1 - c/(1-t)]$.

trivial, but it is reasonable to think that it did contribute to amplifying the shocks incurred by capital owners during the 1914–45 period.

Consider now the more interesting case of a capitalist (or a would-be capitalist) in 1945, and assume that this capitalist is ready to devote a large fraction of her income to capital accumulation. How much can she accumulate in 50 years? The point is that progressive taxation drastically reduces the assets that one can accumulate, including those of capitalists with low living standards (see table 4-2). For instance, with a 5 percent before-tax return rate and a consumption level equal to 40 percent of the before-tax return to the initial capital stock, in 50 years one can accumulate a fortune that is about 5 times as large with a 0 percent tax rate as with a 50 percent tax rate. That is, the initial capital stock is multiplied by 7.3 after 50 years in the absence of taxation, while it is multiplied by 1.5 with a tax rate of 50 percent. The tax rate of 50 percent corresponds approximately to the average effective tax rates faced by fractile P99.99-100 in France since World War II, and the factor of 5 corresponds approximately to the secular decline in the income share of fractile P99.99-100.

These simple simulations do not take into account the impact of the progressive inheritance tax. It should be stressed, nevertheless, that the long-run impact of the progressive inheritance tax on capital accumulation, though important, is probably less drastic than the impact of the progressive income tax. The reason is straightforward: the income tax applies every year and has cumulative effects; an effective tax rate of 50 percent can reduce the size of a fortune by a factor of 5 in 50 years. In contrast, assuming that the inheritance tax is paid once every 50 years, an effective inheritance tax rate of 50 percent reduces the fortune by a factor of 2.

Finally, it is worth emphasizing that it is not easy to find convincing explanations other than the introduction of progressive taxation that can account for the nonrecovery of large fortunes. For instance, explanations based on hypothetical changes in before-tax returns to capital do not seem to work. All capital holders should have been hit by a reduction in returns to before-tax assets. The point is that large fortunes were unable to recover from the 1914–45 shocks, while smaller fortunes recovered perfectly well. We need an explanation that applies to the top of the distribution and nowhere else.

The History since the 1970s: Technological Change versus Institutions

During the post-1970 period, we observe a major divergence between rich countries. While top income shares have remained fairly stable in continental Europe and Japan over the past three decades, they have increased enormously in the United States and other English-speaking countries. In recent years, the rise of top income shares is due not to the revival of top capital incomes but to the very large increases in top wages, especially executive compensation. As a consequence, top executives, or the "working rich," replace top capital owners, or the "rentiers," at the top of the income hierarchy.[28]

To get a sense of magnitude of the upsurge of high incomes in recent years, consider the real income growth displayed by the top 1 percent and the bottom 99 percent, illustrated in table 4-3 for the United States. From 1993 to 2006, average real incomes grew at a 1.9 percent annual rate, or 28 percent over the thirteen-year period. However, if the top 1 percent is excluded, average real income growth is almost halved, to about 1.1 percent per year, or 15 percent over the thirteen-year period. Top 1 percent incomes grew at the much faster rate of 5.7 percent a year, or 105 percent over the thirteen-year period. Consequently, top 1 percent incomes captured about half of the overall economic growth experienced between 1993 and 2006.

A distinction can be made between the 1993–2000 period (Clinton's expansion) and the 2002–06 period (Bush's expansion).[29] During both expansions, the income of the top 1 percent grew extremely quickly, at an annual rate of more than 10.1 percent and 11.0 percent respectively. Nevertheless, while the bottom 99 percent of incomes grew at 2.4 percent a year from 1993 to 2000, they grew less than 1 percent a year from 2002 to 2006. Consequently, during the last expansion the top 1 percent captured three-quarters of all income growth. Moreover, top incomes tax rates went up in 1993, during the Clinton administration, while they went down in 2001, during the Bush administration. Those results

---

28. This is not universal; in the Nordic countries the recent rise is associated with capital incomes.
29. Saez (2008).

Table 4-3. *Real Annual Income Growth by Groups in the United States, 1993–2006*[a]

	Average income	Top 1 percent incomes	Bottom 99 percent incomes
Full period (1993–2006)	1.9	5.7	1.1
Clinton expansion (1993–2000)	3.7	10.1	2.4
Bush expansion (2002–2006)	2.8	11.0	0.9

Source: Piketty and Saez (2003) updated and Saez (2008).

a. Computations are based on family income, including realized capital gains before individual taxes. Incomes are deflated using CPI.

help explain why the dramatic growth in top incomes during the Clinton administration did not generate much public outcry while over the last two years an extraordinary amount of attention has been given to top incomes by the media and in the public debate.

Understanding why top wages have surged in English-speaking countries in recent decades but not in Europe or Japan remains a controversial question that has given rise to three broad views. First, the free market view claims that technological progress has made managerial skills more general and less firm-specific, increasing competition for the best executives from segregated within-firm markets to a single economy-wide market. While that view could account for trends in the United States, it cannot explain why executive pay has not changed in other countries, such as Japan or France, which have gone through similar technological changes. A second view claims that impediments to free markets due to labor market regulations, unions, or social norms regarding pay inequality can keep executive pay below market levels. Such impediments have been largely removed in the United States, but they still exist in Europe and Japan. Under this view, the surge in executive compensation actually represents valuable efficiency gains. Finally, a third view claims that the surge in top compensation in the United States is due to the increased ability of executives to set their own pay and extract rents at the expense of shareholders, perhaps for the same reason as in the second view. In this case, however, there might not be any associated efficiency gains.

It is very hard to explain the dramatic rise of very top wages in the Anglo-Saxon world—especially in the United States, which accounts for a disproportionate share of the rise of top incomes—on the basis of technical change alone. Between 1970 and 2000, the average real compensation of the top 100 CEOs was multiplied by a factor of more than 30, while the average wage in the U.S. economy increased by about 10 percent. Much of the evidence suggests that such a phenomenal increase in executive compensation has more to do with bad governance and lack of control (perhaps due to very dispersed capital ownership) than with the rise of CEO productivity. Investors seem to have realized that CEO compensation was out of control even before the 2008 crash.[30] It is still very difficult to understand why such levels of wage concentration are not observed in Europe. The idea that social norms are an important factor in setting pay is especially plausible for very top wages, given that it is virtually impossible for board members (as well as for economists) to measure precisely the productivity of a CEO. DiNardo, Fortin, and Lemieux argue that changes in institutions such as the minimum wage and unionization account for a large part of the increase in U.S. wage inequality from 1973 to 1992.[31] Acemoglu, Aghion, and Violante emphasize that it is possible that those changes in institutions were triggered by previous technological changes that made it impossible to sustain previous labor market arrangements.[32] It seems unlikely, however, that changes in unionization or in the minimum wage can explain the surge in very top wages. Changing social norms regarding inequality and the acceptability of very high wages might partly explain the rise in Anglo-Saxon top wage shares observed since the 1970s. It is quite telling to read in the survey by Hall and Murphy that their best explanation for the surge in stock-option compensation was that "boards and managers falsely perceive stock options to be inexpensive because of accounting and cash-flow considerations."[33]

Final Remarks

Since the mid 1950s, the Kuznets curve hypothesis has been one of the most debated issues in development economics. This theory has strong and fairly optimistic policy implications: if developing countries are patient enough and do not worry too much about the short-run social costs of development, at some point they should reach a situation in which poverty rates drop sharply while growth and inequality reduction go hand in hand. Today, the Kuznets curve is widely held to have doubled back on itself, especially in the United States and other Anglo-Saxon countries, with a period of falling inequality during the first half of the twentieth century followed by a reversal of the trend since the 1970s. It would be misleading, however, to conclude that Kuznets's hypothesis is no longer of interest, for two reasons. First, many poor and developing countries have not yet

---

30. See Bertrand and Mullainathan (2001) and Krugman (2002).
31. DiNardo, Fortin, and Lemieux (1996).
32. Acemoglu, Aghion and Violante (2001). See also Acemoglu (2002).
33. Hall and Murphy (2004). As shown in Piketty and Saez (2007), the payroll tax burden has increased substantially over the last 25 years in countries such as the United States, France, and the United Kingdom. Because very top incomes are disproportionately composed of business and capital income rather than wage income (especially in France), the overall impact of payroll taxation on tax progressivity is regressive. In France in 2005, the regressivity of the payroll tax system undoes the progressivity of the individual income tax system, so that the resulting tax system is basically flat.

passed the initial industrialization stage. Second, we need to understand why advanced economies went through an initial inverse-U curve.

The reasons why inequality declined in industrialized countries during the first half of the twentieth century do not have much to do with the optimistic process derived from Kuznets's ideas. The compression of income distribution that took place between 1914 and 1945 was due, for the most part, to specific capital shocks—on one hand, the very peculiar conditions of the Great Depression and the stock market crash; on the other, the world wars. Consequently, market forces and historical factors were the leading explanations for the observed facts before 1945. Progressive income and estate taxation likely explain to a great extent why capital concentration did not regain the high levels observed during the first part of the twentieth century. Here, public policy took the lead.

The fact that capital shocks played the leading role between 1914 and 1945 and that progressive taxation is associated with the nonrecovery of top capital incomes after the end of World War II does not imply that the technical change view of inequality dynamics has no relevance. After all, the idea that technological waves have a major impact on labor market inequality is extremely sensible. However, in practice, the impact of technology on inequality depends on a large number of factors, which vary greatly over time and across countries; they include educational institutions, labor market conditions, corporate governance, social norms, and other country-specific factors.

In addition, government policy plays an important role in shaping the dynamics of inequality. Current debates about policy reform in developing countries often focus on improving the delivery of social services, the design of market-friendly economic institutions, the effectiveness of poverty reduction programs, and the role of trade and market liberalization. Perhaps surprisingly, they rarely deal explicitly with tax reform and the need to develop modern income tax systems in those countries. That is unfortunate for at least three reasons. First, developing countries often rely excessively on highly distortionary tax instruments, such as taxes on trade or indirect taxes on specific consumer goods. Second, income taxation can help increase the tax revenues needed to finance public goods. Third, many developing countries witnessed a sharp rise in income inequality during the recent period; progressive taxation is one the least distortionary policy tools available to control the rise in inequality by redistributing the gains from growth.

References

Aarberge, R., and A. B. Atkinson. 2010. "Top Incomes in Norway." In A. B. Atkinson and T. Piketty, *Top Incomes over the Twentieth Century,* vol. 2, *A Global Perspective.* Oxford University Press.

Acemoglu, D., P. Aghion, and G. Violante. 2001. "Deunionization, Technical Change, and Inequality." CEPR Discussion Papers 2764. Washington: Center for Economic and Policy Research.

Acemoglu, D. 2002. "Technical Change, Inequality, and the Labor Market." *Journal of Economic Literature* 40, no. 1: 7–72.

Alvaredo, F. 2009. "Top Incomes and Earnings in Portugal: 1936–2005."*Explorations in Economic History* 46, no. 4: 404–17. (A longer version can be found in A. B. Atkinson and T. Piketty, *Top Incomes over the Twentieth Century,* vol. 2, *A Global Perspective.* Oxford University Press, 2010.)

————. 2010a. "The Rich in Argentina over the Twentieth Century: 1932–2004." In A. B. Atkinson and T. Piketty, *Top Incomes over the Twentieth Century,* vol. 2, *A Global Perspective.* Oxford University Press.

————. 2010b. "A Note on the Relationship between Top Income Shares and the Gini Coefficient." Unpublished paper. Department of Economics, Oxford University.

Alvaredo, F., and E. Pisano. 2010. "Top Incomes in Italy: 1974–2004." In A. B. Atkinson and T. Piketty, *Top Incomes over the Twentieth Century,* vol. 2, *A Global Perspective.* Oxford University Press.

Alvaredo, F. and E. Saez. 2009. "Income and Wealth Concentration in Spain from a Historical and Fiscal Perspective." *Journal of the European Economic Association* 7, no. 5: 1140–167. (A longer version can be found in A. B. Atkinson and T. Piketty, *Top Incomes over the Twentieth Century,* vol. 2, *A Global Perspective.* Oxford University Press, 2010.)

Atkinson, A. B. 2005. "Top Incomes in the United Kingdom over the Twentieth Century." *Journal of the Real Statistical Society* (Series A) 168, no. 2: 325–43.

————. 2007a. "Measuring Top Incomes: Methodological Issues." In A. B. Atkinson and T. Piketty, *Top Incomes over the Twentieth Century: A Contrast between European and English-Speaking Countries.* Oxford University Press.

————. 2007b. "The Distribution of Top Incomes in the United Kingdom: 1908–2000." In A. B. Atkinson and T. Piketty, *Top Incomes over the Twentieth Century: A Contrast between European and English-Speaking Countries.* Oxford University Press.

————. 2010. "Top Incomes in a Rapidly Growing Economy: Singapore." In A. B. Atkinson and T. Piketty, *Top Incomes over the Twentieth Century,* vol. 2, *A Global Perspective.* Oxford University Press.

Atkinson, A. B., and A. Harrison. 1978. *Distribution of Personal Wealth in Britain.* Cambridge University Press.

Atkinson, A. B., and A. Leigh. 2007a. "The Distribution of Top Incomes in Australia." In A. B. Atkinson and T. Piketty, *Top Incomes over the Twentieth Century: A Contrast between European and English-Speaking Countries.* Oxford University Press.

————. 2007b. "The Distribution of Top Incomes in New Zealand." In A. B. Atkinson and T. Piketty, *Top Incomes over the Twentieth Century: A Contrast between European and English-Speaking Countries.* Oxford University Press.

————. 2008. "Top Incomes in New Zealand: 1921–2005: Understanding the Effects of Marginal Tax Rates, Migration Threat, and the Macroeconomy." *Review of Income and Wealth* 54, no. 2: 149–65.

Atkinson, A. B., and T. Piketty. 2007a. *Top Incomes over the Twentieth Century: A Contrast between European and English-Speaking Countries.* Oxford University Press.

————. 2007b. "Towards a Unified Data Set on Top Incomes." In A. B. Atkinson and T. Piketty, *Top Incomes over the Twentieth Century: A Contrast between European and English-Speaking Countries.* Oxford University Press.

————. 2010. *Top Incomes over the Twentieth Century,* vol. 2, *A Global Perspective.* Oxford University Press.

Atkinson, A., T. Piketty, and E. Saez. 2009. "Top Incomes in the Long Run of History." Working Paper 15408. Cambridge, Mass: National Bureau of Economic Research.

Banerjee, A., and T. Piketty. 2005. "Top Indian Incomes: 1922–2000." *World Bank Economic Review* 19, no.1: 1–20.

Bertrand, M., and S. Mullainathan. 2001. "Are CEOs Rewarded For Luck? The Ones without Principals Are." *Quarterly Journal of Economics* 116, no. 3: 901–32.

Burkhauser, R., and others. 2009. "Recent Trends in Top Income Shares in the USA: Reconciling Estimates from March CPS and IRS Tax Return Data." Working Paper 15320. Cambridge, Mass.: National Bureau of Economic Research.

Dell, F., T. Piketty, and E. Saez. 2007. "Income and Wealth Concentration in Switzerland over the Twentieth Century." In A. B. Atkinson and T. Piketty, *Top Incomes over the Twentieth Century: A Contrast between European and English-Speaking Countries.* Oxford University Press.

Dell, F. 2007. "Top Incomes in Germany throughout the Twentieth Century: 1898–1998." In A. B. Atkinson and T. Piketty, *Top Incomes over the Twentieth Century: A Contrast between European and English-Speaking Countries.* Oxford University Press.

DeLong, B. 1998. "Robber Barons." Unpublished paper. Department of Economics, University of California–Berkeley.

DiNardo, J., N. Fortin, and T. Lemieux. 1996. "Labor Market Institutions and the Distribution of Wages, 1973–1992: A Semiparametric Approach." *Econometrica* 64, no. 5: 1001–44.

Feenberg, D., and J. Poterba. 1993. "Income Inequality and the Incomes of Very High Income Taxpayers: Evidence from Tax Returns." In *Tax Policy and the Economy,* vol. 7, edited by Poterba, pp. 145–77. MIT Press.

Guilera, J. 2008. "Top Income Shares in Portugal over the Twentieth Century."Document de Treball de la Facultat de Ciènces Econòmiques i Empresarials E08/195. Universitat de Barcelona.

Hall, B., and K. Murphy. 2004. "The Trouble with Stock Options." *Journal of Economic Perspectives* 17, no. 3: 49–70.

Jäntti, M., and others. 2010. "Trends in Top Income Shares in Finland." In A. B. Atkinson and T. Piketty, *Top Incomes over the Twentieth Century,* vol. 2, *A Global Perspective.* Oxford University Press.

Kopczuk, W., and E. Saez. 2004. "Top Wealth Shares in the United States, 1916–2000: Evidence from Estate Tax Returns." *National Tax Journal* 57, no. 2: 445–87.

Krugman, P. 2002. "For Richer." *New York Times* (October 20).

Kuznets, S. 1953. *Shares of Upper-Income Groups in Income and Savings.* NewYork: National Bureau of Economic Research.

———. 1955. "Economic Growth and Income Inequality." *American Economic Review* 45, no. 1: 1–28.

Lampman, R. 1962. *The Share of Top-Wealth Holders in National Wealth: 1922–1956.* Princeton University Press.

Landais, C. 2007. "Les Hauts Revenus en France (1998–2006): Une Explosion des Inegalités?" Unpublished paper. Paris School of Economics.

Leigh, A., and P. van der Eng. 2010. "Top Incomes in Indonesia: 1920–2004." In A. B. Atkinson and T. Piketty, *Top Incomes over the Twentieth Century,* vol. 2, *A Global Perspective.* Oxford University Press.

Moriguchi, C., and E. Saez. 2008. "The Evolution of Income Concentration in Japan, 1886–2005: Evidence from Income Tax Statistics." *Review of Economics and Statistics* 90, no. 4: 713–34.

Nolan, B. 2007. "Long-Term Trends in Top Income Shares in Ireland." In A. B. Atkinson and T. Piketty, *Top Incomes over the Twentieth Century: A Contrast between European and English-Speaking Countries.* Oxford University Press.

Olivera, J. H. G. 1967. "Money, Prices, and Fiscal Lags: A Note on the Dynamics of Inflation." *Banca Nazionale del Lavoro Quarterly Review*, vol. 20 (September): 258–67.

Perrot, M. 1961. *Le Mode de Vie des Familles Bourgeoises: 1873–1953*. Paris: Armand Collin.

Piketty, T. 2001. *Les Hauts Revenus en France au 20eme Siècle: Inegalités et Redistributions, 1901–1998*. Paris: Éditions Grasset.

———. 2003. "Income Inequality in France: 1901–1998." *Journal of Political Economy* 111, no. 5: 1004–42.

Piketty, T., and E. Saez. 2003. "Income Inequality in the United States: 1913–1998." *Quarterly Journal of Economics* 118, no. 1: 1–39. (An updated version can be found in A. B. Atkinson and T. Piketty, *Top Incomes over the Twentieth Century: A Contrast between European and English-Speaking Countries*. Oxford University Press, 2007.)

———. 2007. "How Progressive in the U.S. Federal Tax System? A Historical and International Perspective." *Journal of Economic Perspectives* 21, no.1: 3–24.

Piketty, T. and N. Qian. 2009. "Income Inequality and Progressive Income Taxation in China and India: 1986–2015." *American Economic Journal: Applied Economics* 1, no. 2: 53–63.

Piketty, T., G. Postel-Vinay, and J. Rosenthal. 2006. "Wealth Concentration in a Developing Economy: Paris and France, 1807–1994."*American Economic Review* 96, no. 1: 236–56.

Roine, J., and D. Waldenström. 2008. "The Evolution of Top Incomes in an Egalitarian Society: Sweden 1903–2004." *Journal of Public Economics* 92, nos. 1–2: 366–87.

Saez, E. 2008. "Striking It Richer: The Evolution of Top Incomes in the United States." *Pathways Magazine* (Stanford Center for the Study of Poverty and Inequality) (Winter): 6–7. (An updated version can be found in E. Saez, unpublished paper, Department of Economics, University of California–Berkeley.)

Saez, E., and M. Veall. 2005. "The Evolution of Top Incomes in Northern America: Lessons from Canadian Evidence." *American Economic Review* 95, no. 3: 831–49. (A longer version can be found in A. B. Atkinson and T. Piketty, *Top Incomes over the Twentieth Century: A Contrast between European and English-Speaking Countries*. Oxford University Press, 2007.)

Salverda, W., and A. B. Atkinson. 2007. "Top Incomes in the Netherlands over the Twentieth Century." In A. B. Atkinson and T. Piketty, *Top Incomes over the Twentieth Century: A Contrast between European and English-Speaking Countries*. Oxford University Press.

Székely, M., and M. Hilgert. 1999. "What's behind the Inequality We Measure: An Investigation using Latin American Data." Working Paper 409. Washington: Research Department, Inter-American Development Bank.

Tanzi, V. 1978. "Inflation, Real Tax Revenues, and the Case for Inflationary Finance: Theory with an Application to Argentina." *Staff Papers IMF*, vol. 25, no. 3: 417–51.

5

A Distribution in Motion:
The Case of Argentina

LEONARDO GASPARINI AND GUILLERMO CRUCES

A ll of the available empirical evidence suggests that income inequality in Argentina substantially increased from the mid-1970s to the mid-2000s. Figure 5-1 presents a summary of this disappointing story: the Gini coefficient of the distribution of household per capita income for Greater Buenos Aires (GBA) soared from 0.344 in 1974 to 0.487 in 2006.[1] Inequality did not increase at a uniform rate over time, however. Figure 5-2 depicts short intervals of relative calm as

This is a shortened version of our paper for the UNDP project "Markets, the State, and the Dynamics of Inequality: How to Advance Inclusive Growth." This work benefited from detailed comments and suggestions by Nora Lustig and Luis Felipe López-Calva, the project directors, and from comments received at project seminars at UNDP headquarters in New York (November 2007) and at UNDP Mexico, Federal District (June 2008). We also wish to thank Alejandro Bonvecchi, Roxana Maurizio, and Martín Tetaz for their valuable input; Sebastián Etchemendy and Alberto Porto for discussions on the topics covered in this chapter's concluding remarks; and Mariellen Malloy Jewers for her excellent editorial suggestions. We are grateful to Sergio Olivieri and Gabriel Facchini (from CEDLAS) for outstanding research assistance.

1. The microdata behind the figures in this chapter come from Argentina's main official household survey, Encuesta Permanente de Hogares (EPH), which covers Argentina's major urban areas. The EPH started in the 1970s as a survey for Greater Buenos Aires, which accounts for one-third of Argentina's population. It was gradually extended, and since the early 1990s the EPH has covered all urban areas with more than 100,000 inhabitants, which represent two-thirds of Argentina's total population. The income concept used to measure inequality is monetary current per capita income. It does not include the value of imputed rent or auto-consumption or capital gains; it does include monetary transfers, both private and public. The EPH does not make explicit whether reported income is before or after taxes and social security contributions, but the authors presume that for salaried workers, income reported in the EPH is probably net of both. Income data were not adjusted for nonsampling errors, such as underreporting. The appendix of our

Figure 5-1. *Distribution of Household Per Capita Income, Greater Buenos Aires, 1974–2006*

Gini coefficient

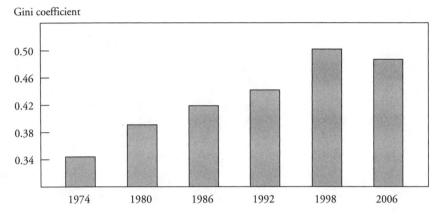

Source: Authors' calculations based on microdata from the Encuesta Permanente de Hogares (EPH) (INDEC, various years).

well as intervals of surges in inequality.[2] Although an inequality series from the mid-1970s can be estimated only for Greater Buenos Aires, which contains roughly one-third of Argentina's total population, the trends described can be extrapolated to the whole urban population. During the period from the mid-1970s to the mid-2000s, the increase in inequality in Argentina was significantly larger than increases in inequality in most other countries worldwide (Gasparini, Gutiérrez, and Tornarolli 2007). The difference between the extent of inequality in Argentina and more unequal economies, like those of Brazil, Chile or Mexico, shrank substantially in the last couple of decades. Argentina's once proud "European" income distribution, with a large middle class, had moved closer toward a "Latin American" income distribution, with high levels of inequality.[3]

companion paper (Gasparini and Cruces 2008) provides more detailed information about the methodology and coverage of the EPH.

2. This upward trend in inequality is robust to the geographic coverage of the data source, to the choice of indicator, and to methodological aspects regarding the underlying income variable. The trend also is apparent using alternative data sources. The confidence intervals for the Gini coefficient show that observed changes in inequality are, for the most part, statistically significant. Moreover, Gasparini (2005b) shows that this trend is robust to a host of methodological issues in household surveys, including nonresponse, misreporting of income, inclusion of nonmonetary income, inclusion of implicit rent from homeownership, accounting for family structure through equivalization, and adjustment for regional prices, among others. The trends also are similar when including or excluding the impact of social expenditure and taxes on household income.

3. We know that surveys underestimate top incomes. Argentina is at present the only Latin American country for which we can have an idea of the extent to which top incomes are underestimated. In chapter 4, Alvaredo and Piketty, using data from tax returns, estimate that the Gini for 2004 could have ranged between .52 and .57, depending on whether it is assumed that the top .1 percent or the top 1 percent,

Figure 5-2. *Variation in Gini Coefficient of Distribution of Household Per Capita Income and Per Capita GDP, 1974–2006*[a]

Index

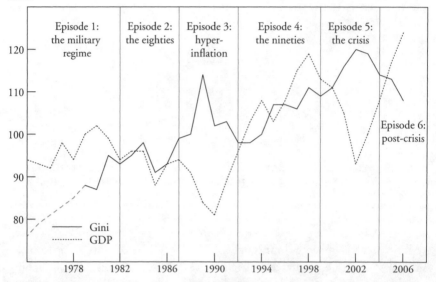

Source: Authors' calculations based on microdata from the Encuesta Permanente de Hogares (EPH) (INDEC, various years).

a. Mean index = 100.

This chapter focuses on early 1990s and the mid-2000s, a period characterized by a sharp increase in inequality until the early 2000s and a decline thereafter. The period covers two contrasting economic policy regimes. In the 1990s, Argentina went through far-reaching, market-oriented reforms in a context of weak labor market institutions and limited social protections. In the 2000s, state intervention in the economy became more pervasive, labor market institutions were stronger, and social protection schemes redistributed income to unskilled and semi-skilled workers.

The chapter begins with a presentation of the main trends in Argentina's income distribution from the mid-1970s to the mid-2000s in terms of six distinct historical episodes, then explores the changes in inequality during noncrisis years by means of microeconometric and sectoral decompositions. Next it examines the relative contribution of three major factors in Argentina's evolution of inequality—trade liberalization, technological change, and macroeconomic adjust-

---

respectively, were not included in the survey data. The survey-based Gini was estimated at .49. The trend for the series with top incomes differs slightly from that for the series based on household surveys between 2001 and 2004. While both show a declining trend, the magnitude is small or negligible in the series with top incomes (see table 4-1 in Alvaredo and Piketty).

ment—and covers other contributing factors for which empirical analysis is scarce, such as demographic factors, privatization, and unionization. The chapter then investigates the distributional impact of social spending and its financing through the tax system; examines poverty and inequality during macroeconomic crises; and analyzes the decline in inequality experienced during Argentina's economic recovery following the 2001–02 crisis.

An Episodic Story of Inequality

As stressed by Atkinson (1997), inequality changes can be analyzed from a long-term perspective or by dividing time into episodes. The episodic story of Argentina's changes in inequality seems to be more compelling than the long-term story. One reason for choosing an episodic story is that intense economic shocks and policy changes have affected Argentina's income distribution in different ways. Likewise, the logic behind Argentina's changes in inequality is different at different intervals of time. Therefore, taking a long-term perspective would miss much of the action and probably would be unhelpful in thinking about the future.

The first episode starts in 1974, since data from the Encuesta Permanente de Hogares (EPH) are available from that year onward, and the following 32 years are divided into six episodes (see table 5-1).[4] The first episode covers the years from 1974 to 1982, encompassing the last two years of a democratic government (1974–76) and an entire dictatorial military regime. The first episode is characterized by several factors: weak labor institutions, with almost no role for unions; a sweeping trade liberalization reform; and a sharp overall increase in inequality. The second episode comprises most of the 1980s (1983–87), and it is characterized by other factors: the return to democratic rule; a substantially more closed economy; increased union activity and stronger labor institutions (minimum wage enforcement, collective bargaining); macroeconomic instability; and a rather stable income distribution. The third episode (1988–91) corresponds to the macroeconomic crisis of the late 1980s, which included two hyperinflations. This episode is characterized by a sharp increase and a subsequent sudden fall in inequality after the economy stabilized in 1991. The fourth episode, which includes most of the 1990s (1992–99), is characterized by several factors: relative macroeconomic stability;[5] a currency board with an exchange rate fixed to the

4. In March 1976, by means of a coup d'état, a military regime came into power. Although, arguably, the first episode should start at that point, information from the EPH is available first for 1974, and then from 1980 onward. Episode 1 thus starts in 1974, although most of the observed distributional changes are attributed to developments under the military regime.

5. This stability refers mainly to the curbing of inflation, which was linked to the fixed exchange rate regime (currency board) set in place in 1991. The opening of the economy to capital flows implied a high degree of exposure to international fluctuations and to flow reversals, as witnessed by the impact of the successive crises in Mexico, Southeast Asia, Russia, and Brazil. See the discussion of macroeconomic crises below for more details.

Table 5-1. *Episodes*

Factor	Episode 1 Military regime 1974–82	Episode 2 The 1980s 1983–87	Episode 3 Hyperinflation 1988–91	Episode 4 The 1990s 1992–99	Episode 5 The crisis 2000–04	Episode 6 Post-crisis 2005–06
Macro situation	Low growth and crisis	Stagnation	Crisis and recovery	Growth	Crisis and recovery	Growth
Import competition	High (not always)	Low		High		Low
Technological change	Low	Low		High		Moderate
Labor institutions	Weak	Strong		Weak		Strong
Social protection (cash)	Low	Low	Low	Low	High since 2002	Moderate
Inequality	Increase	Stable	Increase and fall	Increase	Increase and fall	Fall
Poverty	Stable	Increase	Increase and fall	Increase	Increase and fall	Fall

Source: Authors' assessment.

U.S. dollar; deep structural reforms, which implied a much more open and flexible economy; and weaker labor institutions. Finally, in the fourth episode, the income distribution during the 1990s became substantially more unequal than it ever had been in Argentina's history. The fifth episode, covering the period from 2000 to 2004, includes the deep macroeconomic crisis of 2001–02, which was followed by an economic meltdown and the devaluation of the currency. The fifth episode, similar to the fourth, is characterized by a sharp increase in inequality and a subsequent substantial decline in inequality after economic stabilization. The sixth episode, under way at the time of writing, started around 2005 with rapid growth in the aftermath of the macroeconomic crisis of 2001–02. This episode's main characteristics include the adjustment of economic agents to the new relative prices introduced by Argentina's currency devaluation in 2002, stronger labor institutions, and a more extensive safety net than in prior episodes. Inequality fell to precrisis levels during this episode. Figure 5-2 reproduces the pattern of the Gini coefficients and GDP per capita marking the six episodes.[6]

Like any other modeling exercise, the episodic story tries to highlight the main aspects of a very complex stream of phenomena.[7] Table 5-1 characterizes the episodes in terms of five elements: macroeconomic situation; import competition; technological change and physical capital accumulation; unions and labor institutions; and social protection. Naturally, changes in Argentina's income distribution are the result of a vast array of factors, so any simple classification excludes potentially relevant explanations. The five elements in table 5-1 were chosen because they have two important qualities in common: according to theory, they are closely linked to changes in income distribution, and they have been extensively reviewed in the distributional literature on Argentina.

The six proposed episodes can be classified into three types: type-1 episodes, distinguished by serious macroeconomic crisis (episodes three and five); type-2 episodes, distinguished by liberalization with weak labor institutions (episodes one and four); and type-3 episodes, distinguished by low import penetration and stronger labor institutions (episodes two and six). Inequality seems to have fluctuated widely in type-1 episodes, increased in a rather permanent way in type-2 episodes, and decreased or remained stable in type-3 episodes.

A word of caution is necessary before proceeding with the analysis. It is not easy to derive policy conclusions even from this stylized story, since it is very difficult

6. In chapter 3 of this volume, James Robinson discusses how the dynamics of income distribution in Argentina over the entire twentieth century are closely related to movements backward and forward between authoritarian and democratic regimes. While the type of regime undoubtedly influenced the dynamics of inequality in particular through the weakening or strengthening of labor unions, the relationship is not a one-to-one relationship by far. Robinson also notes that in Argentina there have been episodes in which inequality increased under democratic rule.

7. This episodic review is necessarily simplified, and some aspects, in particular the limits between episodes, are somewhat arbitrary. The reader is referred to Gerchunoff and Llach (2004) and the references therein for a complete account of the period under discussion.

to assess the long-run general equilibrium effects of policies. For example, a given combination of policies or circumstances may be associated with low inequality and poverty in the short run but might contribute substantially to a future crisis in which all the distributional improvements are undone. In that sense, the above classification and the analysis that follows are mostly descriptive.

Exploring the Proximate Determinants of Inequality Changes

Examining only noncrisis years allows one to assess the relevance of proximate factors—that is, not to take into account behavioral changes—in Argentina's inequality trend. We begin by showing the results of a microdecomposition that highlights the main factors contributing to the increase in inequality from 1992 to 1998. Next, we present evidence of a widening gap between the wages of skilled workers and those of unskilled workers, which is a key factor in the surge in inequality. We end with an assessment of the impact of labor supply and sectoral changes on the wage gap.

Microdecomposition Exercises

The first exercise consists of a microeconometric decomposition of the changes in the Gini coefficient for the distribution of hourly wages, earnings, and household income. The methodology closely follows that of Gasparini, Marchionni, and Sosa Escudero (2004). The basic idea of the microsimulations is to find the counterfactual distribution of individual earnings that would be generated in a given period t_1 if some of the determinants of earnings took the observed values in t_2 and the rest remained at their values in t_1. The difference between the real distribution in time t_1 and the counterfactual distribution in time t_2 is equal to the distributional impact of the factors modified in the simulation.[8] By modeling the determinant of wages and hours worked, the microsimulations incorporate behavioral factors into the analysis, at the cost of sometimes having substantial unexplained residuals.

Table 5-2 presents the results for Greater Buenos Aires, which is the only region for which data that go back to 1980 are available.[9] The table shows the impact of six counterfactual exercises on the distribution of hourly wages, earnings, and household income. The simulations include changes in the returns to education in terms of hourly wages; the returns to education in terms of hours worked; the gender wage gap; the distribution of unobservable factors (for example, ability, connections, quality of education); the determinants of employment; and the distribution of education. For each period, table 5-2 reports the actual

8. Since the outcomes are path-dependent, the tables corresponding to the microsimulations report the mean of the results obtained by changing the base year in each simulation.

9. It is difficult to extend the microsimulation to 1974, since the data set for that year includes fewer variables.

change in the Gini coefficient, along with six counterfactual changes corresponding to various simulated effects. For example, column 2 shows the change in the
Gini resulting from changing only the returns to education in terms of hourly
wages (that is, the coefficients of the educational dummies in the hourly wage
equation), keeping everything else constant. The change in the coefficients of the
educational dummies in the hourly wage equation has a direct effect on the counterfactual distribution of hourly wages. Naturally, changing the educational dummies' coefficients also affects earnings and hence equivalized income.

Inequality in hourly wages and earnings diminished in the 1980s (ignoring the
macroeconomic crisis of the late 1980s), driven by a fall in the returns to education in terms of hourly wages. In contrast, during the 1990s the returns to education in terms of hourly wages contributed to higher inequality in hourly wages
and earnings. From 1992–98 the overall effect of the returns to education on the
distribution of hourly wages and earnings accounted for 4.6 points of the
8.4 point increase in the Gini for the equivalized household income distribution
from 1992–98. In addition, unobservable factors were responsible for 1.5 points
of the increase in the Gini. Those results suggest that unskilled workers—both in
terms of formal education and in terms of unobservable factors—lost relatively
more than skilled workers in terms of hourly wages and hours of work during the
1990s. Any story of inequality changes in Argentina should pay particular attention to that phenomenon.

The decomposition can also shed some light on the debate on the contribution of unemployment to the surge in inequality. The increase in inequality in the
1990s occurred simultaneously with unprecedented growth in unemployment.
The unemployment rate rose substantially—from around 3 percent in the 1970s
to 15 percent in the late 1990s—in years of relative macroeconomic stability.
According to figure 5-3, the labor market was rather quiet until the 1990s, when
two combined phenomena generated a shock to the unemployment rate: a significant increase in the labor participation rate (from 40 percent in 1990 to
46 percent in 1999) and a fall in the employment rate driven by the macroeconomic shocks and the adjustments after various structural changes. Nonetheless,
by the end of the 1990s the employment rate recovered, meaning that most of the
increase in unemployment rate can be accounted for by the large increase in labor
market participation. Women and youths joined the labor market in large numbers but faced an economy with a rigid employment rate.

When unemployment is mostly a consequence of increased labor market participation instead of falling employment, its effect on inequality or poverty is less
obvious. For instance, if a youth enters the labor force but is unable to find a job,
the unemployment rate goes up but the income distribution remains unchanged.
The direct distributional impact of employment issues can be assessed by means
of counterfactual distributions derived from changing the coefficients of the variables in a labor participation equation. As reported in column 6 of table 5-2, this

Table 5-2. Changes in the Gini Coefficient between periods, Actual and Simulated

Period	Actual change (1)	Returns to education on		Gender wage gap (4)	Unobservables (5)	Employment (6)	Education (7)	Rest (8)
		Wages (2)	Hours worked (3)					
1980–86								
Hourly wages	-1.5	-2.2		0.7	-2.8		1.1	1.7
Earnings	0.7	-1.4	0.0	1.0	-1.6	0.2	1.3	1.3
Equivalized income	3.1	-2.1	0.5	0.0	-1.6	-0.1	0.6	5.7
1986–92								
Hourly wages	-2.5	-1.6		-0.6	0.5		0.0	-0.8
Earnings	-1.7	-1.1	-0.4	-1.1	0.5	0.0	0.0	0.4
Equivalized income	0.7	0.9	-1.0	0.1	0.4	0.0	0.1	0.0
1992–98								
Hourly wages	5.5	3.0		-0.4	2.6		0.8	-0.5
Earnings	7.1	2.3	2.5	-0.5	1.8	-0.1	0.8	0.1
Equivalized income	8.4	2.7	1.9	0.0	1.5	0.2	0.7	1.4
1998–2006								
Hourly wages	-1.1	0.2		0.1	0.6		0.6	-2.6
Earnings	-1.5	0.1	-1.0	0.3	0.3	0.3	0.6	-2.0
Equivalized income	-1.7	-0.9	0.1	-0.2	0.3	-0.2	0.5	-1.4

Source: Authors' calculations based on microdata from the Encuesta Permanente de Hogares (EPH) (INDEC, various years).

Figure 5-3. *Labor Market Indicators*

Percent

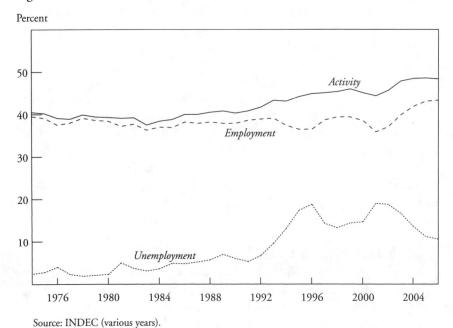

Source: INDEC (various years).

employment effect has been small, even during the years of increasing unemployment (1992–98). As discussed, this exercise provides just an estimate of the *direct* effect of changes in the extensive margin of the labor market; we elaborate on the possible indirect effects of a higher unemployment rate on wages later in the chapter.

Supply Factors

In a typical simple equilibrium model, the wage gap between skilled and unskilled workers is driven by changes in their relative supply and demand. The evidence reveals a strong increase in the relative supply of semi-skilled (high school graduates) and skilled (college graduates) workers, compared with unskilled workers (those with less than a high school degree). While 78.6 percent of adults aged 20 to 65 years were unskilled in GBA in 1974, that share fell significantly, to 47.1 percent, in 2006. In contrast, from 1974 to 2006 semi-skilled workers' share of adults aged 20 to 65 years in GBA climbed from 17.6 percent to 37 percent and skilled workers' share grew from 3.8 percent to 15.9 percent. Those patterns are valid for all urban areas in Argentina. Furthermore, the increases in semi-skilled and skilled workers are even more pronounced when the share in employment or in aggregate labor (total weighted hours of worked) is considered.

Given the strong increase in the relative supply of college graduates, the wage premium would have been bound to fall if factor demand had not changed. In fact, that appears to have happened in the 1980s, though not in the 1990s, when the college wage premium jumped instead. That suggests an increase in the demand for skilled workers (especially for college graduates), which more than offset the downward pressure from the increased supply of skilled workers.

Sectoral Changes

Argentina's economy experienced large changes in its productive and employment structure over the period under study (1974–2006). The most noticeable change in the labor structure since the 1970s has been the fall in employment in the manufacturing industry and the increase in skilled services (public sector as well as professional and business services). From 1974 to 2006, employment in manufacturing industries dropped from 39 percent to just 17 percent. On the other hand, the share of employment in the more skill-intensive sectors of professional and business services and the government increased from 21 percent in 1974 to 41 percent in 2006. Those trends do not vary substantially when the population of workers is divided by skill level.

With skilled-biased technological change, the increase in the stock of more educated workers can be easily absorbed in each sector. In contrast, with constant production technologies, increases in skilled labor can be absorbed by either the relative growth of skilled-labor-intensive sectors, with no changes in the intensity of factor use, or an increase in the use of skilled workers in unskilled tasks. The evidence presented in our companion paper (Gasparini and Cruces 2008) is consistent with Argentina's having experienced a strong increase in the intensity of use of skilled labor in most sectors of the economy (that is, skill-biased technological change). The skill upgrading in production processes was especially strong in basic and high-tech manufacturing sectors and also in commerce and public administration.

To further explore the potential distributional impact of changes in employment, table 5-3 presents an update of the decomposition in Gasparini (2005a) of changes in the share of each type of labor in total aggregate labor. Formally, the table reports

$$\Delta\left[\frac{N_i}{N}\right] = \underbrace{\sum_s \frac{N_{ist}}{N_{st}} \Delta\left[\frac{N_s}{N}\right]}_{\text{Between effect}} + \underbrace{\sum_s \frac{N_{st'}}{N_{t'}} \Delta\left[\frac{N_{is}}{N_s}\right]}_{\text{Within effect}},$$

where N is labor input (number of workers multiplied by efficiency hours of work), i indexes the type of labor (unskilled, semi-skilled, and skilled), s indexes the economic sectors, and t indexes time. The first term of the decomposition (the "between" effect) captures the impact of transformations in the structure of employment sectors (for example, changes in the production structure driven by

Table 5-3. *Sectoral Decomposition of Changes in Labor*

Education	1974–80	1980–86	1986–92	1992–98	1998–2006
Between effect					
Less than high school	−1.6	−0.5	−3.8	−1.9	−0.3
High school graduate	0.5	0.3	0.8	0.6	−0.2
College graduate	1.1	0.2	3.0	1.3	0.6
Within effect					
Less than high school	−2.2	−7.3	−5.6	−5.4	−6.9
High school graduate	1.8	4.4	2.0	−0.3	4.9
College graduate	0.4	2.9	3.6	5.7	2.0
Overall effect					
Less than high school	−3.8	−7.8	−9.4	−7.3	−7.3
High school graduate	2.4	4.7	2.8	0.3	4.7
College graduate	1.4	3.1	6.6	7.0	2.6

Source: Authors' calculations based on microdata from the Encuesta Permanente de Hogares (EPH) (INDEC, various years).

trade liberalization) on the relative employment of factor *i*. The second term (the "within" effect) captures changes due to variations in the intensity of use of different types of labor within each sector (for example, changes due to biased technological change).

Over time, changes across sectors benefited skilled workers primarily (and slightly benefited semi-skilled workers). The between effect for college graduates is always positive (table 5-3). In contrast, the between effect for unskilled workers is negative; they suffered from employment reallocations away from unskilled-labor-intensive sectors. The numbers in the second panel of table 5-3 suggest that the changes within sectors implied increased use of skilled labor. The highest within effect for college graduates is for the 1990s, a fact consistent with the story of capital incorporation and skilled-biased technological change after Argentina's reforms during that time. It is interesting to note that the values in the second panel are generally higher than those in the first panel, suggesting that within effects have been stronger than between effects.

Rising Inequality in the 1990s

Here we deepen the analysis of inequality changes in Argentina by studying the three main hypotheses that have been laid out in the inequality literature: trade liberalization, technological change and capital incorporation, and macroeconomic adjustment. In each case we start by sketching the main arguments linking these phenomena with inequality and then summarize the contributions that provide empirical evidence of those links.

Trade Liberalization

Although Argentina witnessed a series of reforms in almost all aspects of economic life from the mid-1970s to mid-2000s, most of the literature highlights trade liberalization as one of the key factors behind the increase in Argentina's income inequality. While that is due in part to the constraints on data availability for testing competing hypotheses, this line of research is motivated also by the salience of trade in the debate on increasing returns to skills in developed economies (Katz and Autor 1999).

The conventional wisdom in economic theory and some policy circles seemed to be that unskilled labor, a relatively abundant factor in developing economies, would benefit from trade reform and that thus inequality would fall in developing countries with increased trade liberalization (Perry and Olarreaga 2006). However, as documented in the thorough reviews in Goldberg and Pavcnik (2004, 2007), reality seldom corresponded to that "naïve view" of the equalizing impact of trade reform in developing countries. A host of reasons for the discrepancy between the naïve view and reality are described below.

In light of Argentina's status as a middle-income country and its abundance of natural resources, which are complementary to capital and skilled labor,[10] the impact of trade liberalization on inequality in Argentina was not clear-cut ex ante. However, the evidence for Argentina suggests overwhelmingly that trade liberalization led to an increase in inequality. Galiani and Sanguinetti (2003) was among the first studies to find evidence of an unequalizing effect of trade reform during the 1990s. The authors found that in those sectors in which import penetration was deeper, the wage gap between skilled and unskilled workers increased; however, this effect can explain only a minor fraction of the increase in inequality over the period. Galiani and Porto (2008) found that from 1974 to 2001, trade liberalization episodes in Argentina reduced wages on average and that reductions in industry tariffs increased the wage premium for skilled workers. Taken together, this evidence suggests that trade liberalizations increased skill premiums and thus contributed to higher overall income inequality in Argentina.

The general conclusion from the studies on the distributive impact of trade liberalization in Argentina is that more openness produced a wider gap between the wages of skilled and those of unskilled workers and thus higher levels of overall inequality. However, its impacts on the wage premium were small and can explain only a relatively small fraction of the total increase in the wage premium.

10. The relevant factors of production and trade partners that determine Argentina's relative abundance in the international trade arena is not a settled issue. Galiani and Sanguinetti (2003) argues that Argentina is abundant in unskilled labor compared with major trade partners like the United States and the European Union. Galiani and Porto (2008) highlights that Argentina is well-endowed in skills relative to the other countries in Latin America with which it trades. Cristini (1999) and Keifman (2006) consider Argentina a country abundant in land and skilled labor, while Berlinski (1994) shows specialization in natural resources and skilled labor when Argentina is compared with Brazil, its major partner within the region.

Technological Change and Capital Incorporation

A complementary explanation for the large fall in the relative demand for unskilled workers relies on the importance of skilled-biased technological change (SBTC) and capital incorporation in Argentina. Technological and organizational changes that increase the relative productivity of skilled workers translate into wider wage gaps. In addition, with labor market rigidities, those changes also translate into lower employment for unskilled workers. An increase in the use of physical capital in the production process increases inequality through two channels. First, if capital goods incorporate embedded technological change, an increase in investment in new machinery and equipment can accelerate the adoption of new technologies. Second, even without technological innovation, physical capital usually is more complementary to skilled labor, being then a source of an increasing productivity gap across workers with different education levels.

A SHOCK IN PHYSICAL CAPITAL, TECHNOLOGY, AND ORGANIZATION. For decades Argentina was a relatively closed economy with low investment rates; in the 1990s, however, a new scenario emerged. Argentina was experiencing macroeconomic stability and had instituted a set of market-oriented policies, including a massive process of privatization and deregulation, along with measures leading toward capital account liberalization. In addition, appreciation of the real exchange rate and large tariff reductions substantially reduced the relative price of physical capital and favorable international financial conditions contributed to the massive inflow of foreign capital to Argentina.

Private investment as a proportion of GDP increased 44 percent between the 1980s and the 1990s. In particular, foreign direct investment as a share of GDP increased from an average of 0.4 percent of GDP during 1970–90 to 1.6 percent in 1991–97. The physical capital stock (excluding the public sector) grew by 20 percent between 1992 and 1999, and the average age of capital stock decreased from 8.8 to 5.2 years. The rapid increase in physical capital, particularly of imported machinery and equipment, was a vehicle of technological modernization in Argentina after decades of backwardness.

The deregulation of many domestic markets and the removal of barriers to international trade forced private firms to seek the productivity gains necessary to stay in business. In addition, the increased openness of the Argentine economy occurred at a time of increasing globalization and diffusion of new communication and information technologies, inducing firms to adopt state-of-the-art production technologies. Production processes in many sectors underwent radical changes, incorporating information technology, computers, robots, and modern assembly lines within just a few years.

Changes took place not only at the production stage but also at the organizational level. The scenario described above contributed to an extraordinary transformation in the property structure of firms—from public to private, from domestic to foreign, and from small owners to large owners. The new structure favored changes toward larger production scales (for example, from small grocery stores to large supermarkets) and toward a more efficient use of production factors (for example, eliminating excess workers in the public sector).

Both technological and organizational changes implied lower relative demand for unskilled and semi-skilled workers than for skilled workers. Had those changes been adopted gradually or in the context of strong social protections, the impacts on unskilled and semi-skilled workers would have been milder. But that was not the case; the modernization of Argentina's economy took place in just a few years in the context of weak labor institutions and in the midst of labor deregulation.

THE EVIDENCE. One of the main arguments in favor of the technological change explanation is the difficulty of finding alternative plausible hypotheses to account for the co-movements of relative wages and skill intensity. As already mentioned, there was a substantial increase in the wage premium in the 1990s alongside an increase in the relative use of skilled labor across all economic sectors. Those observations are hard to reconcile with the predictions of most models that ignore skill-biased technological change.[11]

The sectoral decomposition of changes in the share of employment by educational groups described earlier in the chapter suggests that the fall in the relative employment of unskilled labor is accounted for mainly by a drop in the intensity of use of unskilled labor within all economic sectors. This "within" effect is especially relevant from 1992 to 1998, and it is consistent with the story of technological/organizational shock in the 1990s. García Swartz (1998) shares that conclusion, although the author's analysis covers just the beginning of the reforms.

The changes in the returns to education and unobservable factors documented previously are also compatible with the SBTC/capital accumulation hypothesis. First, in Argentina both the returns to education and unobserved skills increased substantially in the 1990s (and not in the 1980s), a fact that is consistent with a technological shock driving changes in both returns. Second, the change in the returns to education in Argentina implied substantial and increasing gains for college graduates compared to the rest of the population, without any clear change in the gap between unskilled and semi-skilled workers. That is compatible with a pattern in which a new technology is strongly complementary to nonroutine cognitive tasks (typical of highly skilled workers) and mostly a substitute for the routine tasks found in many traditional middle-wage jobs (like those in the manufacturing sector typical of semi-skilled or unskilled workers).

Acosta and Gasparini (2007) presents evidence for the relationship between capital accumulation and the wage structure by taking advantage of the variability of wage premiums and capital investment across industries in Argentina's man-

---

11. Explanations based on skilled workers performing unskilled tasks, which are consistent with these co-movements, are treated later in the chapter.

ufacturing sectors. The authors find that sectors that accumulated more physical capital in the 1990s were those in which the wage premium grew the most. Using a technology survey with longitudinal data, Bustos (2006) assesses the impact of trade and foreign investment on technology and skill upgrading at the firm level. The study shows that firms that upgraded technology faster also upgraded their need for skilled workers faster.

As discussed, the direct effect of trade liberalization on wage inequality seems to have been small. However, as argued above, it is likely that the profound trade and capital account liberalization process was key in fostering the rapid adoption of new technologies through various channels (see Acemoglu 2003, Atolia 2007, and Yeaple 2005).

The greater relevance of the capital/technology and trade/technology channels over the "pure" trade channel is also found in studies for other countries. Behrman, Birdsall, and Székely (2003) combines policy indices with household survey micro-data on wage differentials by schooling level for eighteen Latin American countries. The authors fail to find a significant effect of trade reform on wage differentials, but they do find an impact of the share of technology exports, which they use as a proxy for technology adoption, on wage differentials. Sánchez-Páramo and Schady (2003) reaches a similar conclusion using repeated cross-sections of household surveys for a series of Latin American countries. The authors stress an important point: although the direct effect of trade on wage inequality may be small, trade is an important mechanism for technology transmission.

Macroeconomic Adjustment

We have highlighted the relevance of the increased skill premium to wage inequality in Argentina and discussed the relevance of trade liberalization, capital incorporation, and technological change as plausible causes behind the increase in wage inequality and the ensuing increase in income inequality. Another strand of the literature sees the impact of macroeconomic adjustment and the resulting reduction in the aggregate demand for labor as a central argument for the increase in inequality in the 1990s.

That argument states that under falling aggregate demand for labor and an increasing supply of skilled workers, more educated workers take the occupations of unskilled workers, who are displaced and become either unemployed or underemployed. That adjustment reduces the mean wage of the skilled workers through a composition effect. However, at the same time, the labor market becomes even tougher for unskilled workers, who lose their jobs or work fewer hours, hence raising inequality. The higher intensity of use of skilled workers in production is then attributed to skilled workers displacing unskilled workers and not to the higher productivity of skilled labor. That argument is often linked to the concept of "credentialism": the same occupations are now performed by more qualified workers, although they have the same job description and basically the same productivity.

Maurizio (2001) finds some evidence of that phenomenon in Argentina, which the author argues was behind the increase in the educational level of the labor force in the 1990s.[12] The finding of devalued educational credentials, however, can be considered a complement to, not a substitute for, the trade, capital, and technology explanations. The question thus relies on its quantitative relevance, which might be relatively minor except for during some periods of employment contraction (for example, 1993–96).

Other studies have emphasized the link between adjustment, unemployment, and inequality by stressing macroeconomic factors rather than the credentialism hypothesis (González and Menéndez 2000; Altimir, Beccaria, and González 2002; Damill, Frenkel, and Maurizio 2003; and Beccaria 2006). However, as argued in the discussion that follows this, the *direct* distributional effect of the increased unemployment in the 1990s seems small, as it is accounted for mainly by the rise in labor market participation. The increase in unemployment may have depressed wages for the employed, especially among unskilled and semi-skilled workers, who bore the largest increase in joblessness, and that might have contributed to a higher wage premium and increased inequality. However, there is no systematic evidence on the strength of that phenomenon in Argentina.

In summary, some explanations stress the relevance of trade liberalization, technological change, and capital incorporation as the driving forces behind the increase in the relative demand for skilled labor. In contrast, the credentialism and macroeconomic adjustment arguments stress the negative impact of structural changes and the macroeconomic climate on the relative demand for unskilled labor. As argued above, the factors behind these explanations are not mutually exclusive and might even be complementary. That implies that the question of their relative merit needs to be answered empirically, although it is not easy to distinguish between the two sets of hypotheses with the data at hand.

Other Contributing Factors

Here we discuss factors that we did not cover previously, not because they are less noteworthy than the topics already presented but because data are lacking or identifying their effects is difficult. This short discussion will not do justice to these factors, but it provides some of the key references for further research.[13]

The first factor, demographic trends, had only a small impact on the income distribution. Marchionni and Gasparini (2007) develops a microdecomposition analysis that finds that a higher average number of children in middle- and low-income households in the period 1980–92 is associated with higher levels of poverty and inequality in equivalized household income. The same study shows

12. Gasparini and Cruces (2008) provides an alternative hypothesis for these findings.
13. A longer and more detailed discussion of these topics is presented in Gasparini and Cruces (2008).

that during 1992–98 household size decreased for most income groups, resulting in a small reduction in poverty and negligible effects on inequality.

Although less extensively reviewed than trade and capital account liberalization, further structural reforms occurred during the 1990s, such as privatization, decentralization, and labor deregulation. Several studies provide partial evidence of their distributive effects.

Until the beginning of the 1990s, the Argentine economy was characterized by the presence of large state-owned enterprises, especially in the utilities, oil, minerals, and financial sectors. In some sectors (especially utilities), privatization was successful in increasing efficiency and broadening service availability. However, its impact on prices means that the overall distributional effect of privatization has to be assessed on a case-by-case basis.

The main pro-poor argument in favor of privatization, the second factor, emphasizes the equalizing benefits from increased access to and supply of public services (Ennis and Pinto 2002). Galiani, Gertler, and Schargrodosky (2005) reports that during the 1990s municipalities that privatized water provision experienced a significant reduction in infant mortality rates (about 8 percent), which points to important equalizing effects in terms of welfare. On the other hand, the removal of implicit subsidies and investment finance resulting from privatization may generate higher prices for services, which could imply higher inequality. Ennis and Pinto (2002) reports that the share of a household's budget spent on telecommunications, natural gas, water, and electricity rose sharply after privatization and that the increases were significantly higher for households living below the median of the income distribution. Galiani and others (2004) argues that large efficiency gains from privatization did not translate into lower prices and that better regulation might have helped reduce prices in public utilities.

Given that most of the efficiency gains in privatized companies were achieved through layoffs, privatization also significantly affected Argentina's labor market. Privatization accounted for 13 percent of the increase in unemployment between 1987–90 and 1997. Layoffs affected as many as 67 percent of workers in the national railway company and 83 percent in Yacimientos Petrolíferos Fiscales (YPF), the state-owned oil company (Ennis and Pinto 2002). While the layoffs generated large losses for the affected workers, it is likely that they represented lower welfare losses for society as a whole. As noted in Galiani and Sturzenegger (2008), laid-off workers from YPF experienced a sharp fall in post-displacement earnings, which is compatible with the presence of rents related to employment in state-owned companies.

The decentralization of health services and secondary education (devolved from the central government to the provinces) was another important component of the 1990s reforms. Decentralization might affect human capital accumulation through health and educational outcomes; therefore, from a distributional perspective, it is related to the long-term distribution of well-being. Despite the arguments in favor of decentralization, Cetrangolo and Gatto (2002) contends that in Argentina these reforms were driven by fiscal considerations. Likewise, they were usually rushed through without ensuring that provinces had sufficient funds and administrative capacity to provide quality health and education services. Galiani, Gertler, and Schargrodsky (2008) analyzes the 1992–94 transfer from the central government to provincial authorities of responsibility for all secondary schools. The authors find positive and significant effects of decentralization on standardized tests but that gains were concentrated in richer municipalities. That implies that this specific decentralization policy increased average quality but also increased the inequality in educational outcomes.

The third factor is labor unions, another factor in the labor market that has profound distributional implications. On one hand, unions tend to compress the distribution of wages within a sector; on the other hand, they also amplify the wage differentials between covered and uncovered workers (or insiders and outsiders). The Argentine labor market has been characterized by the presence of strong, industry-wide unions that played a significant role in shaping the country's social, economic, and political outlook, mainly through their relationship with the Peronist Party. Despite the importance of unions in the Argentine economy, there is little empirical evidence of their impact on wages and income, mostly because of lack of data.[14] While consistent time-series data on union membership are not available, the evolution of union coverage and strength from 1970 to 1983 can be deduced from qualitative sources (Marshall 2002). In broad terms, Argentina's unions were only somewhat weakened by the authoritarian governments at the beginning of the 1970s, but they were greatly weakened by the 1976–83 military regime. Unions regained substantial political and formal power with Argentina's return to democratic rule in 1983. According to data on strikes, union activity increased sharply from 1984 onward (Murillo 1997; Etchemendy and Collier 2007). The figures show a high degree of union activity and volatility during the 1980s; union activity then diminished greatly from 1991 to 1995 and grew again after 2001. Moreover, union membership also declined between 1990 and 2001 (Marshall 2005). The decline in union activity coincides with reforms such as privatization, trade liberalization, and price stabilization in the 1990s, which reduced the power of unions through the dissipation of rents from inefficient state-owned enterprises, protective tariffs, and inflation-induced rents. The decline in union activity during the 1990s thus coincided with a period of rising wage inequality and with factors that, according to the evidence reviewed, contributed to the rise in wage inequality. However, there is no estimate of the impact that a decline in union activity might have had on inequality.

14. The EPH, an otherwise fine labor force survey, has never routinely collected information on union membership.

Finally, it should be noted that from the mid-1990s a new form of organization emerged, representing the "outsiders"—or in more general terms, the disenfranchised—those who traditionally did not have union or political representation. Garay (2007) describes the surge of grassroots groups of unemployed and informal workers, which played an important role in the late 1990s and in the establishment of the 2002 emergency cash transfer program, Programa Jefes y Jefas de Hogar Desocupados (PJJHD). Those organizations strengthened their power and gained political leverage, mostly through protest and through their ability to mobilize beneficiaries. By giving voice and representing the interests of those usually excluded, the groups tend to reduce their exclusion from the democratic process and thus to moderate political inequality.

The Distributional Impact of Government Social Policies

Although monetary income reported in household surveys includes some forms of monetary government transfers, the bulk of the government impact on individual well-being is ignored. In particular, the value of all in-kind subsidies, like education or health, is not included in the welfare proxy (household income) used for distributional analysis. The same is true for most of the tax system; monetary income includes only direct taxation, which has a minor role in Argentina, at least when compared with that in high-income OECD countries.

The results discussed here adjust inequality measures to account for the impact of social public policies, focusing on public benefits that are financed through general revenues and are not linked to contributions. The social policies analyzed include those concerning education, health, water, sanitation, poverty alleviation, housing, employment, and most municipal services (for example, street lighting and garbage collection).[15] Pension benefits are not included; because they are tightly linked to formal workers' contributions, the pension system is not a significant redistributive social public program. In theory, the exercise is simple: starting with the original income distribution reported in the survey, cash transfers are subtracted to get a "market" income distribution, to which the income value of in-kind social transfers is added and the burden of the tax system that finances social spending is subtracted.

The main results of the exercise are summarized in table 5-4. For spending, a higher concentration index means that more spending is directed toward higher-income people. Concentration indices for social public expenditures (SPE) are negative, indicating a mild pro-poor bias. Naturally, SPE is then progressive (column 4); the incidence of SPE is less concentrated on the rich than the income

---

15. See our companion paper (Gasparini and Cruces 2008) for details on the methodology and sources of information.

Table 5-4. *Distributional Impact of Social Spending and Taxes*

| | Concentration index | | | Kakwani progressivity index | | | | | |
	SPE (1)	Taxes (2)	Gini-pre (3)	SPE (3) – (1) (4)	Taxes (2) – (3) (5)	Total (4) + (5) (6)	SPE/DI[a] (7)	Redistributive impact (6) * (7) (8)	Gini-post (3) – (8) (9)
1980	−0.144	0.361	0.391	0.535	−0.030	0.505	0.149	0.075	0.316
1981	−0.120	0.356	0.428	0.549	−0.072	0.476	0.143	0.068	0.360
1982	−0.116	0.362	0.421	0.537	−0.060	0.477	0.098	0.047	0.374
1983	−0.130	0.363	0.431	0.561	−0.068	0.493	0.118	0.058	0.373
1984	−0.131	0.351	0.440	0.572	−0.089	0.483	0.135	0.065	0.375
1985	−0.131	0.369	0.410	0.541	−0.040	0.501	0.141	0.070	0.339
1986	−0.139	0.366	0.420	0.559	−0.054	0.505	0.158	0.080	0.340
1987	−0.129	0.371	0.445	0.574	−0.074	0.500	0.168	0.084	0.361
1988	−0.115	0.374	0.454	0.569	−0.080	0.489	0.143	0.070	0.384
1989	−0.129	0.405	0.516	0.646	−0.111	0.534	0.126	0.068	0.449
1990	−0.115	0.376	0.462	0.577	−0.087	0.491	0.137	0.067	0.395
1991	−0.129	0.367	0.463	0.593	−0.096	0.496	0.147	0.073	0.390

Year									
1992	-0.122	0.340	0.452	0.574	-0.112	0.462	0.151	0.070	0.382
1993	-0.129	0.344	0.446	0.575	-0.102	0.473	0.169	0.080	0.366
1994	-0.133	0.350	0.455	0.588	-0.105	0.483	0.173	0.083	0.371
1995	-0.129	0.353	0.483	0.612	-0.130	0.482	0.168	0.081	0.402
1996	-0.135	0.358	0.487	0.622	-0.129	0.493	0.157	0.077	0.410
1997	-0.141	0.356	0.485	0.626	-0.129	0.497	0.160	0.080	0.405
1998	-0.138	0.362	0.504	0.642	-0.141	0.501	0.166	0.083	0.421
1999	-0.140	0.368	0.493	0.634	-0.125	0.509	0.184	0.094	0.400
2000	-0.142	0.379	0.507	0.648	-0.128	0.521	0.178	0.093	0.414
2001	-0.145	0.384	0.525	0.670	-0.141	0.529	0.188	0.099	0.425
2002	-0.172	0.391	0.554	0.725	-0.163	0.563	0.148	0.083	0.471
2003	-0.182	0.400	0.544	0.725	-0.144	0.582	0.141	0.082	0.461
2004	-0.175	0.390	0.518	0.693	-0.128	0.565	0.146	0.083	0.435
2005	-0.171	0.393	0.512	0.683	-0.119	0.564	0.158	0.089	0.423
2006	-0.165	0.392	0.493	0.659	-0.101	0.558	0.171	0.095	0.398

Source: Authors' calculations based on various sources (see text).
a. SPE/DI = Social public expenditure/Disposable income.

distribution. For taxes, a higher concentration index means higher-income people pay more taxes. Although taxes show a positive concentration index, according to column 5 they are not progressive. At least in this exercise, in which adjusted current (not permanent) income is the welfare proxy, the tax system, in contrast to SPE, is slightly regressive.

Two factors explain the increasing progressivity of SPE in Argentina. First, SPE's targeting of the poor has increased over time, especially since the implementation of large conditional cash transfer programs in 2002. However, Argentina's increasing income inequality is a second, unintended factor in the rising progressivity of SPE. If an income distribution becomes more unequal (as has been happening in Argentina), a fixed spending structure will become increasingly progressive.

Taxes are more concentrated in the upper-income strata, as reflected by their positive concentration index. Tax concentration rose in the 1990s but not at the same speed as income concentration, turning the tax system increasingly regressive, as shown by the increasingly negative progressivity index. That pattern changed in the 2000s as inequality started to decline after the 2001–02 crisis and significant changes in the tax structure favored the more progressive export and financial levies.

That point deserves further discussion. The government encouraged a large devaluation of the peso in 2002 and tried to sustain a higher exchange rate in the ensuing period. The devaluation implied a substantial fall in real wages and hence a potentially large impact in increasing inequality. On the other hand, the real devaluation of the peso, along with a surge in the price of agricultural commodities, created large rents to land. A fraction of those rents were extracted through progressive export taxes, which financed large poverty-alleviation programs. Therefore, the regressive devaluation was a key element that allowed Argentina to build and afford a substantially more equalizing fiscal system. It should also be noted that excise duties (or *retenciones*) had another indirect distributive impact. They kept local prices of traded goods below the international level, which was very important in a context of increasing international prices (the so-called commodity price boom). That effect is not included in these calculations, but it is discussed in Gasparini and Cruces (2008). Given the opposing effects in play, the net distributional impact of the peso devaluation is difficult to estimate.

Figure 5-4 shows that although Argentina's fiscal policy reduced inequality, it did not have a significant effect on the pattern of inequality over the last decades, primarily because the impact of fiscal policy on Argentina's income distribution was small compared with that of "market" forces on inequality.

The Impact of Macroeconomic Crises on Inequality

Unfortunately, macroeconomic crises have been a recurrent factor in the Argentine economy since at least the mid-1970s. The series in figure 5-2 depict sudden and large falls in GDP per capita associated with macroeconomic crises. There

Figure 5-4. Gini Coefficient, Before and After Social Policy

Gini coefficient

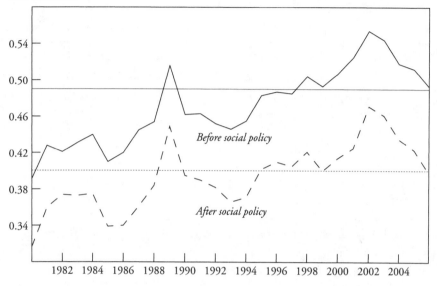

Source: Authors' calculations.

seems to be a clear correlation between the evolution of GDP and distributional indicators during the episodes of crisis and recovery. There also appear to be sharp falls in inequality associated with macroeconomic stabilization. In what follows we analyze those trends and their potential determinants in Argentina.

The Crises

Several large crises occurred in Argentina in 1980–81, beginning with a banking crisis in 1980 followed by a large devaluation of the peso. In 1981, Argentina experienced a reversal in capital flows as a result of the collapse of a managed exchange rate system set up by the military government. The situation deteriorated further in 1982, when Mexico announced that it would default on its external debt. Mexico's default triggered an "external debt" crisis throughout the region. The devaluation of 1981 and the liquidity difficulties of 1982 (fueled also by the confidence crisis after the Malvinas conflict) resulted in a fall of around 5 percent in 1982 in Argentina's annual output. From 1980 to 1981, the Gini coefficient increased significantly (by about 3 points) and poverty rose by 2 percentage points. From 1981 to 1982, the Gini fell almost 1 point. The poverty headcount ratio, however, continued to increase by 3 percentage points during the year; by 1982 it rose above 10 percent.

Argentina's second big crisis took place in the mid-1980s. It began with the 1985 recession, which preceded the Austral stabilization plan. Although the

Austral stabilization plan initially managed to reduce inflation, the effects were not permanent. Inflation accelerated again during 1985–88, culminating in two hyperinflation attacks: one in mid-1989 and one in the first quarter of 1990. Output fell 11 percent between 1988 and 1990, and annual inflation rates were 343 percent in 1988, 3080 percent in 1989, and 2314 percent in 1990. Hyperinflation had a very large distributional impact: poverty increased by 25 percentage points and the Gini coefficient increased by 6.3 points between 1988 and 1989 (although it should be noted that inequality had been increasing steadily between the 1985 stabilization and the 1989 hyperinflation-induced jump).

In April 1991, the country adopted a currency board with a fixed exchange rate regime, the convertibility plan, which managed to curb inflation successfully. The convertibility plan was accompanied by a series of far-reaching structural reforms. The Argentine economy grew fast, fueled by growing public and private indebtedness from the liquidity in international capital markets, until 1994. A currency crisis in Mexico at the end of 1994 triggered capital flight from the region and a financial crisis that severely affected the Argentine economy. The currency board sustained the drain of reserves, but the so-called "Tequila crisis" implied a fall in Argentina's GDP of around 4 percent in 1995. Argentina's growth bounced back quickly from the contagion of the Mexican financial crisis. Nonetheless, the Tequila crisis had a large distributional impact: poverty increased by 5 percentage points and the Gini went up by 2.7 points in a year.

The effects of the crisis are also visible in the national urban unemployment rate, which soared from 10.7 in May 1994 to 18.4 percent in May 1995. The hike was probably partially a consequence of the reforms; it already had been increasing steadily, from 6 percent in October 1991 (the first measure before the implementation of the convertibility plan). But unemployment jumped with the Tequila crisis and remained in double digits until the second half of 2006. The crisis also generated a set of changes in the structure of employment, the most notable being an increase in the labor force participation of women and secondary workers. A second change was the implementation of the Plan Trabajar, a workfare program, which would form the basis for future cash transfer initiatives. However, neither inequality nor the unemployment rate fell during the recovery, as they did in the period after the hyperinflation crisis.

It is possible that the financial crisis acted as a catalyst that accelerated and amplified the adverse effects of the reforms, which were bound to produce large sectoral reallocations of employment. Households and small firms were especially vulnerable in the context of an overvalued exchange rate, increased competition, and almost no compensatory policies to ease the transition (Plan Trabajar was implemented after the crisis, not during the initial reforms). The Tequila crisis probably exacerbated what was going to be, in any case, a difficult transition. While the crisis had long-lasting effects on the income distribution (and on unemployment levels), it is likely that they were partially due to the acceleration and worsening of a process that was already under way.

While growth resumed fairly strongly from 1996 to 1998, inequality fell only slightly. The continuing exposure to international capital flows brought about by the currency board regime and capital account liberalization hit the Argentine economy at the end of the millennium. As a result of the 1997 financial crisis in Southeast Asia and the 1998 crisis in Russia, in January 1999 Brazil, Argentina's largest trading partner, devalued its currency. The Argentine economy entered a period of recession, which culminated in a major economic, banking, and financial crisis. In December 2001, the currency board system collapsed, after restrictions were imposed on withdrawal of funds from the banking system. From 2000 to 2002, Argentina's GDP per capita fell 17 percent. The difference is even greater when comparing 2002 with 1998, when the recession started; over that five-year period Argentina's GDP per capita fell 22 percent.

The recession and the subsequent economic crisis in 2001 had a large impact on poverty, which rose 26 percentage points between 1999 and 2002. It also had a significant negative effect on inequality: the Gini coefficient increased 4 points from 1999 to 2002. The most dramatic effect was the combination of increasing prices (due to the devaluation) and falling nominal incomes (due to the sharp fall in economic activity), which instigated a jump in Argentina's official poverty rate from 38.3 percent in October 2001 to 53 percent in May 2002. Nonetheless, by 2003 the economy began to recover, and from 2003 to 2007 it grew at very high rates (above 8 percent per year).

LARGE MACROECONOMIC CRISES: THE IMPACTS OF HYPERINFLATION ON INCOME DISTRIBUTION. From the macroeconomic-distribution perspective, the two largest crises (1989 and 2001–02) represent the most interesting episodes in the years under study. Both crises precipitated unusually large falls in GDP and simultaneous large negative impacts on Argentina's income distribution.

Given the fiscal origin of most bouts of high inflation and hyperinflation (Heymann and Leijonhufvud 1995), it is not surprising that the literature concentrates on the differential incidence of the inflation tax.[16] Ahumada and others (1993) and Canavese, Sosa Escudero, and González Alvaredo (1999) quantify the distributional effects of inflation in Argentina from a tax-incidence perspective. Both studies estimate Argentina's aggregate monetary demand functions and aggregate inflation tax and seigniorage collection and include a re-weighted consumer price index by quintile. Canavese, Sosa Escudero, and González Alvaredo (1999) finds that, except for the hyperinflation during 1989 and 2001–02, quintile-specific inflation rates did not differ significantly over time. However, from 1980 to 1990, the infla-

---

16. Inflation constitutes by definition a proportional tax on nominal balances, but its effect on the income distribution is neutral only if all households face the same inflation rate, if all households have the same income elasticity in their demand for money, or if they all have access to the same "protection" technologies, such as currency substitution or indexed contracts.

tion tax as a proportion of income was about twice as large for households in the poorer quintile as for those in the richer quintile. The impact of the inflation tax on aggregate inequality indicators was comparatively small for high-inflation periods, with increases of about 1 to 1.5 points in the Gini for 1980–88 and 1990. In contrast, in 1989 the inflation tax produced an increase of 3.4 points in the Gini coefficient. The inequality-increasing impact of hyperinflation, however, was short lived. Stabilization programs reduced the inflation tax, as witnessed by the 1991–93 downward trend in the Gini coefficient (figure 5-2).

LARGE MACROECONOMIC CRISES: THE DISTRIBUTIVE EFFECTS OF THE 2001–02 MELTDOWN. The crisis induced by the implosion of the currency board regime in December 2001 was unusually virulent, even by Argentine standards. The origins and consequences of the crisis have been analyzed extensively, and a selection of the existing studies is covered in the following discussion.

Using a survey implemented by the World Bank in the midst of the crisis (June and July 2002), Fiszbein, Giovagnoli, and Adúriz (2003) found that almost half of households suffered a fall in nominal income. They also documented a change in household roles, with respect to the labor market, with higher employment among secondary workers as a strategy to complement the fall in income from primary workers who were unemployed or working reduced hours. As in other crises in Latin America, the extremely high level of unemployment meant that school enrollment did not fall significantly among younger children and only slightly among those aged 16 to 18 years.

One key component of the crisis was a large bank deposit freeze, which in principle has an ambiguous direct distributional effect.[17] Halac and Schmukler (2004) finds that the probability of having savings was positively and significantly associated with measures of income. Interestingly, however, the authors found that among those with savings, the less educated and those with lower incomes had a larger probability of being affected by the bank deposit freeze. That finding suggests that the measure probably did have an inequality-increasing effect.

McKenzie (2004) examines the labor market responses to the 2001-02 crisis based on the panel structure of the EPH. They found that most of the fall in households' real income was due to the fall in the real wages of individuals remaining in the same jobs. Because unemployment was already at very high levels from the 1999–01 recession, it only rose 3 percentage points during the crisis. Cruces (2005), using the same panel feature of the EPH data, found that households exposed to the 2001–02 crisis experienced significant increases in income variability (70 percent).

PERMANENT EFFECTS OF THE CRISES. The available evidence clearly shows that in Argentina the poor were more affected by crises than the non-poor. How-

---

17. While no empirical analysis has attempted to link the two phenomena, it is widely believed that the restrictions on withdrawing cash from banks had a poverty- and inequality-increasing effect by starving the cash (or informal) economy.

ever, most of the inequality-increasing factors mentioned here tend to dissipate relatively quickly through increases in employment and income levels as the economy recovers. In the two large crises, inequality first jumped but then fell drastically right after economic stabilization. There is a debate on the existence of hysteresis effects on inequality from the crises (Lustig 2000), but there does not seem to be definitive empirical evidence for Argentina. While the Tequila crisis had permanent effects on the income distribution, it is likely that they were due to the acceleration of the negative aspects of the underlying reform process. Moreover, any permanent effects of the 2001–02 crisis are difficult to evaluate, since they are confounded with the strong recovery from 2003 onward. Given the aforementioned evidence that school enrollment did not decline during the crisis, the typical argument of a permanent reduction in the stock of general human capital does not seem to apply for the 2001–02 crisis. However, other more subtle mechanisms might have influenced inequality, like losses of firm-specific human capital for the newly unemployed, who were for the most part unskilled workers. Those impacts, and the psychological costs of long-term unemployment, are some of the questions on the impact of the 2001–02 crisis that merit further research.

The Fall in Inequality during the Post-Crisis Recovery: 2003–07

A new episode unfolded in Argentina after the peak of the crisis in 2002. Between 2003 and 2007, the average annual growth rate was an unprecedentedly high 8 percent and the unemployment rate plummeted from more than 20 percent to 8 percent. Inequality fell sharply from 2003, and by 2006 it had descended to approximately the same level as in the second half of the 1990s, before the start of the 1999–2001 recession and the subsequent crisis.

The strong devaluation of the peso in 2002 generated a new structure of relative prices that propitiated the economic recovery. The fall in real wages increased the competitiveness of Argentina's products and deterred imports. New taxes and a default on the government's debt obligations allowed for a fiscal surplus that helped stabilize the economy. The new and stronger government from the traditional Peronist Party (2002–03) curbed the social unrest and the political instability of 2001–02 with the help of a large cash transfer program, which achieved unprecedented coverage. Moreover, Argentina saw a large increase in the prices of commodities that it exported during those years, and the exceptional conditions in the international markets were also a key factor in the recovery.

Reasons for the fall in inequality

Several factors combined to create a scenario in which inequality fell: the recovery from the crisis of 2001–02; realignments after the devaluation of the peso; strong expansion of employment; productive changes after new relative prices;

slower technical upgrading; stronger labor institutions and labor policies; and a more extensive safety net.

As discussed previously, major macroeconomic crises, which seriously disrupt the economy, are associated with large jumps in inequality. When economic life returns to some level of normality, inequality always falls. Although the 2001–02 crisis was considered one of the worst in Argentina's history, by 2004 the economy had fully recovered, with GDP levels similar to those in pre-crisis years. Some of the drop in inequality after 2002 was driven by the recovery and rebuilding of business and economic relationships after such a large shock.

After years of pegging the Argentine peso to the dollar at a clearly overvalued rate, in January 2002 the currency board regime was abandoned, and as a result the nominal exchange rate increased threefold in only a few months. That dramatic devaluation implied a sudden fall in real wages, and hence inequality rose. As in many devaluation episodes, the full impact of the shock in 2002 started to dissipate as nominal wages increased, and the nominal exchange rate recovered from its initial "overshooting." The increase in nominal wages originated from workers' demands to recover part of the large real losses in purchasing power due to the devaluation. A substantial part of the fall in inequality since 2002 can be attributed to those realignments.

The strong recovery of the economy meant higher demand in a labor market with depressed real wages. The share of adults employed jumped from 35 percent in 2001 to 43 percent in 2006. Accordingly, the unemployment rate fell from around 20 percent in 2001–02 to 10 percent in 2006. By 2006 unemployment had finally declined to a level lower than in most of the 1990s. The expansion in employment was surely another contributing factor to the fall in inequality. Employment affected inequality through both the direct channel of rising incomes for the formerly non-employed and the wage-increasing pressures on the labor market.

The change in relative prices due to the devaluation benefited industries that relied on unskilled labor (such as the textile industry), which had faced strong import competition under the previously overvalued exchange rate. For the reasons discussed previously, it is likely that the trade channel (through import substitution) also contributed to lower inequality. Unfortunately, the evidence on the distributive effects of trade-induced changes is fragmentary.

As argued above, the Argentine economy in the 1990s experienced substantial changes in the organization of production. In the 2000s, the rate of technology adoption and capital investment is believed to have been slower than during the 1990s for several reasons. A large upgrading increase already had taken place in the previous decade. Firms also resorted to idle capacity after the crisis. Finally, investment might have slowed because of the uncertainty of the social unrest brought about by the crisis, because of an atmosphere of distrust following the default on the country's debt, and because of some perceptions that the government was sending signals that were unfriendly to markets. The literature typically finds inequality overshooting after skill-biased technical shocks because it takes time for displaced unskilled workers to be reallocated in the economy,[18] and the initially strong unequalizing impact of the technological shock of the 1990s should have lost strength over time. That adjustment after the production shock was interrupted by the recession of the late 1990s and the crisis of the early 2000s, but it likely resumed during the recovery, with the ensuing equalizing consequences.

Beginning in 2002, Argentina's governments took a more active role in the labor market by increasing the minimum wage, mandating lump-sum increases in wages (which compresses their distribution), taking a pro-union stance, and promoting collective bargaining. The government also implemented active policies, ranging from subsidies to firms to export taxes on agricultural products, to keep the prices of utilities and foodstuffs low. While export taxes that introduce a gap between domestic and international prices have all sorts of leakages to the non-poor and inefficiency costs, in the short run they have an equalizing effect given the higher share of foodstuff in the consumption bundle of the poor.

As discussed above, the economic expansion and new price structure improved the redistributive impact of fiscal policy. Social spending rose, taxes became somewhat more progressive (mostly because of export levies), and the increased revenues went in part to sustain a large system of pro-poor cash transfers. The Programa Jefes y Jefas de Hogar Desocupados, which covered 2 million households in 2003, was still running in 2007, and new cash transfer programs were being implemented. The impact of the PJJHD lost strength as the economy recovered because beneficiaries left the program to work but also because the cash subsidy remained fixed in nominal terms in a context of increasing inflation.

Finally, it is interesting to notice that although inequality fell substantially with respect to the crisis levels, inequality in 2006 was not significantly different from that of the mid- to late 1990s, despite the fact that per capita GDP and employment were higher, labor institutions were stronger, and a massive cash transfer program was implemented. That rigidity is probably due, at least in part, to the fall in the relative productivity of unskilled workers that followed the modernization of the economy in the 1990s. The main challenge for distributive policies in the long run in Argentina is to raise the productivity of this group of workers and of their offspring, allowing them to share the benefits of economic growth.

Concluding Remarks

This chapter describes the level and evolution of inequality in Argentina from the mid-1970s to the mid-2000s by reviewing the empirical evidence behind a series of determinants of that evolution. Along the way, it also attempts to pinpoint which of the factors contributing to the dynamics of inequality can be attributed

---

18. See, for example, the discussion by Jaime Kahhat in chapter 2 of this volume.

to market forces, to state action, to sociopolitical influences, or to different combinations of those elements.

Only time will tell whether the reforms implemented will have a positive impact on welfare through the growth channel and whether a trade-off exists between short-term inequality and long-term growth. Too many factors are in play to construct clean counterfactuals, but the evidence on the poverty- and inequality-reducing effects of government action seems to suggest an excessive increase in inequality after macroeconomic shocks and reforms, with real welfare costs. Those costs might have been mitigated by the presence of ex-ante policies for coping with shocks and by compensation and income-smoothing mechanisms to ease the transitions after reforms.

Some of the factors that account for the long-term trends in inequality can be attributed to government acts and others to market forces, but most of the distributional factors covered in this chapter correspond to a mix of both that might be ultimately impossible to disentangle—for instance, trade liberalization corresponds to the operation of market forces following a change in government policy, while most other changes occur within the government's regulation of an economy. The evidence, however, has shown that government intervention can have powerful effects on the distribution of welfare, and the government role in managing and compensating losers during transitions must not be underestimated.

References

Acemoglu, Daron. 2003. "Patterns of Skill Premia." *Review of Economic Studies* 70, no. 2: 199–230.

Acosta, Pablo, and Leonardo Gasparini. 2007. "Capital Accumulation, Trade Liberalization, and Rising Wage Inequality: The Case of Argentina." *Economic Development and Cultural Change* 55, no. 4 (July): 793–812.

Ahumada, Hildegart, and others. 1993. "Efectos distributivos del impuesto inflacionario: Una estimación para el caso argentino." Serie Seminarios. Buenos Aires: Instituto T. Di Tella.

Altimir, Oscar, Luis Beccaria, and Martín González Rozada. 2002. "La distribución del ingreso en Argentina: 1974–2000." *Revista de la Cepal* 78 (December): 55–86.

Atkinson, Anthony B. 1997. "Bringing Income Distribution in from the Cold." *Economic Journal* 107, no. 441 (March): 297–321.

Atolia, Manoj. 2007. "Trade Liberalization and Rising Wage Inequality in Latin America: Reconciliation with HOS theory." *Journal of International Economics* 71, no. 2: 467–94.

Beccaria, Luis. 2006. "Notas sobre la evolución de la distribución de las remuneraciones en la Argentina." *Estudios del Trabajo* 32. Buenos Aires: Asociación Argentina de Especialistas en Estudios del Trabajo.

Behrman, Jere R., Nancy Birdsall, and Miguel Székely. 2003. "Economic Policy and Wage Differentials in Latin America." Working Paper 29. Washington: Center for Global Development.

Berlinski, Julio. 1994. "Post Trade Liberalization Institutional Issues in Argentina." Working Paper 182. Buenos Aires: Instituto Di Tella.

Bustos, Paula. 2006. "Rising Wage Inequality in the Argentinean Manufacturing Sector: The Impact of Trade and Foreign Investment on Technology and Skill Upgrading." Unpublished paper. Barcelona: CREI.

Canavese, Alfredo, Walter Sosa Escudero, and Facundo González Alvaredo. 1999. "El efecto de la inflación sobre la distribución del ingreso: el impuesto inflacionario en la Argentina en la década del ochenta." In *La Distribución del Ingreso en la Argentina*. Buenos Aires: FIEL (Fundación de Investigaciones Económicas Latinoamericanas).

Cetrangolo, Oscar, and Francisco Gatto. 2002. "Descentralización fiscal en Argentina: restricciones impuestas por un proceso mal orientado." Unpublished paper. Buenos Aires: CEPAL (Comisión Económica para America Latina y el Caribe).

Cristini, Marcela. 1999. "Apertura económica, política comercial, y la distribución del ingreso: ¿Qué aporta el caso argentino al debate?" In *La Distribución del Ingreso en la Argentina*. Buenos Aires: FIEL (Fundación de Investigaciones Económicas Latinoamericanas).

Cruces, Guillermo. 2005. "Income Fluctuations, Poverty, and Well-Being over Time: Theory and Application to Argentina." Distributional Analysis Research Programme Working Paper 76. STICERD (Suntory and Toyota International Centres for Economics and Related Disciplines), London School of Economics and Political Science.

Damill, Mario, Roberto Frenkel, and Roxana Maurizio. 2003. "Políticas macroeconómicas y vulnerabilidad social: La Argentina de los años noventa." Serie Financiamiento del Desarrollo CEPAL 135. Buenos Aires.

Ennis, Huberto, and Santiago Pinto. 2002. "Privatization and Income Distribution in Argentina." Unpublished paper. West Virginia University.

Etchemendy, Sebastián, and Ruth Collier. 2007. "Down but Not Out: Union Resurgence and Segmented Neocorporatism in Argentina: 2003–2007." *Politics and Society* 35, no. 3: 363–401.

Fiszbein, Ariel, Paula Giovagnoli, and Isidoro Adúriz. 2003. "Argentina's Crisis and Its Impact on Household Welfare." *CEPAL Review* 79.

Galiani, Sebastian, and Guido Porto. 2008. "Trends in Tariff Reforms and Trends in the Structure of Wages." Social Science Research Network Working Paper (http://ssrn.com/abstract =1083908).

Galiani, Sebastian, and Pablo Sanguinetti. 2003. The Impact of Trade Liberalization on Wage Inequality: Evidence from Argentina. *Journal of Development Economics* 72, no. 2: 497–513.

Galiani, Sebastian, and Federico Sturzenegger. 2008. "The Impact of Privatization on the Earnings of Restructured Workers." *Journal of Labor Research* 29, no. 2: 162–76.

Galiani, Sebastian, Paul Gertler, and Ernesto Schargrodsky. 2005. "Water for Life: The Impact of the Privatization of Water Services on Child Mortality." *Journal of Political Economy* 113, no. 1: 83–120.

———. 2008. "School Decentralization: Helping the Good Get Better, but Leaving the Poor Behind." *Journal of Public Economics* 92: 2106–120.

Galiani, Sebastian, and others. 2004. "The Benefits and Costs of Privatization in Argentina: A Microeconomic Analysis." In *Benefits and Costs of Privatization in Latin America*, edited by Alberto Chong and Florencio López-de-Silanes. Stanford University Press.

Garay, Candelaria. 2007. "Social Policy and Collective Action: Unemployed Workers, Community Associations, and Protest in Argentina." *Politics and Society* 35, no. 2: 301–28.

Garcia Swartz, D. 1998. "General-Equilibrium Perspectives on Relative Wage Changes in an Emerging-Market Economy: Argentina between 1974 and 1995." Ph.D. dissertation, University of Chicago.

Gasparini, Leonardo. 2005a. "El fracaso distributivo de Argentina: El papel de la integración y las políticas públicas." In *Debate sobre el impacto de la globalización en los mercados de trabajo de América Latina*, edited by Gustavo Márquez. Washington: Inter-American Development Bank.

———. 2005b. "Poverty and Inequality in Argentina: Methodological Issues and a Literature Review." Unpublished paper. CEDLAS and World Bank.

Gasparini, Leonardo, Mariana Marchionni, and Walter Sosa Escudero. 2004. "Characterization of Inequality Changes through Microeconometric Decompositions: The Case of Greater Buenos Aires." In *The Microeconomics of Income Distribution Dynamics,* edited by François Bourguignon, Francisco H. G. Ferreira, and Nora Lustig. Washington: World Bank and Oxford University Press.

Gasparini, Leonardo, Federico Gutiérrez, and Leopoldo Tornarolli. 2007. "Growth and Income Poverty in Latin America and the Caribbean: Evidence from Household Surveys." *Review of Income and Wealth* 53, no. 2 (June): 209–45.

Gasparini, Leonardo, and Guillermo Cruces. 2008. "A Distribution in Motion: The Case of Argentina. A Review of the Empirical Evidence." Paper prepared for the UNDP project "Markets, the State, and the Dynamics of Inequality: How to Advance Inclusive Growth," coordinated by Luis Felipe López-Calva and Nora Lustig (http://undp.economiccluster-lac.org/). Also available as Documento de trabajo 78 del CEDLAS-UNLP.

Gerchunoff, Pablo, and Lucas Llach. 2004. *Entre la equidad y el crecimiento.* Buenos Aires: Siglo Veintiuno.

Goldberg, Pinelopi K., and Nina Pavcnik. 2004. "Trade, Inequality, and Poverty: What Do We Know? Evidence from Recent Trade Liberalization Episodes in Developing Countries." *Brookings Trade Forum*, pp. 223–69.

———. 2007. "Distributional Effects of Globalization in Developing Countries." *Journal of Economic Literature* 45, no. 1 (March): 39–82.

González, Martín, and Alicia Menéndez. 2000. "The Effect of Unemployment on Labor Earnings Inequality: Argentina in the Nineties." RPDS Working Paper 1/00. Princeton University.

Halac, Mariana, and Sergio L. Schmukler. 2004. "Distributional Effects of Crises: The Financial Channel." *Economía: Journal of the Latin American and Caribbean Economic Association* 5, no. 1: 1–67.

Heymann, Daniel, and Axel Leijonhufvud. 1995. *High Inflation*. Oxford: Clarendon Press.

INDEC (Instituto Nacional de Estadística y Censos). Various years. Buenos Aires (www.indec.gov.ar).

Katz, Lawrence F., and David H. Autor. 1999. "Changes in the Wage Structure and Earnings Inequality." In *Handbook of Labor Economics,* vol. 3A, edited by Orley Ashtenfelter and David Card. Amsterdam, Netherlands: North-Holland.

Keifman, Saul. 2006. "Economic Openness and Income Inequality: Deconstructing Some Neoliberal Fallacies." Paper presented at the Jornadas de la AAEP (Anales de la Asociación Argentina de Economía Política). Salta, Argentina.

Lustig, Nora. 2000. "Crises and the Poor: Socially Responsible Macroeconomics." *Economía: Journal of the Latin American and Caribbean Economic Association* 1, no. 1:1-45.

Marchionni, Mariana, and Leonardo Gasparini. 2007. "Tracing Out the Effects of Demographic Changes on the Income Distribution: The Case of Greater Buenos Aires, 1980–2000." *Journal of Economic Inequality* 5, no. 1: 97–114.

Marshall, Adriana. 2005. "Labor Regulations and Unionization Trends: Comparative Analysis of Latin American Countries." Visiting Fellow Working Papers. Cornell University.

———. 2002. "Transformaciones en el empleo y la intervención sindical en la industria: efectos sobre la desigualdad de salarios." *Desarrollo Económico* 42, no. 166: 211–30.

Maurizio, Roxana. 2001. "Demanda de trabajo, sobreeducación, y distribución del ingreso." Paper presented at V Congreso Nacional de Estudios del Trabajo, Buenos Aires.

McKenzie, David J. 2004. "Aggregate Shocks and Urban Labor Market Responses: Evidence from Argentina's Financial Crisis." *Economic Development and Cultural Change* 52, no. 4: 719–58.

Murillo, Victoria. 1997. "La adaptación del sindicalismo argentino a las reformas de mercado en la primera presidencia de Menem." *Desarrollo Económico* vol. 37, no.147: 419–46.

Perry, Guillermo, and Marcelo Olarreaga. 2006. "Trade Liberalization, Inequality, and Poverty Reduction in Latin America." Unpublished paper. Washington: World Bank.

Sánchez-Páramo, Carolina, and Norbert Schady. 2003. "Off and Running? Technology, Trade, and Rising Demand for Skilled Workers in Latin America." WP 3015, produced as background paper for the report "Closing the Gap in Education and Technology in Latin America." Washington: World Bank, Office of the Chief Economist for Latin America.

Yeaple, Stephen Ross. 2005. "A Simple Model of Firm Heterogeneity, International Trade, and Wages." *Journal of International Economics* 65, no. 1: 1–20.

6

Markets, the State, and the Dynamics of Inequality in Brazil

RICARDO BARROS, MIRELA DE CARVALHO,
SAMUEL FRANCO, AND ROSANE MENDONÇA

Brazilian income inequality has been the subject of a large number of studies[1] that for more than four decades have shown that Brazil has an extremely high and persistent level of inequality: in 2007, the income shares of Brazil's poorest and richest 10 percent were equal to .9 and 43.5 percent, respectively.[2] However, between 2001 and 2007, the country experienced a sharp and continuous decline in income inequality: the Gini coefficient declined at an average rate of 1.2 percent a year and in 2007, income inequality reached its lowest level in more than 30 years (figure 6-1).[3]

This reduction in income inequality has had significant impacts on the living conditions of the poorest groups in Brazil. From 2001 to 2007, the per capita income of the poorest 10 percent grew 7 percent a year, nearly three times the national average of 2.5 percent. As a result, Brazil has accomplished the first Mil-

The authors are grateful to Nora Lustig for detailed comments on a previous draft and to Mariellen Jewers and Amanda Lintelman for their editorial input.

1. See, among others, Langoni (2005); Hoffmann (1989); Bonelli and Sedlacek (1989); Barros and Mendonça (1992); Ramos (1993); Barros, Henriques, and Mendonça (2000).

2. Income here is total current (no capital gains) monetary income before deductions of taxes and social security (that is, gross income). The survey asks for a "normally" received income, which means that short-run positive (overtime) or negative (furlough) shocks are not captured.

3. As Alvaredo and Piketty show in chapter 4 of this volume, for other countries survey-based inequality measures underestimate the income share at the top, and Brazilian surveys are not exception. Thus, the "true" Gini is likely to be higher than the one reported in figure 6-1.

Figure 6-1. *Evolution of Income Inequality in Brazil,*
Measured by the Gini Coefficient, 1977–2007

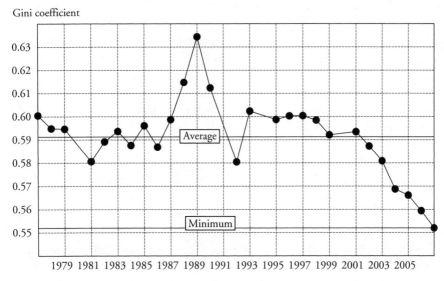

Source: Authors' estimations based on Pesquisa Nacional por Amostra de Domicílios (PNAD), 1977 to 2007.

lennium Development Goal (MDG)—*to reduce by half the proportion of the popu-lation living in extreme poverty*—almost ten years in advance. Not only was the recent decline in extreme poverty three times faster than necessary to achieve the first MDG by 2015, but also, more than 60 percent of the decline was due to the reduction in inequality, demonstrating the importance of the recent decline in inequality for the extremely poor.

Despite the sharp decline in inequality, Brazil still has a level of income inequality well above the world average. Brazil's recent reductions in inequality remain limited because they are a consequence of neither a coherent set of government policies nor properly functioning markets. Indeed, Brazil's success in reducing income inequality is the net result of a social policy that still has serious inconsistencies and a mix of well-functioning markets and market failures. That indicates that there is plenty of room for improving social policy design and the functioning of markets and thus plenty of opportunities to further reduce inequality and poverty.

In this chapter we estimate the contribution of public policy and the performance of markets to the evolution of income inequality. In particular, we focus on four main issues: changes in government transfers; changes in wage differentials by skill level; changes in labor market segmentation; and changes in the minimum wage. Of the main proximate factors influencing the level of inequality (demography, nonlabor income, employment, and productivity), we identify which contributed the most to the recent reduction in inequality. Finding that nonlabor income plays a central role in reducing inequality, we provide a detailed analysis of its various components, in particular public transfers. We then address the contribution of changes in labor income—in particular the connection between education expansion and the decline in wage inequality—and how and to what extent the growing integration of labor markets has contributed to the reduction in labor income inequality. Finally, we analyze the impact of changes in the minimum wage on income distribution and compare their impact with what could be achieved if the same amount of resources were allocated to an expansion of the conditional cash transfer program Bolsa Família.

In Brazil, inequality has declined sharply and continuously since 2001. From 2001 to 2007, the Gini coefficient declined from 0.593 to 0.552, an average rate of 1.2 percent a year (figure 6-1). Of the seventy-four countries for which we have data, less than one-fourth were able to reduce inequality faster than Brazil. For that period, there is "Lorenz dominance," meaning that the decline is unambiguous and that all inequality measures satisfying the Pigou-Dalton principle show a decline. The fall in inequality also is statistically significant: there is a 1 percent probability or less of having observed the decline in the Gini if the "true" change were no change (Barros and others 2009a).

However, if we break the 2001–07 period into subperiod 2001–04 and subperiod 2004–07, during the latter period the Lorenz curves cross, so the fall in inequality is not unambiguous. The growth rate in income for the bottom 5 percent was below the overall average for all percentiles and less than half of the growth rate corresponding to the second quintile. That change is especially clear when attention is focused on 2006–07. Even though the Gini coefficient held to its historical path in 2007 and overall per capita income increased almost 3 percent from 2006 to 2007, the average income of the bottom 5 percent declined by 14 percent and, as a consequence, their income share declined.

Poverty reduction can occur when there is balanced economic growth and/or a reduction in inequality. If inequality had not changed between 2001 and 2007, both the income of the rich and that of the poor would have grown at the national rate: 2.6 percent a year. Since the income of the poorest 10 percent actually grew 7.0 percent a year—that is, 4.4 percentage points above the overall average—almost two-thirds of the income growth of this group came from declines in inequality. For the poorest 20 percent, 60 percent of the growth in income also originated from declines in inequality. As a result, levels of poverty and extreme poverty, measured by all three basic indicators (headcount ratio, poverty gap, and severity of poverty)[4] declined between 25 percent and 40 percent from 2001 to 1007.[5]

4. We used regionalized poverty and extreme poverty lines.
5. The reductions in poverty and extreme poverty are robust regardless of the poverty line used and may be considered substantial according to at least two criteria. First, the reduction in extreme poverty is three times faster than would be necessary to comply with the first MDG. At the current pace, it would be pos-

As a result of the sharp reduction in rates of poverty and extreme poverty and despite population growth, the number of poor and extremely poor people in Brazil declined, as did the amount of resources necessary to alleviate all poverty and extreme poverty. Indeed, the population living in extreme poverty declined by 11 million and the number of poor people (extremely and moderately poor) was reduced by 13 million; likewise, the resources needed to alleviate all poverty and extreme poverty in Brazil declined from R$63 to R$45 billion a year. Because of the reduction in the volume of resources necessary to alleviate poverty and the growth in overall income, alleviating poverty in Brazil has become an even more viable goal. While in 2001 at least 7 percent of total household income was needed to eliminate (extreme and moderate) poverty,[6] in 2007 only 4 percent was required. If inequality had not declined, the poverty headcount would have gone down by 5.3 percentage points; since the headcount declined by almost 11 percentage points, half of the reduction in the headcount can be attributed to the decline in inequality. The impact of inequality reduction on extreme poverty was greater: 62 percent of the decrease in extreme poverty was due to the reduction in inequality.

The faster income growth for the poor is characteristic of an equitable growth process. Whenever growth is accompanied by a reduction in inequality, the income of the poor grows above the average. Almost two-thirds of the income growth among the poorest 10 percent from 2001–07 resulted from the decline in inequality. That equitable growth process also led to a significant reduction in the level of absolute poverty. The proportion of people living in extreme poverty declined 7 percentage points from 2001 to 2007, a rapid pace of poverty reduction in Latin America that trails only Mexico's. Brazil has experienced previous episodes of poverty decline; however, declines were due solely to economic growth. In this recent episode, unlike in previous ones, at least half of the decrease in poverty and extreme poverty was due to the reduction in inequality.

From these results we can extract two basic implications. First, the impressive rate at which poverty has been declining serves as evidence of the importance of Brazil's recent decline in inequality. The results demonstrate that reductions in inequality can be an extremely effective instrument for reducing poverty. In fact, in order to achieve the same reduction in extreme poverty without the recent decline in inequality, it would have been necessary for Brazil's overall per capita income to have grown an extra 4 percentage points a year. From the point of view of the extremely poor, a 1.0 percentage point reduction in the Gini coefficient is equivalent to 4.2 percentage points higher growth in per capita income.

---

sible to reduce extreme poverty in Brazil by half in 8 years, while the MDGs establish a period of 25 years to reach that goal. Second, these reduction rates are greater than those observed in all Latin American countries for which information is available, with the exception of Mexico.

6. Total household income as recorded in the PNAD (Pesquisa Nacional por Amostra de Domicílios) surveys and not in the National Accounts.

Proximate Determinants of the Decline in Income Inequality

To identify and quantify the proximate determinants that contributed to Brazil's recent decline in inequality we relied on a series of counterfactual simulations. The proximate determinants considered in our analysis are ratio of adults to total number of members in the household; household nonlabor income (which includes government transfers) per adult; proportion of adults working to total number of adults in the household; and labor income per working adult. Attention is given to both changes in the distribution of each of those factors and changes in their association or correlation. It is worth emphasizing that here our analysis is limited to the proximate determinants of inequality. It is important to emphasize that although the analysis is limited to the identification of the proximate determinants, this is only a first step[7] to identify the factors that contributed the most to Brazil's decline in inequality and therefore deserve a more in-depth analysis. However, each proximate determinant is, in turn, the result of behavioral and external processes that are not modeled here.

The empirical analysis presented here is based on the following sequence of identities:

(1) $$y = a.r$$
(2) $$r = o + t$$
and
(3) $$t = u.w$$
Hence,
(4) $$y = a.(o + u.w)$$

Identity (1) expresses household per capita income, y, as a product of the proportion of adults in the household, a, and household income per adult, r. Identity (2) expresses household income per adult, r, as the sum of household nonlabor income per adult, o, and household labor income per adult, t. Identity (3), labor income per adult, t, is expressed as the product of the proportion of working adults, u, and the labor income per working adult in the household, w. Identity (4) relates per capita household income, y, to its four proximate determinants: the proportion of adults in the household, a; household nonlabor income per adult, o; proportion of working adults, u; and labor income per working adult in the household, w. Visually, the identities are presented in figure 6-2.

It is important to point out that because the expression is an identity, any changes in the income distribution must be related to changes in the joint distribution of the four proximate determinants. Thus, here we identify all the proximate channels that lead to reductions in inequality.

7. For a more detailed analysis of the role of demographic factors, see Wajnman, Turra, and Agostinho (2006); for an analysis of the contribution of changes in the distribution of nonlabor income see Barros, Carvalho, and Franco (2007) and Barros and others (2006d); and for an analysis of the role of the changes in the distribution of labor income, see Barros, Franco, and Mendonça (2007a, 2007b).

Figure 6-2. *Household Per Capita Income and Its Determinants*

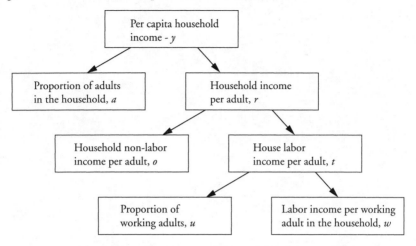

Source: A similar figure can be found in Barros, Foguel, and Ulyssea (2006) and Herrán (2005).

Barros and others (2006b) presents the methodology for decomposing varia-tions in the level of inequality due to variations in the marginal distribution of each determinant and its correlation with other determinants. The results can be found in tables 6-1a through 6-1c. Two inequality measures were used to assess the recent decline in inequality: the Gini coefficient and the ratio between the income of the richest 20 percent and the poorest 20 percent. To facilitate the interpretation of the results, in table 6-2 we present the evolution of each proximate determinant fac-tor's average and the level of inequality associated to its distribution.[8]

The importance of demographic factors and income per adult

Table 6-1a shows that recent changes in the distribution of the proportion of adults in the household were responsible for 8 percent of the overall reduction in income inequality from 2001 to 2007. Its relatively small contribution can be explained by the nature of the demographic changes that occurred during that period. As shown in table 6-2, although the proportion of adults in the household increased by 5 per-cent between 2001 and 2007, the inequality in the distribution of the proportion of adults declined by only 5 percent to 6 percent. In contrast, the decline in income inequality was 4 to 5 times larger using the same inequality measure.[9]

8. In this table we use an additional inequality measure: the ratio between the top 10 percent and the bottom 60 percent. It was necessary to introduce that measure because a large fraction of the population does not receive any income from nonlabor income. In this case, the average income for the bottom 20 per-cent or 40 percent is null and measures such as the ratio between the top and bottom 20 percent could not be obtained.

9. It is worthwhile to point out that this assessment takes into account only the direct contribution of demographic factors. Inasmuch as the changes in the distribution of income per adult could also result from demographic factors, the total contribution (direct and indirect) of these factors may be higher.

Table 6-1a. *Contribution of the Proportion of Adults in the Household, Household Income per Adult, and Associations to Explain Income Inequality Reduction between 2001 and 2007*

Counterfactual simulations	Inequality (Gini coefficient)	Contribution to the inequality reduction (percent)	Inequality (ratio 20+/20–)	Contribution to the inequality reduction (percent)	Determinants
Original situation in 2001	59.3	...	26.9	...	
If the distribution of household income per adult and the proportion of adults were the same in 2007 as in 2001	59.5	–4	27.0	–1	Association between the proportion of adults in the household and household income per adult
If the distribution of household income per adult was the same in 2007 as in 2001	59.2	7	26.4	8	Proportion of adults in the house
Original situation in 2007	55.2	97	20.2	93	Distribution of household income per adult

Source: Authors' estimations based on the Pesquisa Nacional por Amostra de Domicílios (PNAD), 2001 and 2007.

Table 6-1b. *Contribution of Labor and Nonlabor Income per Adult and Associations to Explain Income Inequality Reduction between 2001 and 2007*

Counterfactual simulations	Inequality (Gini coefficient)	Contribution to the inequality reduction (percent)	Inequality (ratio 20+/20–)	Contribution to the inequality reduction (percent)	Determinants
Original situation in 2001	59.3	...	26.9	...	
If the distribution of household income per adult and the proportion of adults were the same in 2007 as in 2001	59.5	–4	27.0	–1	Association between the proportion of adults in the household and household income per adult
If the distribution of household income per adult was the same in 2007 as in 2001	59.2	7	26.4	8	Proportion of adults in the household
If the distributions of labor income per adult and nonlabor income per adult were the same in 2007 as in 2001	58.8	10	25.7	11	Association between labor income per adult and nonlabor income per adult
If the distribution of labor income per adult was the same in 2007 as in 2001	57.1	40	22.3	51	Distribution of household nonlabor income per adult
Original situation in 2007	55.2	46	20.2	31	Distribution of household labor income per adult

Source: Authors' estimations based on the Pesquisa Nacional por Amostra de Domicílios (PNAD), 2001 and 2007.

Table 6-1c. *Contribution of the Percentage of Working Adults, Labor Income per Adult Worker, and Associations to Explain Income Inequality Reduction between 2001 and 2007*

Counterfactual simulations	Inequality (Gini coefficient)	Contribution to the inequality reduction (percent)	Inequality (ratio 20+/20–)	Contribution to the inequality reduction (percent)	Determinants
Original situation in 2001	59.3	...	26.9	...	
If the distribution of household income per adult and the proportion of adults were the same in 2007 as in 2001	59.5	–4	27.0	–1	Association between the proportion of adults in the household and household income per adult
If the distribution of household income per adult was the same in 2007 as in 2001	59.2	7	26.4	8	Proportion of adults in the household
If the distributions of labor income per adult and nonlabor income per adult were the same in 2007 as in 2001	58.8	10	25.7	11	Association between household labor income per adult and household nonlabor income per adult
If the distribution of labor income per worker was the same in 2007 as in 2001	57.1	40	22.3	51	Distribution of household nonlabor income per adult
If the distribution of labor income per worker and the proportion of working adults were the same in 2007 as in 2001	57.4	–7	23.2	–13	Association between the proportion of working adults and household labor income per worker
If the distribution of labor income per workerwas the same in 2007 as in 2001	57.3	2	23.0	3	Proportion of working adults
Original situation in 2007	55.2	52	20.2	41	Distribution of labor income per adult worker in the household

Source: Authors' estimations based on the Pesquisa Nacional por Amostra de Domicílios (PNAD), 2001 and 2007.

Table 6-2. *Evolution of Per Capita Income Distribution and Its Determinants, Brazil, 2001 and 2007*

	2001			2007			Percent variation (2007–01)		
Determinant	*Average*	*Inequality (ratio 20+/20–)*	*Inequality (ratio 10+/60–)*	*Average*	*Inequality (ratio 20+/20–)*	*Inequality (ratio 10+/60–)*	*Average*	*Inequality (ratio 20+/20–)*	*Inequality (ratio 10+/60–)*
Per capita household income[a]	459	26.9	2.5	533	20.2	2.0	16	–25	–20
Proportion of adults in the household (15 years and more)	71	2.5	0.3	75	2.4	0.3	5	–5	–6
Household income per adult	617	19.4	2.1	687	14.6	1.7	11	–25	–20
Nonlabor income per adult	122	...	214	146	...	26	19	...	–88
Labor income per adult	494	59.4	2.8	541	55.6	2.3	9	–6	–15
Proportion of working adults	62	6.1	0.4	64	5.9	0.4	4	–4	–5
Labor income per working adult	829	21.0	2.1	862	17.3	1.7	4	–18	–17

Source: Authors' estimations based on the Pesquisa Nacional por Amostra de Domicílios (PNAD), 2001 and 2007.
a. Income is expressed in 2007 reais (R$).

The association between proportion of adults in the household and household income per adult did not contribute to explaining the decline in income inequality from 2001 to 2007. In fact, the impact of the correlation on inequality was negative (table 6-1a), indicating that changes in this correlation were unequalizing. If the correlation between the proportion of adults and income per adult had been held constant, the decline in income inequality would have been greater. As table 6-1a reveals, practically all the recent decline in income inequality was caused by changes in the distribution of household income per adult. According to table 6-2, the recent changes in that distribution were profound. Between 2001 and 2007, the household income per adult increased by 11 percent and the inequality in its distribution was reduced by the same magnitude as the inequality in per capita household income (20 percent to 25 percent).

The relative importance of labor income and nonlabor income

Given the importance of changes in the distribution of income per adult, the next step is to decompose its contribution. As already mentioned, household income per adult can be expressed as the sum of nonlabor and labor income per adult, . Thus, the total contribution of income per adult results from changes in the distribution of o and t as well as from changes in the correlation between them.

The estimates presented in table 6-1b show that depending on the measure of inequality, between 40 and 50 percent of the recent decline in income inequality was due to changes in the distribution of nonlabor income per adult. The impact of its distribution on income inequality resulted from both a large reduction in the level of inequality and growth in its share in the total household income[10] (see table 6-2).[11]

Changes in the distribution of labor income per adult can explain 31 percent to 46 percent of the decline in inequality (see table 6-1b). Table 6-2 shows that this contribution resulted from both considerable growth in labor income per adult (9 percent in the period) and a moderate reduction in the level of inequality (6 percent to 15 percent). The change in the association between labor and nonlabor income per adult also was of some importance, explaining 11 percent of the recent reduction in inequality.[12]

10. This high contribution is also found in Barros, Carvalho, and Franco (2007). Meanwhile, other authors, such as Hoffmann (2006a, 2006b, 2006c) and Soares and others (2007), find much smaller contributions. The difference is due to corresponding differences in methodology. As Barros, Carvalho, and Franco (2007) argues, the methodology that we use has a number of advantages over the one used by Hoffmann (2006a, 2006b, 2006c) and Soares and others (2007) and so should produce more reliable results.

11. We investigate this contribution and the role of expansions in government transfers in particular in greater detail later in the chapter.

12. See Barros, Carvalho, and Franco (2007) for a more detailed analysis of the reduction in this association and its contribution to the decline in inequality.

*The importance of the proportion of working adults
and the labor income per worker*

As shown, almost half of the recent decline in income inequality resulted from changes in the distribution of labor income per adult. Because labor income per adult is the product of the proportion of working adults and the labor income per working adult in the household ($t = u.w$), its overall contribution is derived from changes in the marginal distribution of those two factors or from changes in the correlation between them.

As shown in table 6-2, from 2001 to 2007, despite the sizable increase (4 percent) in the proportion of working adults, the reduction in inequality of access to jobs was very limited: between 4 to 6 times smaller than the corresponding reduction in overall income inequality. Consequently, changes in the distribution of the proportion of working adults (with a contribution of below 5 percent) were not important in explaining the decline in income inequality (see table 6-1c).

Changes in labor income per working adult in the household, however, were significant, showing important effects on overall income inequality. Depending on the inequality measure, 40 to 50 percent of the recent decline in income inequality resulted from changes in the distribution of labor income per working adult. That important contribution came, essentially, from a substantial reduction in inequality of labor income among workers. According to table 6-2, between 2001 and 2007, the decline in labor income inequality among workers was very similar to the one observed for per capita income. Indeed, measured by the ratio of the top 20 percent of income to the bottom 20 percent of income, inequality in labor income per worker declined by 18 percent; using the same measure of inequality, per capita income inequality declined by 25 percent. In contrast, changes in the correlation between the proportion of working adults and household labor income per worker were unequalizing. The fact that changes in the correlation between those two determinants had negative impacts on overall inequality, despite the recent large employment increase, indicates that workers from relatively poor households were not among those who benefited the most from job creation during 2001–07.

The Contribution of Changes in Public Transfers to the Fall in Income Inequality

As shown, at least half of the recent sharp decline in inequality is related to changes in the distribution of nonlabor income.[13] Between 2001 and 2007, the proportion of Brazilians living in households receiving some nonlabor income rose from

---

13. See Barros and others (2006a, 2006d); Hoffman (2006a, 2006d); Soares and others (2007), among others.

42 percent to 52 percent (see table 6-3). It is worth mentioning that despite the sharp increase in coverage, the share of nonlabor income in total household income increased only slightly, from 22 percent (in 2001) to 23 percent (in 2007).

Although methodological differences generate some disagreement in the literature about the magnitude of the impact of these changes,[14] there is consensus that a sizable fraction of the recent decline in inequality originated from changes in nonlabor income.[15] In chapter 3 of this volume, James Robinson argues that the "surge" in public transfers is associated with the PT (a Social Democratic leftist party) winning the presidential elections. However, regardless of the political economy dynamics that produced this result, the first thing to know is the extent to which expansion of the coverage and benefits of programs targeting the poor accounted for the observed decline in inequality. Here we decompose the impact of nonlabor income by source in order to isolate the contribution of changes in the distribution of income from the following nonlabor income sources: assets (rents, interest, and dividends); private transfers (for example, remittances); and public transfers. Since public transfers account for more than 80 percent of households' nonlabor income (see table 6-4)[16] and the percentage of the population in households with at least one beneficiary has increased by 10 percentage points since 2001 (see table 6-3), public transfers will receive priority in our analysis. We use a procedure proposed by Barros and others (2007) to decompose the contribution of changes in nonlabor income by source.

We decomposed nonlabor income into seven sources. Two are from assets (rents; interest and dividends); two from private transfers (transfers from nonresidents; other pensions); and three from public transfers (pensions and other standard contributory social security benefits; Benefício de Prestação Continuada; Bolsa Família and similar programs (see figure 6-3).[17] Benefício de Prestação Continuada (BPC) is a transfer based on the constitutional right of people age 65 or older and disabled people to independent living. The benefit, equal to a monthly payment of one minimum wage, is managed by the Ministry of Social Development and Combating Hunger (MDS) and is fully funded by the National Fund of Social Assistance

14. See Barros, Carvalho, and Franco (2007) for a discussion regarding these methodological differences.

15. The impact estimates for the 2001–05 period vary from 20 percent, according to Hoffmann (2006d), to 50 percent, according to Barros and others (2006a, 2006d). For the 2001–04 period, Hoffman (2006a) finds a contribution of 25 percent and Soares and others (2007) finds 27 percent.

16. The composition of household income varies according to the source of information. Given the PNAD's larger underestimation of income from assets, the contribution of public transfers tends to be larger in this source than in Pesquisa de Orçamentos Familiares (POF). For a comparative analysis of the composition of nonlabor income using these two surveys and the National Accounts, see Barros, Cury, and Ulyssea (2006).

17. Among similar programs are Bolsa Escola, Bolsa Alimentação, Cartão Alimentação, Auxílio Gás, and Programa de Erradicação do Trabalho Infantil (PETI). Unfortunately, this breakdown of nonlabor income does not follow immediately from the PNAD data set. The methodology used to construct this income aggregate is adapted from the one proposed by Barros, Carvalho, and Franco (2007).

(FNAS).[18] Bolsa Família, managed by the same ministry, is a conditional cash transfer provided to poor families on condition that they ensure that children and adolescents attend school and that they meet basic health care requirements, such as having children under the age of 6 years vaccinated and, in the case of pregnant women and lactating mothers, attending pre- and postnatal care sessions. The program attempts both to reduce short-term poverty by direct cash transfer and to fight long-term poverty by investing in the human capital of the poor. The benefits paid by the program range from R$20 to R$182, depending on monthly income per person in the family and the number of children and adolescents up to the age of 17 years. It reaches 11 million families, more than 46 million people, a large proportion of the country's low-income population.[19]

Table 6-3 shows that according to PNAD (Pesquisa Nacional por Amostra de Domicílios) (2007), almost 25 percent of total household income comes from nonlabor sources, of which transfers, especially public transfers, are the most important.[20] Indeed, as table 6-4 shows, public and private transfers together represent 90 percent of all nonlabor income. The remaining nonlabor income is constituted by rents (6 percent) and interests and dividends (3 percent).[21]

Analyzing transfers in more detail (see tables 6-3 and 6-4), we find that 90 percent are public. Pensions and retirements represent 95 percent of all public transfers; Bolsa Família and Benefício de Prestação Continuada benefits each represent less than 0.5 percent of total household income and around 3 percent of all public transfers. Together, BPC and Bolsa Família benefits account for only 1 percent of total household income and 5 percent of public transfers.[22]

Identifying recent changes in nonlabor income

As already mentioned, about half of the recent decline in income inequality was due to changes in the distribution of nonlabor income. Later in the discussion we estimate and analyze the individual contribution of each of the seven nonlabor income sources in reducing inequality. Meanwhile, in order to make the outcome

18. For more information, see Benefício de Prestação Continuada de Assistência Social (BPC) (www.mds.gov.br/programas/rede-suas/protecao-social-basica/beneficio-de-prestacao-continuada-bpc).

19. For more information, see Programa Bolsa Família (www.mds.gov.br/bolsafamilia/o_programa_bolsa_familia). In 2007, the number of extremely poor people was 18.4 million (10.2 percent) and the total number of poor people (extremely plus moderately poor) was 50.6 million (28 percent). Poverty figures were estimated using an extreme poverty line equal to R$87.6 a month and a moderate poverty line equal to R$175.1 a month. Brazil does not have official poverty lines. Barros and others (2009b).

20. According to Pesquisa de Orçamento Familiar (POF) and Contas Nacionais (National Accounts), the contribution of labor income is smaller. A significant fraction, however, is due to imputed rents for households living in houses that they own. See Barros, Cury, and Ulyssea (2006).

21. The income from assets is clearly underestimated in PNAD. Barros, Cury, and Ulyssea (2006) estimated that the aggregate value of asset income is four times larger in according to National Accounts than according to PNAD.

22. It is worth emphasizing that because PNAD does not take sporadic sources of income into consideration, it also ends up not capturing some important public transfers, such as Seguro Desemprego and Abono Salarial. PNAD therefore underestimates the total value of public transfers.

Table 6-3. Decomposition of Household Per Capita Income by Source, Brazil, 2001 and 2007

Source of income	Per capita income (in R$ per month)		Percent variation (2007–01)	Percent of total household income		Variation (2007–01, in percentage points)	Percentage of people in households that receive nonlabor income		Variation (2007–01, in percentage points)
	2001	2007		2001	2007		2001	2007	
Total income	458.8	532.6	16	100	100	...	...	...	...
Labor income	357.3	409.7	15	77.9	76.9	–1.0	...	...	...
Nonlabor income	101.4	122.9	21	22.1	23.1	1.0	42.4	52.1	9.7
Income from assets	11.8	11.4	–4	2.6	2.1	–0.4	5.7	5.7	0.1
Rents	8.8	7.7	–13	1.9	1.4	–0.5	3.7	3.3	–0.4
Interest and dividends	3.0	3.7	26	0.6	0.7	0.1	2.2	2.6	0.4
Transfers	89.6	111.5	24	19.5	20.9	1.4	39.3	48.8	9.5
Private	9.8	10.5	7	2.1	2.0	–0.2	7.2	7.5	0.3
Aid from nonresidents	3.1	2.9	–8	0.7	0.5	–0.1	3.0	2.5	–0.5
Pensions and retirements	6.7	7.6	13	1.5	1.4	0.0	4.4	5.2	0.8
Public	79.8	101.0	27	17.4	19.0	1.6	34.5	44.5	10.0
Pensions and retirements	78.5	95.6	22	17.1	17.9	0.8	29.3	29.5	0.2
Benefício de Prestação Continuada	0.3	2.7	715	0.1	0.5	0.4	0.5	2.5	2.0
Bolsa Família and related programs	0.9	2.8	195	0.2	0.5	0.3	6.5	16.9	10.4

Source: Authors' estimations based on the Pesquisa Nacional por Amostra de Domicílios (PNAD), 2001 and 2007.

Table 6-4. *Decomposition of Household Nonlabor Income by Source, Brazil, 2001 and 2007*
Percent

Income source	Nonlabor per capita income			Per capita income from transfers			Per capita income from public transfers		
	2001	2007	Variation (2007–01, in percentage points)	2001	2007	Variation (2007–01, in percentage points)	2001	2007	Variation (2007–01, in percentage points)
Nonlabor income	100	100	...	...	...	.	...	...	.
Income from assets	11.6	9.3	–2.4	...	...	...	...	...	—
Rents	8.7	6.2	–2.5	...	...	...	...	...	...
Interest and dividends	2.9	3.0	0.1	...	...	...	...	...	...
Transfers	88.4	90.7	2.4	100	100	...	...	...	...
Private	9.7	8.6	–1.2	11.0	9.4	–1.6	...	...	...
Transfers from nonresidents	3.1	2.3	–0.7	3.5	2.6	–0.9	...	...	...
Pensions	6.6	6.2	–0.4	7.5	6.8	–0.7	...	...	...
Public	78.6	82.2	3.5	89.0	90.6	1.6	100	100	...
Pensions	77.4	77.8	0.4	87.6	85.7	–1.9	98.4	94.6	–3.8
Benefício de Prestação Continuada	0.3	2.2	1.8	0.4	2.4	2.0	0.4	2.6	2.2
Bolsa Família and related programs	0.9	2.3	1.3	1.1	2.5	1.4	1.2	2.8	1.6

Source: Authors' estimation based on Pesquisa Nacional por Amostra de Domicílios (PNAD), 2001 and 2007.

Figure 6-3. *Source of Total Income*

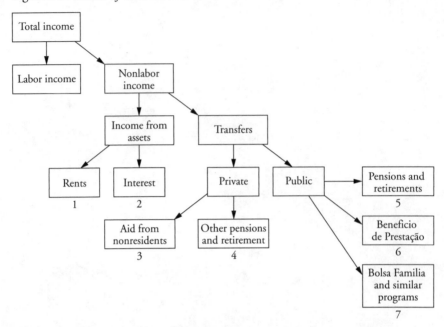

Source: A similar figure can be found in Barros, Foguel, and Ulyssea (2006) and Herrán (2005).

of this decomposition more transparent, and facilitate its interpretation, we present a short description of the changes that took place in the distribution of each one of these seven nonlabor income sources since 2001.

—*Coverage.* Despite the fact that nonlabor income represents only one-fourth of total household income, it is not concentrated in a few households. On the contrary, more than half of all Brazilians (52 percent) live in households that receive some sort of nonlabor income. Public transfers are the main factor in that broad coverage: 45 percent of all Brazilians live in households that receive some sort of public transfer (see table 6-3).

Of public transfers, contributory social security has the largest coverage—about 30 percent of the Brazilian population lives in households receiving contributory social security benefits. However, since 2001, the percentage of the population living in households benefiting from Bolsa Família (a noncontributory benefit) increased steadily, reaching 17 percent in 2007. Although the amount of resources transferred through BPC is similar to the amount transferred by Bolsa Família, the number of Brazilians in households that benefit from Bolsa Família is 7 times greater than the number in households that receive BPC (table 6-3). From 2001 to 2007, the coverage rate of nonlabor income grew 10 percentage points, increasing from 42 percent to 52 percent. Essentially all growth came from Bolsa Família. The percentage of population in households receiving BPC increased only slightly, by

2 percentage points, and the coverage of contributory social security benefits remained virtually unchanged (table 6-3).

—*Average value of the benefit income among recipients.* The impact of a change in an income source on total inequality strongly depends on its share in total income. Indeed, changes in income sources with a relatively small share in total income do not generate significant impacts on total inequality.

A given income source's share in total income depends on its coverage (percentage of households with some income from that source) and the average benefit among those receiving it. We previously reviewed the recent evolution of coverage of contributory social security, BPC, and Bolsa Família; here we analyze the average benefit among recipients of income from each of those sources.

As table 6-5 shows, contributory social security or pensions (R$324 per capita) is the nonlabor income source with the highest per capita value among households with at least one recipient. Bolsa Família (R$15–R$16 per capita) is the nonlabor income source with the lowest per capita value. The average benefit from Bolsa Família is much smaller even when compared with other noncontributory transfers, like BPC. As a matter of fact, the per capita BPC benefit among households with at least one recipient is 6 times greater than the corresponding benefit from Bolsa Família.

During the 2001–07 period, the amount of all public transfers increased, particularly among those indexed to the minimum wage (BPC and contributory social security benefits). As table 6-5 reveals, per capita BPC and per capita social security benefits among households with at least one beneficiary increased by 55 percent and 21 percent, respectively. The per capita benefits from Bolsa Família also increased, but by only 13 percent. In contrast, per capita income among households with at least one recipient did not increase significantly for all other nonlabor income sources. Transfers from nonresidents were an exception; they increased 10 percent.

—*Income share.* All nonlabor income sources, particularly public transfers, increased as shares of total income, except for rents and private transfers. Since the share of an income source is determined by its average value per beneficiary and its coverage rate, any increase in its share in total nonlabor income can be decomposed into two components: one component due to the increase in coverage and a second component due to the increase in the average value of the benefit/income received per beneficiary. Table 6-5 presents this decomposition for each nonlabor income source.

The table reveals that from 2001 to 2007 most nonlabor income sources increased their share of total income by expanding coverage. In fact, the increase in the share of overall nonlabor income in total income—and particularly the share of public transfers in total income—was generated by expanding coverage. Between 80 percent and 90 percent of the increase of the share of noncontributory public transfers (like BPC and Bolsa Família) in total income was caused by expanding

Table 6-5. *Evolution of Nonlabor Income (Average and Share), Brazil, 2001–07*

Income source	Per capita value of nonlabor income sources among households with at least one recipient			Decomposing the share evolution of each nonlabor income source		
	2001	*2007*	*Percent variation (2007–01)*	*Due to coverage*	*Due to average benefit*	*Total*
Nonlabor income	239	236	–1	>100	<0	100
Income from assets	208	198	–5	<0	>100	100
Rents	236	232	–2	88	12.4	100
Interest and dividends	136	142	4	81	18.8	100
Transfers	228	229	0	99	0.8	100
Private	137	139	2	72	28.1	100
Transfers from nonresidents	104	115	10	>100	<0	100
Pensions	153	147	–4	>100	<0	100
Public	231	227	–2	>100	<0	100
Pensions	268	324	21	4.00	96.0	100
Benefício de Prestação Continuada	69	107	55	79.1	20.9	100
Bolsa Família and related programs	15	16	13	88.6	11.4	100

Source: Authors' estimations based on the Pesquisa Nacional por Amostra de Domicílios (PNAD), 2001 and 2007.

Table 6-6. *Contribution of Nonlabor Income Sources to Overall Income Inequality Decline, Brazil, 2001–07*

Income source	2007 Gini coefficient	2007 Gini with the distribution of the source complement of 2001 Gini	2001 Gini coefficient	Percent contribution of each income source
Total income	0.552		0.593	
Labor income		0.568		62
Nonlabor income		0.572		51
Income from assets		0.592		4
Rents		0.593		1
Interest and dividends		0.592		3
Transfers		0.573		49
Private		0.593		1
Aid from nonresidents		0.594		−1
Pensions and retirements		0.593		2
Public		0.573		49
Pensions and retirements		0.582		28
Benefício de Prestação Continuada		0.589		10
Bolsa Família and related programs		0.588		13

Source: Authors' estimations based on the Pesquisa Nacional por Amostra de Domicílios (PNAD), 2001 and 2007.

coverage. The only important exception to this rule was pensions and retirements. Almost the entire increase in social security's share of total income was a consequence of greater benefit generosity. Social security coverage remained essentially the same, but the real value of benefits increased by 20 percent.

Contribution from nonlabor sources to the fall in income inequality

Here we analyze the impact that changes in each component of nonlabor income had on the recent decline in inequality.[23] We compare the Gini coefficients for 2001 and 2007 with counterfactual simulations designed to capture what would have happened if the distribution of each nonlabor income source had not changed during that time. From the difference between the actual decline in inequality and the decline in the counterfactual scenarios, we obtain estimates of the impact of each nonlabor income source on the reduction in overall inequality. The results are presented in table 6-6.

Confirming the results obtained previously, the estimates reveal that half of the recent decline in inequality (over the 2001–07 period) was due to changes in the

23. All estimates are based on the methodology described in Barros, Carvalho, and Franco (2007).

distribution of nonlabor income. That is a very significant result, considering that nonlabor income represents only one-fourth of total household income.

The decomposition by type of nonlabor income source is even more revealing. As expected, the impacts of changes in the distribution of income from assets (rents; interest and dividends) and private transfers were limited. Most of the impact of nonlabor income on the reduction of overall income inequality was due to the recent changes in the distribution of public transfers, which explain 49 percent of the total decline in inequality. Although both contributory and noncontributory transfers were important factors, the role of contributory transfers was predominant. The recent changes in social security benefits explain almost 30 percent of the overall reduction in income inequality. The increasing coverage of noncontributory benefits like BPC and Bolsa Família also were important. Despite representing just a tiny fraction of total household income (0.5 percent), each of these noncontributory benefits explains about 10 percent of the overall decline in income inequality.

Labor Earnings Inequality and Education

As shown, the fall in labor income inequality accounted for about half of the reduction in overall income inequality. The fall in labor income inequality, in turn, was due primarily to the fall in inequality in the distribution of labor income per working adult. One factor that may explain that trend could be changes in access to education. The last decade was marked by the accelerated expansion of access to education in Brazil, an expansion that occurred more than twice as fast as the one that occurred in the 1980s.[24] In chapter 3 in this volume, James Robinson argues that the massive expansion of education is related to the restoration of democracy in 1985.

Here we analyze the relationship between the expansion of education in Brazil and the recent decline in income inequality.[25] Expansion in education may influence income inequality through the following mechanisms: a decline in fertility; an increase in female labor force participation; and a reduction in labor earnings inequality. We focus here only on the impact of the expansion in education on the distribution of labor earnings.[26] As shown previously, half of the recent decline in inequality is due to changes in the distribution of labor earnings.[27] Hence, the

24. Estimates from PNAD show that in the last decade average schooling of the Brazilian labor force increased by almost two completed grades, while in the previous decade it increased by only 0.7 of a completed grade.

25. Foguel and Azevedo (2007) and Menezes-Filho, Fernandes, and Picchetti (2007) also investigate this issue. However, we wish to investigate the causes of inequality associated with the distribution of the population according to household per capita income, and those studies investigate only the impact on labor earnings inequality.

26. For an analysis on the impact of demographic changes, see Wajnman, Turra, and Agostinho (2006).

27. See also Hoffmann (2006c, 2006d); Soares and others (2007); Barros and others (2006c, 2006d), and Barros, Carvalho, and Franco (2007).

accelerated expansion of education over the last decade may have played an important role in reducing overall inequality.[28]

A large literature[29] emphasizes that education affects the distribution of labor earnings through two channels: *quantity effect* and *price effect*. First, earnings (returns to education) tend to increase as workers' education increases; thus, the greater the inequality in education, the greater the inequality in labor earnings (quantity effect). Moreover, given a level of inequality in education, the larger the earnings differentials by education, the greater the inequality in labor income (price effect). In other words, labor markets "translate" educational inequality into labor earnings inequality depending on the shape of the curve of returns to education. The magnitude of the inequality translated from education to labor earnings is determined by two factors: the magnitude of the inequality in education and the sensitivity of the "translator" used to transform education inequality into labor earnings inequality. The sensitivity of the translator is the steepness of the correlation between earnings and education; the more sensitive earnings are to workers' education level, the greater the eventual labor earnings inequality. Here we evaluate both the joint and the individual contribution of these two channels.

Evidently, the magnitude and nature of changes in the education distribution (quantity effects) and changes in the steepness of earnings-education correlation (price effects) determine the impact of those changes on overall inequality. Therefore we describe the magnitude and nature of changes in quantity effects and price effects of education before estimating their impact on overall inequality. The following discussion may be of considerable use in interpreting the results.[30]

The relation between labor earnings and education

The typical form of the correlation between educational attainment and monthly labor earnings in Brazil initially is concave and then becomes convex. Hence, the first years of schooling (literacy) and the last (higher education) have the greatest

---

28. See the theoretical discussion on the role of educational expansion on the supply of skills and its impact on labor earnings inequality in chapter 2 by Jaime Kahhat.

29. See Langoni (2005); Tinbergen (1956, 1975); Becker and Chiswick (1966); Sattinger (1993); and Barros and Mendonça (1993, 1996), among others.

30. The methodology used here to estimate the contribution of educational expansion to reducing income inequality is based on Barros, Franco, and Mendonça (2007a). It extends the available literature in three dimensions. First, this methodology, similar to that in Bourguignon and Ferreira (2004) and Barros, Ganuza, and Vos (2002), investigates the impact on inequality in household per capita income, while most of the others procedures are limited to investigating the impact on earnings inequality; see Menezes-Filho, Fernandes, and Picchetti (2007); Foguel and Azevedo (2007); and Cortez and Firpo (2007). Second, it isolates the impact of education from the impact of other human capital dimensions. Other methodologies allow us to obtain only the joint impact of changes in all dimensions of human capital; see Menezes-Filho, Fernandes, and Picchetti (2007); Foguel and Azevedo (2007). Finally, it allows us to isolate for each type of human capital the contribution of changes in the distribution of human capital (quantity effect) from the impact of changes in the sensitivity of earnings to human capital (price effect). All the other available methodologies allow isolating the price and quantity effects only for all changes in the distribution of human capital combined; see, again, Menezes-Filho, Fernandes, and Picchetti (2007) and Foguel and Azevedo (2007).

Figure 6-4. *Evolution of the Differentials in Labor Earnings between Education Levels, Brazil, 1995–2007*[a]

Percent differential in labor earnings

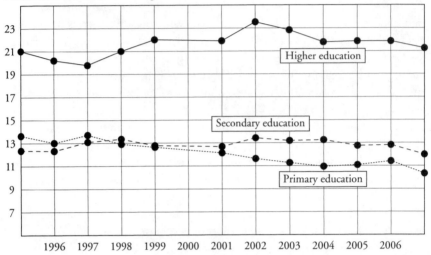

Source: Authors' estimations based on Pesquisa Nacional por Amostra de Domicílios (PNAD), 1995 to 2007.

a. The y-axis equals {Exp [(average of the logarithmic of labor earnings of workers with X years of education) – (average of the logarithmic of labor earnings of workers with Y years of education) / (X – Y)]} – 1. The returns are estimated controlling for age, sex, race, and location of residence.

impact on labor earnings. The impact of in-between years of schooling is especially limited. Since 1995 labor earnings differentials by education level have declined at all levels.[31] As shown in figure 6-4 that reduction is much clearer after 2002, particularly for secondary and higher education. The decrease in the labor earnings differential by education level has been, unquestionably, one of the factors contributing to the recent decline in inequality in Brazil.

The correlation between earnings and education is responsible for translating education inequality into labor earnings inequality. Indeed, if all workers had the same level of education, there would be no education inequality to translate into labor earnings inequality and education would not contribute to labor earnings inequality, regardless of the steepness of the correlation between earnings and education. Over the last decade education inequality shows an inverted U shape. It increased until the end of the twentieth century and has continuously declined since then. This recent decline in education inequality is one of the factors responsible for the decline in overall income inequality.

31. In order to facilitate their interpretation, they all have been transformed into percentage changes per additional grade successfully completed.

Figure 6-5. *Education Inequality among Workers, Brazil, 1995–2007*

Standard deviation

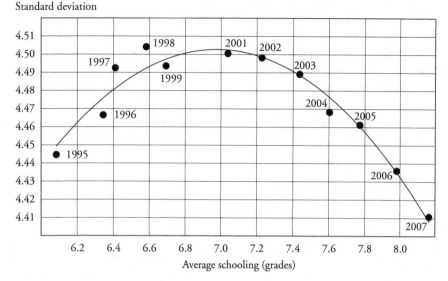

Source: Authors' estimations based on Pesquisa Nacional por Amostra de Domicílios (PNAD), 1995 to 2007.

It is worth pointing out that the inverted U shape of the evolution of education inequality was not unexpected. On the contrary, it is the natural consequence of the corresponding inverted U shape of the correlation between average education and inequality, which is known as the Kuznets curve (see figure 6-5). According to the behavior of Kuznets' curve, education inequality begins to decline whenever average schooling exceeds some threshold level, which typically is around seven completed grades. As shown in figure 6-5, education inequality in Brazil starts to decline precisely when average schooling reaches seven completed grades.

This figure has important implications for the future impact of education on income inequality. The concavity implies that, from now on, education inequality should decline at increasing rates. Moreover, the inverse correlation implies that the faster education expands, the faster education inequality and, consequently, earnings inequality will decline.

But labor income inequality is not determined only by the magnitude of education inequality. It also depends on how labor markets translate educational differences into labor earnings differences (price effects). In some markets, small educational differences lead to small differences in earnings, while in other markets small educational differences lead to substantial earnings differentials. Given two labor markets with equal education inequality, the one with the flatter correlation between education and earnings will reveal less income inequality. Conversely, given two labor markets with equally steep earnings-education correlations, the market with lower education inequality will reveal less income inequality.

As a consequence, for education to contribute to reducing income inequality, it is necessary to have either a decline in the inequality of education or a flattening of the correlation between labor earnings and education, or both. As already seen, throughout the 2001–07 period, both a decline in education inequality and a flattening of the correlation between labor earnings and education have occurred; thus, both have contributed to the recent decline in income inequality. According to Barros, Franco, and Mendonca (2007a), quantity (price) effects together contributed to 50 (29) percent of the decline in total labor income inequality between 2001 and 2007; the price effect was larger, accounting for 35 (23) percentage points of the 50 (29) percent.

Contributions of quantity and price effects

Education (that is, changes in earnings differential by educational level and the distribution of education) was responsible for 50 percent of the recent decline in labor earnings inequality and for almost 30 percent of the decline in household per capita income inequality. The breakdown of its contribution reveals that the reduction in the steepness in the returns to education (price effect) was by far the more important factor, constituting 35 percent of the decline in labor earnings inequality and 23 percent of the decline in per capita income inequality. The direct contribution of changes in the distribution of education (quantity effect) was smaller, representing 11 percent of the decline in earnings inequality and only 3 percent of the decline in per capita income inequality.

Earnings Inequality and Labor Market Segmentation

As shown previously, a sizable fraction of the recent decline in income inequality came from changes in the distribution of labor earnings, in particular from a sharp decline in labor market earnings inequality.[32] Half of the decline in labor earnings inequality was caused by the combined effect of a fall in the inequality of education and a fall in the returns to education; the former was a result of the large expansion in educational access that took place in Brazil over the last decade.[33] What remains to be explained is the cause of the other half of the decline in labor earnings inequality.

As emphasized in Barros and Mendonça (1993, 1996), there are essentially two basic sources of differences in labor income. On one hand, earnings differentials may simply reflect preexisting intrinsic differences in productivity among workers;

---

32. See Hoffmann (2006a, 2006b); Barros, Carvalho, and Franco (2007); Soares and others (2007); Rocha (2007); Lavinas, Matijascic, and Nicoll (2007); Cury and Leme (2007); Bourguignon, Ferreira, and Leite (2007); Camargo and Cortez (2007).

33. See, for example, Herrán (2005).

if so, they are not generated but only revealed by labor markets. Those intrinsic differences were the source of inequality treated previously (that is, more educated workers have higher productivity and therefore command higher wages). On the other hand, some earnings differentials result from labor market imperfections, such as discrimination and segmentation. In that case, earning differences among equally productive workers are created by the failures in the labor market. Indeed, not all differences in earnings result from intrinsic differences in workers' productivity. A sizable fraction of earnings inequality is found among workers perfectly substitutable in production—workers whose productivity does not change even when they switch jobs with one another. In that case, the labor market rewards workers with the same intrinsic productivity differently and therefore certainly generates new inequalities.

The labor market generates inequality both when it unequally remunerates men and women or whites and blacks with the same productivity and when there are earning differences between perfectly substitutable workers from different labor market segments (for example, from markets in different geographic locations or from formal and informal labor markets). In the first case, the differentials are said to come from discrimination; in the second, they are said to come from labor market segmentation.

We focus here on the relationship between labor market segmentation and income inequality in order to evaluate the degree of segmentation of the Brazilian labor market, to analyze the extent to which it has become more integrated over the last decade, and to identify the impacts of its increasing integration on the recent decline in income inequality. Specifically, we analyze the contribution of three types of segmentation: spatial segmentation;[34] segmentation between the formal and informal segments of the labor market; and segmentation between economic sectors.

Before we begin, it is important to recognize that there is a strong interaction between inequality revealed by labor markets and inequality generated by labor markets. In general, it is not possible to add those components without incurring some double counting. When workers and jobs are heterogeneous and their allocation is not random, the best jobs may be assigned to workers with higher educational levels. In that case, there are two gains from education. First, a higher educational level elevates intrinsic productivity and hence elevates earnings, regardless of the kind of job a worker may end up with. Second, a higher education level leads to higher earnings whenever it gives priority access to better jobs. The second advantage will exist only as long as the labor market is segmented (generating better and worse jobs); workers are educationally heterogeneous; those with higher educational levels have priority access to better jobs. Thus, by nature, labor earnings inequality is an interaction

---

34. In this analysis we focus on the contribution of changes in the degree of labor market segmentation to the decline in overall income inequality. For an analysis of the relation between the level of regional disparities and the level of income inequality in Brazil, see Savedoff (1995) and the extensive literature reviewed there.

between inequality revealed by the labor market and inequality generated by the labor market.

Given the interaction between revealed and generated inequalities, we must be cautious when aggregating contributions. It is not possible simply to add the contribution of a segmentation decrease and the contribution of a reduction in earnings differentials by education level; there are overlaps. Part of the decline in earnings differentials by educational level comes from the decrease in labor market segmentation. When jobs become more homogeneous (similar earnings for similar jobs in different locations, for example), the benefits of a higher educational level decline.

Spatial segmentation

Here we consider three types of spatial segmentation: differentials among federal states; differentials between metropolitan areas and nonmetropolitan municipalities;[35] and differentials between urban and rural areas. In order to evaluate the degree of labor market segmentation among federal states, we divided the country into twenty-one territories, of which nineteen represent federal states and two represent conglomerates of smaller states in the Amazon region.[36] Since the twenty-one territories lead to 210 earnings differentials, we simplify the analysis of their evolution by using their average.[37] Since 1995 labor earnings differentials among states have shown a declining trend that undoubtedly contributed to Brazil's recent income inequality decline.

The PNAD does not identify the municipality where each of the workers in the sample resides or works, but it does identify whether workers live in a metropolitan area, in a nonmetropolitan area (including both small and medium municipalities), or in a small or medium municipality. The evolution of the level of labor market segmentation among these three geographical areas is presented in figure 6-6.

Figure 6-6 shows a continuous reduction in earnings differentials among these three segments of the labor market over the entire period. The reduction was especially sharp over the 2001–07 period, throughout which the differential between metropolitan areas and nonmetropolitan medium-size municipalities declined by 4 percentage points. The differential between metropolitan areas and nonmetropolitan small municipalities declined even more, about 6 percentage points. Also, the increasing integration of metropolitan and nonmetropolitan labor markets is certainly among the factors that have contributed to the country's recent decline in income inequality.

35. In the case of nonmetropolitan municipalities we work with two groups: self-representative nonmetropolitan municipalities (medium municipalities) and small municipalities. To simplify the analysis, we refer throughout the text only to the differential between metropolitan and nonmetropolitan areas.

36. See Barros, Franco, and Mendonça (2007b).

37. Obtained from the formula $C_{21;2} = \dfrac{21!}{2!(21-2)!} = \dfrac{21.20.19!}{2!19!} = \dfrac{21.20}{2} = 210.$

Figure 6-6. *Evolution of Labor Earnings Differential among Metropolitan and Nonmetropolitan Areas, Brazil, 1995–2007*

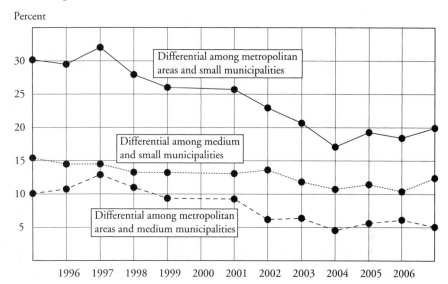

Percent

Differential among metropolitan areas and small municipalities

Differential among medium and small municipalities

Differential among metropolitan areas and medium municipalities

Source: Authors' estimations based on Pesquisa Nacional por Amostra de Domicílios (PNAD), 1995 to 2007.

Within municipalities, earnings disparities persist among workers with similar productive characteristics. The most salient disparity is the earnings gap between workers in urban and rural areas. In 2007, urban workers' labor earnings were 10 percent above earning for rural workers in similar jobs and with similar observed characteristics. The level of integration between urban and rural labor markets increased since 2001. Despite the significant increase of urban-rural differentials between 2003 and 2006, the urban-rural earnings gap for the entire 2001–07 period declined 2 percentage points, contributing to the recent decline in income inequality.

Segmentation between the formal and informal sectors

The segmentation between formal and informal employees and between formal employees and self-employed workers are among the most visible forms of segmentation in the Brazilian labor market.[38] Typically, informal and self-employed workers receive lower wages than those received by formal workers with the same productive characteristics.

38. Informal employees are those who do not have a formal labor contract (*carteira de trabalho assinada*). Formal employees are those who have a formal labor contract or are public employees.

Figure 6-7. *Evolution of Formal-Informal Labor Earnings Differentials, Brazil, 1995–2007*

Percent

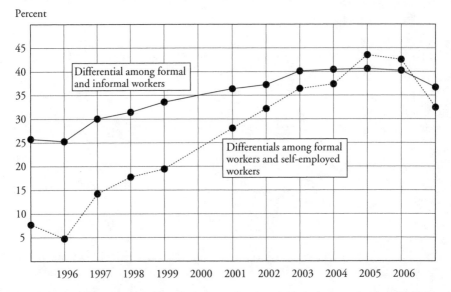

Source: Authors' estimations based on Pesquisa Nacional por Amostra de Domicílios (PNAD), 1995 to 2007.

Despite the decline in the degree of informality over the last decade, wage differentials between formal employees and self-employed workers increased significantly.[39] As figure 6-7 shows, despite a sharp decline in 2007, the differential between formal employees and self-employed workers is still 4 percentage points higher than in 2001 while the differential between formal and informal wage-earners has remained relatively stable since 2001. Given the lack of progress, labor market segmentation between formal and informal workers cannot have been a positive force in the recent decline in income inequality.

Segmentation by economic sector

To evaluate the degree of labor market segmentation by economic sector, we consider twelve economic sectors, leading to sixty-six intersectoral earnings differentials. Again, to simplify the analysis of the evolution of these differentials, we compute a synthetic measure that represents the average intersectoral differential. Over the last decade, the differentials between economic sectors declined by 2 percentage points, with half of the decline occurring after 2001. Hence, the reduction in

39. The degree of informality is defined as the proportion of the labor force that can be found in the informal sector (informal employees and self-employed workers). According to the PNAD, the degree of informality decreased 4 percentage points (from 50 percent in 1995 to 46 percent in 2007).

the level of sectoral segmentation is among the factors that contributed to the recent decline in income inequality.

Integration and inequality reduction

We previously described how labor market segmentation in Brazil evolved over the last decade along several dimensions, demonstrating that the Brazilian labor market—with the exception of the formal-informal sectors—became increasingly integrated. That growing integration certainly contributed to the recent reduction in income inequality.

To evaluate the magnitude and importance of its contributions, we apply a procedure, similar to that proposed in Langoni (2005),[40] that consists in predicting what each worker's labor income would have been in 2007 if the level of labor market segmentation were the same as in 2001. The results are presented in tables 6-7a and 6-7b.

We calculated the Ginis under the 2007 column by assuming that labor market segmentation for the corresponding dimensions remained as it was in 2001. These simulated Ginis are calculated by replacing the 2007 coefficients with the corresponding ones in 2001 in the earnings regressions.[41] The contribution is calculated by taking the difference between the 2007 Gini and the Gini that we assumed had no change in the particular source of segmentation and dividing it by the difference between the actual Ginis in the two points in time. So, for example, the contribution of labor market segmentation due to variations in labor earnings by economic sector is calculated as $(.528 - .531)/(.528 - .564) = .08$.[42]

As shown previously, all three types of spatial segmentation (among federal states, between metropolitan and nonmetropolitan areas, and between urban and rural areas) have declined from 2001 to 2007. The combined impact of those decreases in segmentation (geographic location) on the declines in labor earnings inequality and per capita household income inequality was 10 percent and 5 percent, respectively. Although all three types of spatial segmentation contributed to declines in earnings and per capita household income inequality, the contribution of the decline in the metropolitan-nonmetropolitan areas differential was especially important.[43] The reduction of the metropolitan-nonmetropolitan differential explains 6 percent of the decline in labor earnings inequality and 4 percent of the decline in per capita income inequality. The differentials among federal states were

40. See also Barros, Courseuil, and Leite (1999).

41. To keep the average wage in 2007 the same as the actual wage after the coefficients are replaced, one adjusts the intercept.

42. For example, to calculate the contribution of labor market segmentation: $.036 - .032/.036 = 11$ percent.

43. See also Ulyssea (2007) for additional evidence on the contribution of reductions in wage disparities between workers in small towns, in medium metropolitan areas, and in large metropolitan areas. The author shows that this process had a positive contribution for the reduction of inequality, which has become especially stronger in recent years.

Table 6-7a. *Contribution of Labor Market Segmentation to the Recent Decline in Labor Earnings Inequality*[a]

Counterfactual simulations	Inequality measured by the Gini coefficient		Reduction (Gini in 2007 –0.564)	Percent contribution to the reduction in inequality
	2001	2007		
Original distribution	0.564	0.528	0.036	100
Labor market segmentation		0.532	0.032	11
Geographic location		0.532	0.033	10
Federal states		0.529	0.035	4
Urban-rural areas		0.528	0.036	1
Municipality size[b]		0.530	0.034	6
Labor market segments		0.528	0.036	1
Formal-informal		0.525	0.039	–7
Economic sector		0.531	0.033	8

Source: Authors' estimations based on the Pesquisa Nacional por Amostra de Domicílios (PNAD), 2001 and 2007.

a. Table estimates do not include income from imputed rent and adjustments in transfers.

b. Nonmetropolitan municipalities are divided into two groups: self-representative municipalities and small municipalities. To simplify the analysis, we refer throughout the text only to the differential between metropolitan and nonmetropolitan.

Table 6-7b. *Contribution of Labor Market Segmentation to the Recent Decline in Per Capita Income Inequality*[a]

Counterfactual simulations	Inequality measured by the Gini coefficient		Reduction (Gini in 2007 –0.593)	Percent contribution to the reduction in inequality
	2001	2007		
Original distribution	0.593	0.552	0.042	100
Labor market segmentation		0.555	0.039	7
Geographic location		0.554	0.039	5
Federal states		0.552	0.041	1
Urban-rural areas		0.552	0.041	1
Municipality size[b]		0.553	0.040	4
Labor market segments		0.553	0.041	1
Formal-informal		0.550	0.043	–4
Economic sector		0.554	0.039	6

Source: Authors' estimations based on the Pesquisa Nacional por Amostra de Domicílios (PNAD), 2001 and 2007.

a. Table estimates do not include income from imputed rent and adjustments in transfers.

b. Nonmetropolitan municipalities are divided into two groups: self-representative municipalities and small municipalities. To simplify the analysis, we refer throughout the text only to the differential between metropolitan and nonmetropolitan.

responsible for almost 4 percent of the decline in earnings inequality but for only 1 percent of the decline in per capita income inequality. Finally, the reduction of the urban-rural earnings gap was responsible for only 1 percent of the reduction in both earnings and per capita income inequality.[44]

As shown, over the last decade there has been an increase in the wage gap between formal and informal workers. Hence, that increasing segmentation could not possibly explain the recent decline in income inequality in the country. Indeed, the simulation results indicate that if the formal-informal earnings gap had not increased over the 2001–07 period, the decline in earnings and per capita income inequality would have been 7 percent and 4 percent greater, respectively (see table 6-7b).

Finally, as shown, intersectoral earning differentials have declined sharply over the last six years, contributing to the overall decline in income inequality. Indeed, that reduction in segmentation was responsible for 8 percent of the decline in earnings inequality and for 6 percent of the decline in per capita income inequality.

The Relative Effectiveness of the Minimum Wage and the Bolsa Família Program

As shown previously, a sizable fraction of the recent decline in income inequality came from increases in the generosity of social security benefits as well as from reductions in earning differentials by skill level, location, and economic sector.[45] The increase in social security benefits is linked to increases in the minimum wage. In Brazil the minimum wage has a double function: it establishes a floor for social security benefits and for the wages of unskilled workers, especially in more traditional sectors. From 2001 to 2007 the minimum wage increased by 35 percent in real terms.[46] It therefore is natural to consider the minimum wage as one of the factors responsible for the greater generosity of government transfers and for the decrease of several earning differentials that, together, have contributed so much to the recent decline in income inequality. Indeed, several studies have argued that the recent increase in the real value of the minimum wage was responsible for a significant portion of the recent decline in income inequality.[47]

There seems to be no doubt that marginal increases in the minimum wage reduce income inequality and therefore that the real increase in the minimum wage

44. It is important to mention that we did not take into consideration spatial disparities in the cost of living (mainly because the information is not available). As a consequence, if the previous decade was marked by a significant spatial convergence in the cost of living, our results are overestimating both the real decline in income inequality and the contribution of increasing spatial labor markets integration to the decline in income inequality.

45. On the association between the recent decline in inequality and the reduction in intersectoral wage differentials as well as between metropolitan and nonmetropolitan areas, see Ulyssea and Foguel (2006) and Barros, Franco, and Mendonça (2007b).

46. This gain refers to the variation between May 1, 2001, and May 1, 2007.

47. In the case of the impact through government transfers, see Soares and others (2007). In the case of the contribution through the labor market, see Cortez and Firpo (2007).

that occurred between 2001 and 2007 must have contributed to overall inequality decline during that period.[48] However, in designing social policy it is not enough to recognize that increases in the minimum wage can reduce inequality; it also is necessary to determine whether the minimum wage is, among the available instruments, the most effective.

To shed some light on this issue, we compare the effectiveness of the minimum wage and one of its main alternatives, the Bolsa Família program.[49] More specifically, we compare the impact that a 10 percent increase in the minimum wage would have on income inequality with the corresponding impact if the same amount of resources were allocated to increase the value of Bolsa Família benefits.[50]

The methodology used is based on counterfactual simulations, and it corresponds to an attempt to have an ex ante evaluation of the impact on income inequality of increasing the minimum wage and of increasing the value of Bolsa Família benefits. This methodology, by its counterfactual nature, has the advantage of allowing a perfect identification of the impact but the disadvantage of being able to consider only a few channels through which the minimum wage and Bolsa Família benefits may influence income inequality. Empirical studies such as Barros and others (2001), Fajnzylber (2001), and Neumark, Cunningham, and Siga (2004) have the advantage of taking into consideration a much wider set of channels through which the minimum wage may operate. Those studies, however, have greater difficulty in isolating the impact of the minimum wage from all other economic factors, such as economic growth and exchange rate devaluation.

Standardizing the magnitude of interventions

At first, nothing prevents us from comparing the cost-effectiveness of programs with different costs and impacts. The existence of economies and diseconomies of scale may, however, make the comparison misleading. If there are diseconomies of scale, the impact of the program will not grow in proportion to the resources allocated to it. In that case, the program with more resources might seem less cost-effective, just because of its scale. The opposite event can also occur if there are economies of scale. For that reason, we compare only the cost-effectiveness of the minimum wage and the Bolsa Família program in situations in which each receives an identical volume of resources. In such cases, since the two alternatives have the same cost, the most cost-effective instrument will be the one with the greatest impact.

48. Of the studies of the impact of the minimum wage on Brazilian income distribution, it is worth mentioning Drobny and Wells (1983); Ramos and Almeida Reis (1995); Barros and others (2000, 2001); Neri (2000); Fajnzylber (2001); Soares (2002); Neumark, Cunningham, and Siga (2004); and Lemos (2005).

49. Barros and Carvalho (2006) also considers the comparison of an increase in minimum wage with an expansion of salário-família benefits.

50. Per beneficiary.

Once we have ensured that comparable amounts of resources have been devoted to an increase in the minimum wage and to Bolsa Família benefits, the relative effectiveness of the two instruments should not depend much on the chosen scale.[51] Thus, in order to facilitate our exposition, we established a 10 percent increase in the minimum wage and increased the Bolsa Família benefits using exactly the same amount of resources. We then simulate what each instrument's impact on income inequality would be.

Admittedly, the minimum wage influences the distribution of income through a variety of channels, some favorable (such as the increase in unskilled workers wages) and others unfavorable (such as a reduction in employment opportunities for unskilled workers or an increase in informality). At the risk of overestimating the effectiveness of the minimum wage, we ignore its negative impact on employment and informality and assume that it is capable of raising wages close to its value in both formal and informal sectors. Since in Brazil the minimum social security benefit is tied to the minimum wage, we take into account that increases in the minimum wage will raise the social security floor by the same amount.

We estimate that a 10 percent increase in the minimum wage would have an annual cost of R$7.4 billion.[52] Of that total, more than half the additional costs are in social security (R$3.9 billion). In order to standardize the amount of resources used, we identified the increase in Bolsa Família benefits that would require the same amount of resources. The same R$7.4 billion needed to raise the minimum wage by 10 percent would allow an increase in Bolsa Família benefits of three times their current value. Such an increase would certainly have a variety of direct and indirect effects on income inequality. In this analysis, however, we consider only its direct impact.[53]

Comparing the effectiveness of the minimum wage with that of the Bolsa Família program

Figure 6-8 presents the impact on the income share of the poorest α% (Lorenz curve) of a 10 percent increase in the minimum wage and the equivalent increase

---

51. If the importance of economies of scale is very distinct for the two instruments, the choice of scale can influence their relative effectiveness. In theory, Bolsa Família could be more effective than the minimum wage for the same scale and less effective for others. In this study, we do not investigate the relative scale sensitivity of the two instruments.

52. This includes the cost to the federal government and private sector employers.

53. To calculate direct impact, we assume an increase in the minimum wage, and, knowing by assumption who will benefit from that (for example, pensioners receiving about the minimum wage, workers earning about the minimum wage, and so on), we estimate how much total income will increase. A 10 percent increase in the minimum wage will increase family income by 7.4 billion reales. Dividing that by the total value of Bolsa Familia transers, we estimate how much the Bolsa Familia benefit must increase to generate the same increase in family income. The number of people who actually receive Bolsa Familia is obtained by checking which households receive an amount of "other income" that is typical of the size of the Bolsa Familia transfer (15, 30, 45, and so forth reales per month).

Figure 6-8. *Impact of Increasing Minimum Wage and Benefits from the Bolsa Familia Program on the Income Share of the Poorest Percentiles*

Percent income share

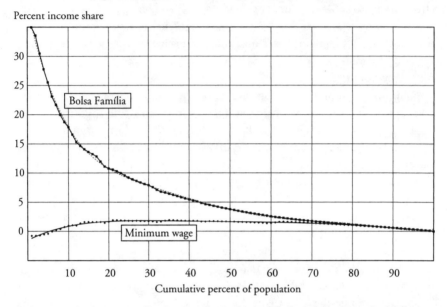

Cumulative percent of population

Source: Authors' estimations based on Pesquisa Nacional por Amostra de Domicílios (PNAD), 2005.

in Bolsa Família benefits. Since the amount of resources being used is identical, this figure allows us to directly evaluate the two instruments' relative effectiveness. The most effective will be the one with the greatest impact.

The increase in Bolsa Família benefits leads to an overall increase in the income share of the poorest $\alpha\%$, regardless of the point chosen in the distribution (α). Therefore, it unambiguously reduces inequality. The increase in the minimum wage, however, has an ambiguous impact on inequality. Indeed, an increase in the minimum wage reduces the income share of the poorest percentiles. Hence, not every measure of inequality will decline as a result of an increase in the minimum wage. For example, a 10 percent increase in the minimum wage would reduce the income share of the poorest 5 percent by 0.7 percentage points. Increasing Bolsa Família benefits is more effective[54] than increasing the minimum wage in raising the income share of the poorest 50 percent, regardless of the point chosen in the distribution. Therefore Bolsa Família is unambiguously more effective than the minimum wage in reducing inequality.

54. The effectiveness is calculated as the ratio between the impact on the income share of Bolsa Familia and an increase in the minimum wage for the corresponding centile.

Conclusion

Since 2000, income inequality in Brazil has been declining steadily and sharply. As a consequence, the per capita income of the bottom 10 percent of the population has been increasing at very high rates (7 percent a year), well above the national average. Extreme poverty has been declining at three times the pace necessary to meet the first Millennium Development Goal, and more than half of the decline came from reductions in income inequality. Never have reductions in inequality played such an important role in fighting poverty. Brazil experienced two previous episodes of large reductions in poverty;[55] in both cases, however, poverty reduction was due entirely to balanced economic growth. The decline in inequality during both previous episodes was minimal.

This analysis seeks to identify the factors responsible for the recent decline in inequality, in particular, the role of market forces, public policy, and institutions. It suggests that the decline resulted from three main factors: an increase in contributory and noncontributory government transfers; a decline in wage differentials by educational level and reductions in the inequality in education caused by accelerated expansion of the educational level of the labor force; and an improvement in spatial and sectoral integration of labor markets, in particular among metropolitan and nonmetropolitan areas.

The greater generosity of government transfers and the fast expansion of education were certainly a direct consequence of public policies implemented over the last 15 years. The reductions in labor earnings differentials and the greater spatial and sectoral integration of labor markets are clearly market responses. It remains debatable, nevertheless, whether the reductions in labor earnings differentials were also influenced by increases in the real value of the minimum wage.

Regardless of the contribution attributed to the increase in the minimum wage, it is undeniable that a shift in the pattern of economic growth toward more balanced regional and sectoral growth must also have contributed to the greater integration of Brazilian labor markets. Indeed, over the last decade, probably in response to the opening up of the Brazilian economy and facilitated by the increase in workers' educational level outside large metropolitan areas, a sizable fraction of Brazil's economic activity moved toward nonmetropolitan areas. According to IPEA, IBGE, and UNICAMP (2002), while the metropolitan areas and large cities (having more than 500,000 inhabitants) lost share in GDP between 2002 and 2005, the medium-size cities (between 100,000 and 500,000 inhabitants) had the best performance, increasing their participation in GDP by more than 1 percentage point.

In addition, government expenditures have likely become less concentrated in the country's more developed areas, particularly due to the increasing importance of targeted government transfers. The shift in government expenditure toward less

---

55. The Brazilian Miracle in the 1970s and more recently the Real Plan are important examples.

developed and remote areas fostered local labor markets, hence promoting regional integration.

Brazil's recent success in effectively reducing inequality and poverty is undeniable. However, despite such progress, the magnitude of inequality in the country is still high. According to this analysis, almost two additional decades of similar progress would be necessary for Brazil's level of inequality to align with the world average. As a result, the recent declines in poverty and inequality can be seen only as a very important first step in a long journey.

The sustainability of this unprecedented equalization process should be of serious concern to Brazilian society and policymakers. Up to this point, income inequality reductions were accomplished alongside increases in government expenditure. Actually, very few hard policy choices had to be faced. For instance, Brazil substantially increased the real value of the minimum wage and basic social security benefits and at the same time implemented a bold noncontributory social assistance program (Bolsa Família). It remains to be seen, therefore, what Brazil's capacity is for making the hard choices necessary to keep equalization going over periods of serious fiscal constraints.

Moreover, the very policies that have been so effective in reducing inequality are now beginning to show increasing signs of exhaustion. Major evidence of this is the decline in the absolute income of the poorest 5 percent in 2007, a year with an otherwise significant increase in overall per capita income and a substantial reduction in the Gini coefficient. Hence, to ensure the sustainability of the equalization process, Brazilian social policy also needs to adjust quickly to challenges posed by the ever-changing face of poverty in the country.

The design of Brazilian social policy is still far from optimum. A very active minimum wage policy continues to be pursued, despite the fact that, as we have shown, increases in the minimum wage are much less effective in reducing inequality than expansions in Bolsa Família benefits. Moreover, poverty is still 10 times greater among children than among the elderly, but the average noncontributory public transfer for an elderly person is at least 20 times greater than the average noncontributory public transfer for a child.[56] This suboptimum nature of Brazilian social policy has two interrelated implications. On one hand, it is one cause of the persistently high levels of inequality and poverty. On the other hand, optimizing social policy design gives Brazilian policymakers plenty of room to further reduce inequality, without the need of additional resources.

Maintaining the recent fast pace of equalization is certainly a major challenge for Brazil. Hard choices leading to better allocation of resources will have to be made if increases in government expenditures are to be contained. Equally important, policymakers will need to redesign existing policies to take into account the

56. In Brazil, households with elderly members generally have no children and households with children have no elderly members, so the transfers to grandchildren are already taken into account in the households with children.

changing face of poverty and maintain the effectiveness of public policy in fighting inequality.

References

Barros, Ricardo Paes de, and Mirela de Carvalho. 2006. "A efetividade do salário mínimo como instrumento para reduzir a pobreza e a desigualdade." In "Uma agenda para o crescimento econômico e a redução da pobreza," edited by Paulo M. Levy and Renato Villela. IPEA Texto para Discussão. Rio de Janeiro: IPEA.

Barros, Ricardo Paes de, Mirela Carvalho, and Samuel Franco. 2007. "O Papel das Transferências Públicas na Queda Recente da Desigualdade de Renda Brasileira." In *Desigualdade de Renda no Brasil: uma análise da queda recente,* vol. 2, edited by Ricardo Paes de Barros, Miguel Nathan Foguel, and Gabriel Ulyssea. Brasília: IPEA.

Barros, Ricardo Paes de, Carlos Henrique Courseuil, and Phillippe Leite. 1999. "Labor Market and Poverty in Brazil." *Revista de Econometria* 19, no. 2: 211–96.

———. 2001. "Uma avaliação dos impactos do salário mínimo sobre o nível de pobreza metropolitana no Brasil." *Revista Economia* 2, no. 1: 111–14.

Barros, Ricardo Paes de, Samir Cury, and Gabriel Ulyssea. 2006. "A desigualdade de renda encontra-se subestimada? Uma análise comparativa usando a Pnad, POF, e Contas Nacionais." In *Desigualdade de Renda no Brasil: uma análise da queda recente,* vol. 1, edited by Ricardo Paes de Barros, Miguel Nathan Foguel, and Gabriel Ulyssea. Brasília: IPEA.

Barros, Ricardo Paes de, Miguel Nathan Foguel, and Gabriel Ulyssea, orgs. 2006. *Desigualdade de Renda no Brasil: uma análise da queda recente.* Nota tecnica. Brasília: IPEA.

Barros, Ricardo Paes de, Samuel Franco, and Rosane Mendonça. 2007a. "A recente queda na desigualdade de renda e o acelerado progresso educacional brasileiro da última década." In *Desigualdade de Renda no Brasil: uma análise da queda recente,* vol. 2, organized by Ricardo Paes de Barros, Miguel Nathan Foguel, and Gabriel Ulyssea. Brasília: IPEA.

———. 2007b. "Discriminação e Segmentação no Mercado de Trabalho e Desigualdade de Renda no Brasil." In *Desigualdade de Renda no Brasil: uma análise da queda recente,* vol. 2, organized by Ricardo Paes de Barros, Miguel Nathan Foguel, and Gabriel Ulyssea. Brasília: IPEA.

Barros, Ricardo Paes de, Enrique Ganuza, and Rob Vos. 2002. "Labour Market Adjustment, Poverty, and Inequality during Liberalization." In *Economic Liberalization, Distribution, and Poverty: Latin America in the 1990s,* edited by Rob Vos, Lance Taylor, and Ricardo Paes de Barros. Massachusetts: Edward Elgar.

Barros, Ricardo Paes de, Ricardo Henriques, and Rosane Mendonça. 2000. "A estabilidade inaceitável: desigualdade e pobreza no Brasil." In *Desigualdade e Pobreza no Brasil,* edited by Ricardo Henriques. Rio de Janeiro: IPEA.

Barros, Ricardo Paes de, and Rosane Mendonça. 1992. "A Research Note on Family and Income Distribution: The Equalizing Impact of Married Women's Earnings in Metropolitan Brazil." *Sociological Inquiry* 62, no. 2: 208–19

———.1993. "Geração e reprodução da desigualdade de renda no Brasil." In *Perspectivas da economia brasileira: 1994,* pp. 471–90. Rio de Janeiro: IPEA.

———. 1996. "Os determinantes da desigualdade no Brasil." In *A economia brasileira em perspectiva: 1996.* Rio de Janeiro: IPEA.

Barros, Ricardo Paes de, and others. 2000. "Uma avaliação dos impactos do salário mínimo sobre o nível de pobreza metropolitana no Brasil.." IPEA Texto para discussão no. 739. Rio de Janeiro: IPEA.

———. 2006a. "Conseqüências e causas imediatas da queda recente na desigualdade de renda brasileira." In *Parcerias Estratégicas:Análise sobre a Pesquisa Nacional por Amostra de Domicílios (Pnad 2004)*. Brasília: Centro de Gestão e Estudos Estratégicos (www.cgee.org.br/parcerias/p22.php).

———. 2006b. "Uma análise das principais causas da queda recente na desigualdade de renda brasileira." *Econômica revista do Programa de Pós-Graduação em Economia da UFF* 8, no. 1: 117–47.

———. 2006c. "A queda recente da desigualdade de renda no Brasil." In *Desigualdade de Renda no Brasil: uma análise da queda recente,* vol. 1, edited by Ricardo Paes de Barros, Miguel Nathan Foguel, and Gabriel Ulyssea. Brasília: IPEA.

———. 2006d. "Determinantes imediatos da queda da desigualdade de renda Brasileira." In *Desigualdade de Renda no Brasil: uma análise da queda recente,* vol. 1, edited by Ricardo Paes de Barros, Miguel Nathan Foguel, and Gabriel Ulyssea. Brasília: IPEA.

———. 2009a. Background paper prepared for the UNDP Project "Markets, the State, and the Dynamics of Inequality: How to Advance Inclusive Growth," coordinated by Luis Felipe López-Calva and Nora Lustig (http://undp.economiccluster-lac.org/).

———. 2009b. "Determinantes da queda na desigualdade de renda no Brasil." Unpublished paper. IPEA.

Becker, Gary S., and Barry R. Chiswick. 1966. "Education and the Distribution of Earnings." *American Economic Review* 56, no. 1-2: 358–69.

Bonelli, Regis, and Guilherme Luis Sedlacek. 1989. "Distribuição de Renda: evolução no último quarto de século." In *Mercado de Trabalho e Distribuição de Renda: Uma Coletânea,* edited by Guilherme Luis Sedlacek, and Ricardo Paes de Barros. Rio de Janeiro: IPEA.

Bourguignon, Francois, and Francisco Ferreira. 2004. "Decomposing Changes in the Distribution of Household Incomes: Methodological Aspects." In *The Microeconomics of Income Distribution Dynamics in East Asia and Latin America*, edited by Francois Bourguignon, Francisco Ferreira, and Nora Lustig, pp. 83–124. Washington: World Bank.

Bourguignon, Francois, Francisco Ferreira, and Phillippe G. Leite. 2007. "Os efeitos do antigo programa Bolsa Escola sobre a pobreza, a desigualdade, a escolaridade e o trabalho infantil: uma abordagem de microssimulação." In *Desigualdade de Renda no Brasil: uma análise da queda recente,* vol. 2, edited by Ricardo Paes de Barros, Miguel Nathan Foguel, and Gabriel Ulyssea. Brasília: IPEA.

Camargo, José Márcio, and Maurício Cortez. 2007. "Transferências e incentivos." In *Desigualdade de Renda no Brasil: uma análise da queda recente,* vol. 2, edited by Ricardo Paes de Barros, Miguel Nathan Foguel, and Gabriel Ulyssea. Brasília: IPEA.

Cortez, Maurício, and Sergio Firpo. 2007. "O salário mínimo e a redução da desigualdade nos rendimentos do trabalho principal: 2001–2004." In *Desigualdade de Renda no Brasil: uma análise da queda recente*, vol. 2, edited by Ricardo Paes de Barros, Miguel Nathan Foguel, and Gabriel Ulyssea. Brasília: IPEA.

Cury, Samir, and Maria Carolina da Silva Leme. 2007. "Redução da desigualdade e os programas de transferência de renda: uma análise de equilíbrio geral." In *Desigualdade de Renda no Brasil: uma análise da queda recente,* vol. 2, edited by Ricardo Paes de Barros, Miguel Nathan Foguel, and Gabriel Ulyssea. Brasília: IPEA.

Drobny, Andres, and John Wells. 1983. "Salário mínimo e distribuição de renda no Brasil: uma análise do setor de construção civil." *Pesquisa e Planejamento Econômico* 13, no. 2: 415–64.

Fajnzylber, Pablo. 2001. "Minimum Wage Effects throughout the Wage Distribution: Evidence from Brazil's Formal and Informal Sectors." Texto para Discussão no. 151. Belo Horizonte: Centro de Planejamento e Desenvolvimento e Planejamento Regional/UFMG.

Foguel, Miguel Nathan, and João Pedro Azevedo. 2007. "Uma decomposição da desigualdade de rendimentos no Brasil: 1984–2005." In *Desigualdade de Renda no Brasil: uma análise da queda recente*, vol. 2, organized by Ricardo Paes de Barros, Miguel Nathan Foguel, and Gabriel Ulyssea. Brasília: IPEA.

Herrán, Carlos Alberto. 2005. *Reduzindo a pobreza e a desigualdade no Brasil.* Brasília: Banco Interamericano de Desenvolvimento.

Hoffmann, Rodolfo. 1989. "Evolução da Distribuição da Renda no Brasil, entre Pessoas e entre Famílias, 1979–86." In *Mercado de Trabalho e Distribuição de Renda: uma coletânea*, edited by G. L. Sedlacek and Ricardo Paes de Barros. Rio de Janeiro: IPEA.

———. 2006a. "Brasil, 2004. Menos pobres e menos ricos." In *Parcerias Estratégicas:Análise sobre a Pesquisa Nacional por Amostra de Domicílios (Pnad 2004)*. Brasília: Centro de Gestão de Estudos Estratégicos (www.cgee.org.br/parcerias/p22.php).

———. 2006b. "Transferências de renda e a redução da desigualdade no Brasil e cinco regiões entre 1997–2004." *Econômica* (Rio de Janeiro) 8, no. 1: 55–81.

———. 2006c. "Queda da desigualdade da distribuição de renda no Brasil, de 1995 a 2005, e delimitação dos relativamente ricos em 2005." In *Desigualdade de Renda no Brasil: uma análise da queda recente*, vol. 1, edited by Ricardo Paes de Barros, Miguel Nathan Foguel, and Gabriel Ulyssea. Brasília: IPEA.

———. 2006d. "Transferências de renda e redução da desigualdade no Brasil e em cinco regiões entre 1997 e 2005." In *Desigualdade de Renda no Brasil: uma análise da queda recente*, vol. 2, edited by Ricardo Paes de Barros, Miguel Nathan Foguel, and Gabriel Ulyssea. Brasília: IPEA.

IPEA, IBGE, and UNICAMP. 2002. "Configuração Atual e Tendências da Rede Urbana." *Série Configuração Atual e Tendências da Rede Urbana.* Instituto de Pesquisa Econômica Aplicada, Instituto Brasileiro de Geografia e Estatística, Universidade Estadual de Campinas, Brasília.

Langoni, C. G. 2005. *Distribuição de Renda e Desenvolvimento Econômico no Brasil.* 3ª edição. Rio de Janeiro: Editora FGV.

Lavinas, Lena, Milko Matijascic, and Marcelo Nicoll. 2007. "Desigualdade de cobertura: a evolução recente do acesso a uma renda mínima via sistema de proteção de social." In *Desigualdade de Renda no Brasil: uma análise da queda recente*, vol. 2, edited by Ricardo Paes de Barros, Miguel Nathan Foguel, and Gabriel Ulyssea. Brasília: IPEA.

Lemos, Sara. 2005. "Minimum Wage Effects on Wages, Employment, and Prices: Implications for Poverty Alleviation in Brazil." Discussion Paper 05/15. Department of Economics, University of Leicester, England.

Menezes-Filho, Naercio A., Reynaldo Fernandes, and Paulo Picchetti. 2007. "Educação e a queda da desigualdade no Brasil." In *Desigualdade de Renda no Brasil: uma análise da queda recente*, vol. 2, edited by Ricardo Paes de Barros, Miguel Nathan Foguel, and Gabriel Ulyssea. Brasília: IPEA.

Neri, Marcelo. 2000. *Efeitos informais do salário mínimo e pobreza.* IPEA Texto para Discussão no. 724. Rio de Janeiro: IPEA.

Neumark, David, Wendy Cunningham, and Lucas Siga. 2004. "The Effects of the Minimum Wage in Brazil on the Distribution of Family Incomes: 1996–2001." Working Paper, Department of Economics, University of California–Irvine.

Ramos, Lauro. 1993. *Distribuição de Rendimentos no Brasil: 1976–85.* Rio de Janeiro: IPEA.

Ramos, Lauro, and José Guilherme Almeida Reis. 1995. "Salário mínimo, distribuição de renda, e pobreza no Brasil." *Pesquisa e Planejamento Econômico* 25, no. 1 (Rio de Janeiro: IPEA).

Rocha, Sonia. 2003. *Pobreza no Brasil: afinal, de que se trata?* Rio de Janeiro: Editora FGV.

————. 2007. "Os "novos" programas de transferência de renda: impactos possíveis sobre a desigualdade no Brasil." In *Desigualdade de Renda no Brasil: uma análise da queda recente*, vol. 2, edited by Ricardo Paes de Barros, Miguel Nathan Foguel, and Gabriel Ulyssea. Brasília: IPEA.

Sattinger, Michael. 1993. "Assignment Models of the Distribution of Earnings." *Journal of Economic Literature* 31, no. 2: 831–80.

Savedoff, William D. 1995. *Wages, Labour, and Regional Development in Brazil*. England: Ashgate Publishing.

Soares, Fabio Véras, and others. 2007. "Programas de transferências de renda no Brasil: impactos sobre a desigualdade." In *Desigualdade de Renda no Brasil: uma análise da queda recente*, vol. 2, edited by Ricardo Paes de Barros, Miguel Nathan Foguel, and Gabriel Ulyssea. Brasília: IPEA.

Soares, Sergei. 2002. "O impacto distributivo do salário mínimo: a distribuição individual dos rendimentos do trabalho." Texto para Discussão no. 873. Rio de Janeiro: IPEA.

Tinbergen, Jan. 1956. "On the Theory of Income Distribution." *Welwirtsch* 77, no. 2: 155–73.

————. 1975. *Income Distribution: Analysis and Policies*. Amsterdam: North-Holland.

Ulyssea, Gabriel. 2007. "Segmentação no mercado de trabalho e desigualdade de rendimentos no Brasil: uma análise empírica." In *Desigualdade de Renda no Brasil: uma análise da queda recente,* vol. 2, edited by Ricardo P. Barros, Miguel Nathan Foguel, and Gabriel Ulyssea. Brasília: IPEA.

Ulyssea, Gabriel, and Miguel Nathan Foguel. 2006. "Efeitos do salário mínimo sobre o mercado de trabalho brasileiro." IPEA Texto para Discussão no. 1168. Rio de Janeiro: IPEA.

Wajnman, Simone, Cássio M. Turra, and Cíntia Agostinho. 2006. "Estrutura Domiciliar e Distribuição da Renda Familiar no Brasil." In *Desigualdade de Renda no Brasil: uma análise da queda recente*, vol. 1, edited by Ricardo Paes de Barros, Miguel Nathan Foguel, and Gabriel Ulyssea. Brasília: IPEA.

7

Mexico:
A Decade of Falling Inequality:
Market Forces or State Action?

GERARDO ESQUIVEL, NORA LUSTIG,
AND JOHN SCOTT

M exico is among the most unequal countries in the world.[1] However, it is
making progress in becoming less unequal: from 1996 to 2006, Mexico's
Gini coefficient fell from 0.543 to 0.498 (or by 0.8 percent a year),[2] and from
2000 to 2006 it fell by 1 percent a year.[3] The decline in inequality coincided with

1. The authors are grateful to participants in the UNDP project "Markets, the State, and the Dynamics of Inequality in Latin America," coordinated by Nora Lustig and Luis Felipe López Calva, as well as to participants in seminars at the United Nations offices in New York and Mexico City, the Latin American and Caribbean Economic Association meeting in Rio de Janeiro (2008), and the Latin American Studies Association meeting in Rio de Janeiro (2009). We also are very grateful to Mary Kwak and anonymous reviewers for their very useful comments and suggestions and to Fedora Carbajal as well as Edith Cortés, Francisco Islas, and Mariellen Malloy Jewers for their outstanding research assistance.

2. The Gini reported in this paragraph is calculated by using total income (which includes monetary income and nonmonetary income, such as the imputed value of owner-occupied housing and auto-consumption, but does not include capital gains). The decomposition of income inequality by source presented in this chapter uses current monetary income (which excludes capital gains and nonmonetary income). The income concept in both cases is assumed to be after monetary transfers, direct taxes, and social security contributions (that is, it is disposable income). For the incidence analysis, the income concept used to rank households is total current income (including nonmonetary income but excluding capital gains) per capita before transfers and indirect taxes but net of direct taxes, as reported in ENIGH, the National Survey of Household Income and Expenditures (see INEGI, various years). The same concept is used for market income when comparing the distribution of total transfers and taxes with market income (to estimate incidence and change in inequality), except that market income in this case is net of all taxes, not just direct taxes.

3. The change in the Gini coefficient between 1996 and 2006, 1996 and 2000, and 2000 and 2006 was found to be statistically significant at the 95 percent level. The confidence intervals were constructed

important changes in Mexico's economic and social policy. In 1994, the North American Free Trade Agreement (NAFTA) with the United States and Canada went into effect, thereby establishing the largest free trade area in the world—and the most asymmetrical in terms of the countries' relative GDP.[4] Mexico also implemented two important government transfer programs: Procampo in 1994 and Progresa (later called Oportunidades) in 1997. Procampo is an income support program for farmers designed to help them face the transition costs resulting from the opening of agricultural trade under NAFTA. Progresa/Oportunidades is a targeted conditional cash transfer program; it is considered Mexico's most important antipoverty program.

The period of declining inequality, which coincided with the period in which NAFTA went into effect, saw significant variation in annual growth rates. The peso crisis that began in December 1994 led to a sharp decline in economic activity during 1995, when per capita GDP fell to the tune of 8 percent.[5] The economy recovered quickly, and between 1996 and 2000 Mexico's per capita GDP grew at a rate of 4 percent a year. However, between 2000 and 2006, per capita GDP growth slowed to 1 percent a year. That low-growth period is precisely when income inequality started to decline more rapidly.

This chapter uses nonparametric decomposition methods to analyze the proximate determinants of the reduction in income inequality between the mid-1990s and 2006. In particular, it looks at the roles played by the reduction in both labor income inequality and nonlabor income inequality. It also analyzes the impact of changes in demographics, such as the numbers of adults and of working adults per household. The chapter examines the extent to which the reduction in labor income inequality was due to a decline in the wage skill premium and explores the influence of changes in labor force composition, in terms of education and experience, on the decline in the wage skill premium; it also examines the relationship between labor force composition and changes in public spending on education.[6] It then analyzes the contribution of changes in government transfers, with particular emphasis on Progresa/Oportunidades, to the reduction in nonlabor income inequality. The chapter concludes with a look at the distributive impact of government redistributive spending and taxes using standard incidence analysis.

---

by applying the bootstrap method with 150 replications. There is Lorenz dominance for the comparisons of 2006 and 1996, 2006 and 2000, and 2000 and 1996.

4. See Tornell and Esquivel (1997) for more details on these issues.

5. For an analysis of the peso crisis, see Lustig (1998).

6. For a theoretical discussion of the relationship between educational expansion, the supply of skills, and labor earnings inequality see, for example, chapter 2, by Jaime Kahhat, in this volume.

Income Inequality after NAFTA: 1994–2006

In this chapter we use the Gini coefficient as our preferred measure of inequality.[7] It has all but one of the desirable properties of an inequality indicator.[8] Also, it is decomposable by proximate determinants as well as income sources.[9] Our analysis uses both total income per capita and total monetary income per capita.[10] All of our estimates use information from the National Survey of Household Income and Expenditures (ENIGH).[11] Comparable surveys are available for the years 1994, 1996, 1998, 2000, 2002, 2004, 2005, and 2006.[12] The surveys capture income net of taxes and contributions to social security and include transfers from Procampo and Progresa/Oportunidades.

Figure 7-1 shows the evolution of the Gini coefficient for 1984–2006, using alternative definitions of income. The figure clearly indicates an inverted-U pattern with its peak in the mid-1990s. After rising by several percentage points between the mid-1980s and mid-1990s, the Gini coefficient for total household per capita income declined from 0.543 to 0.498 (and the Gini for monetary household per capita income declined from 0.539 to 0.506) between 1996 and 2006. The pace of decline accelerated between 2000 and 2006, when the Gini fell at 1 percent a year. Other measures of inequality follow the same general trend as the Gini coefficient, although some differences arise from the fact that the Gini is more sensitive to what happens to the middle of the distribution while the other measures are more heavily influenced by changes at the top and the bottom.[13] For example, although the other measures tend to peak around 1998, the Gini peaks in 1994.[14]

---

7. Other measures of inequality such as the Theil index show trends similar to those described in the text. They are available from the authors on request.

8. These principles are: adherence to the Pigou-Dalton transfer principle; symmetry; independence of scale; homogeneity; and decomposability. The Gini is not additively decomposable.

9. Although it is not additively decomposable, as is the Theil index.

10. *Income* includes *labor income* and *nonlabor income*. The former includes all the income that is reported as labor income in ENIGH, including labor income of the self-employed. Nonlabor income includes income from own businesses; income from assets (including capital gains), pensions (public and private), public tranfers (Oportunidades and Procampo), and private transfers (for example, remittances); and *nonmonetary income* (imputed rent on owner-occupied housing and consumption of own production, common in poor rural areas). Official poverty measures in Mexico use *net current income*—that is, capital gains, gifts, and in-kind transfers to other households subtracted from current total income. *Current monetary income*, the concept used in the decomposition of inequality by source presented below, does not include nonmonetary income and consumption of own production and excludes capital gains.

11. In Spanish, Encuesta Nacional de Ingresos y Gastos de los Hogares (ENIGH).

12. Surveys for 1984 and 1989 are not as comparable, but they are still used for lack of a better alternative.

13. Sen and Foster (1973).

14. See Esquivel (2008).

Figure 7-1. *Gini Coefficients for Alternative Income Definitions, 1984–2006*[a]

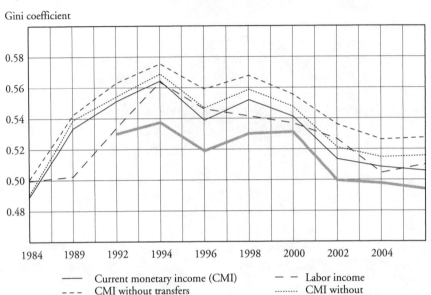

Gini coefficient

Source: Esquivel (2008).
a. Current income excludes capital gains and income from the sale of durable goods.

The evolution of Mexico's income distribution can also be analyzed by using the growth incidence curves (GICs) suggested by Ravallion and Chen.[15] These curves show the percent change in per capita income along the entire income distribution between two points in time. Figure 7-2 shows the GIC for 1996–2006, 1996–2000, and 2000–06, constructed using total per capita income. The negative slope in the first graph shows that the income of the lower deciles grew faster than the income of the upper deciles from 1996 to 2006. For example, income growth for the bottom percentile was more than 4 times that of the top percentile.

Esquivel (2008) provides more detail on trends in inequality by presenting GICs for urban and rural areas for 1994–2006.[16] In urban areas, income growth was pretty flat across the entire distribution except for the top three deciles, which experienced smaller and in some cases even negative income growth rates. In rural areas, the GIC had a negative slope, indicating that the bottom half of the income distribution had higher income growth rates than the top segment of the distribution. Average income growth was greater in rural areas than in urban areas—a pattern that, given the relatively large rural-urban gap, is inequality-reducing.

15. Ravallion and Chen (2003).
16. Esquivel (2008). Rural areas are defined as townships with fewer than 15,000 inhabitants.

Figure 7-2. *National, Urban, and Rural Growth Incidence Curves, 1996–2006*[a]

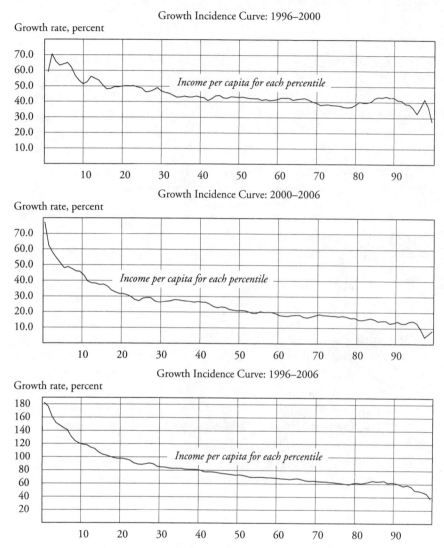

Source: Authors' elaboration based on ENIGH 1996, 2000, and 2006 (INEGI, various years).

a. Growth incidence curves are based on total household per capita income; "rural" refers to households living in townships having a population of less than 15,000.

Breaking out GICs for 1996–2000 and for 2000–06 also provides important details on the overall decline in inequality: in 2000–06 inequality fell at a faster rate, a result of a larger increase in bottom incomes. In both periods, the poorest two deciles of the income distribution experienced an above-average increase in monetary income and the income of the top decile grew at below-average rates; however, the changes at the bottom were more pronounced in the second period.

The increase for the two lowest deciles seems to be associated with income growth in the rural sector. The lackluster growth of income in the top deciles is associated with the dynamics of the urban sector: GICs for urban areas in 1996–2000 and 2000–06 are very flat through most of the income distribution, with the income of the top two deciles growing at the lowest rates.[17] These results suggest that during 2000–06 there must have been some factors that benefited the bottom part of the rural income distribution as well as other factors that hurt—in relative terms—the upper part of the urban income distribution. In the next sections we shall try to identify these factors.

Proximate Determinants of the Decline in Income Inequality: Labor and Nonlabor Income and Demographic Factors

Here we seek to identify the proximate determinants of Mexico's decline in inequality between 1996 and 2006 and quantify each proximate determinant's contribution to the total decline. The proximate determinants considered in our analysis are the ratio of adults to the total number of members in the household; the ratio of working adults to the total number of adults in the household; labor earnings per working adult; and nonlabor income (including government transfers and remittances) per adult.[18]

The contribution of each proximate determinant to the total decline in inequality was quantified by applying the method proposed by Barros and others, which consists of decomposing the change in an inequality measure into the contributions from changes in the distribution of the proximate determinants, taken one at a time, plus the contributions from changes in the interaction (correlation) of proximate determinants with each other.[19] The contributions are estimated through a series of sequential counterfactual simulations that assume that the distribution of the proximate determinant of interest remains the same as in the base year.[20] The method is based on the following sequence of identities:

(1) $y = a.r$

(2) $r = o + t$

and

17. Esquivel (2008).

18. Each proximate determinant is the result of behavioral and external processes that are not modeled here. For example, the first proximate determinant captures the impact of changes in fertility and life expectancy. The second is influenced by decisions to participate in the labor force and the demand for labor. The third and fourth are determined by numerous factors, including market forces and state action affecting the demand for different types of labor; individual decisions (to invest in education and other forms of capital, to participate in the labor market, to migrate, and so on); and government transfers.

19. For a detailed description of the methodology, see Barros and others (2006).

20. Note that although you can apply this method using any inequality indicator, the results will vary depending on the indicator. Also, the results will be sensitive to which year is chosen as the base year and the sequence selected to construct the counterfactual simulations.

Figure 7-3. *Household Per Capita Income and Its Determinants*

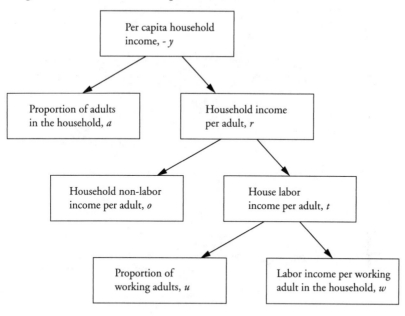

Source: Barros and others (2009).

(3) $$t = u.w$$
(4) $$y = a.(o + u.w)$$

Identity 1 expresses household per capita income, y, as a product of the proportion of adults in the household, a, and household income per adult, r. Identity 2 expresses household income per adult, r, as the sum of household nonlabor income per adult, o, and household labor income per adult, t. Identity 3, household labor income per adult, t, is expressed as the product of the proportion of working adults, u, and the labor income per working adult in the household, w. Identity 4 relates per capita household income, y, to its four proximate determinants: the proportion of adults in the household, a; household nonlabor income per adult, o; proportion of working adults, u; and labor income per working adult in the household, w. These identities are presented in figure 7-3.

Using this method, Alejo and others estimated the contribution of changes in the four proximate determinants mentioned above to the 1.40 percentage point decline in the Gini coefficient from 1996 to 2000 and the 3.07 percentage point decline in the Gini coefficient from 2000 to 2006.[21] Their results are summarized

21. Alejo and others (2009). This decomposition was based on inequality measures calculated using total (monetary plus nonmonetary) income while the next decomposition exercise was based on inequality measures estimated using monetary income only. The results, however, should not be very sensitive to the use of different concepts because both monetary and nonmonetary income followed the same pattern of change.

Table 7-1. *Contribution of the Proximate Determinants to Changes in Income Inequality, 1996–2000 and 2000–06*[a]

Marginal contribution of the proximate factor	Contribution to the change*	Percent	
Years 1996–2000			
Proportion of adults	−0.19	7.7	
Nonlabor income	−0.01	0.4	
Proportion of working adults	−0.12	4.9	
Labor income per working adult	−2.18	87.1	
Subtotal	−2.50	100.0	178.7
All interactions	1.10		−78.7
Total change in Gini coefficient	−1.40		100.0
Years 2000–2006			
Proportion of adults	−0.50	10.3	
Nonlabor income	−0.73	15.1	
Proportion of working adults	−0.44	9.1	
Labor income per working adult	−3.19	65.5	
Subtotal	−4.87	100.0	158.3
All interactions	1.79		−58.3
Total change in Gini coefficient	−3.07		100.0

Source: Authors' calculations based on Alejo and others (2009).

a. The change in Gini coefficient is in percentage points. The asterisk refers to the contribution of the factor to the change in the Gini coefficient, measured in percentage points. The change in the Gini coefficient between 1996 and 2000 and 2000 and 2006 was found to be statistically significant at the 95 percent level. The confidence intervals were constructed applying the bootstrap method with 150 replications. A negative (positive) sign means that a marginal increase in the source is equalizing (unequalizing).

in table 7-1.[22] The reduction in labor income inequality (leaving out the interaction terms) accounted for 87.1 percent of the decline in inequality in 1996–2000 and for 65.5 percent of the decline in 2000–06. Given its relative importance, below we will analyze the factors that explain the reduction in inequality in the distribution of labor income per worker.[23] This discussion will focus on the gap between skilled and unskilled wages and the latter's relationship to trade liberalization and the educational upgrading of the labor force.

The most dramatic change among the four proximate determinants was observed in the impact of changes in the distribution of nonlabor income. In 1996–2000 changes in nonlabor income contributed a meager 0.4 percent to the reduction in inequality. In contrast, in 2000–06 they accounted for 15.1 percent

22. The changes in all of the four proximate determinants reduced inequality, and the changes in all the interactions between the proximate determinants combined increased inequality in both 1996–2000 and 2000–06. The individual interaction terms between pairs of variables all increased inequality too. See Alejo and others (2009).

23. Labor income includes all income that individuals reported as labor income in the ENIGHs, including all wages and salaries as well as income reported by self-employed individuals.

of the total decline in inequality, making nonlabor income the second-most-important contributor to the decline in inequality in this period. Nonlabor income is a very heterogeneous concept. It includes income from the ownership of capital (such as profits, interests, and rents), which tends to be concentrated at the top of the income distribution, but it also includes private transfers (such as remittances), which tend to be more concentrated in the middle and lower-middle ranges of the distribution. Finally, nonlabor income includes government transfers (such as pensions), which are concentrated in the middle and upper-middle ranges of the income distribution, as well as targeted government transfers (such as the conditional cash transfer program Progresa/Oportunidades), which are concentrated in the bottom of the distribution.

The two other proximate determinants were far less significant. Changes in the proportion of adults in the household (which measures the dependency ratio) accounted for 7.7 percent of the decline in inequality in 1996–2000 and 10.3 percent of the decline in 2000–06. Changes in the proportion of working adults in total adults (which reflects both supply-side and demand-side conditions in the labor market) accounted for 4.9 percent of the decline in inequality in 1996–2000 and 9.1 percent of the decline in 2000–06.[24]

In order to get a more detailed picture of how different forms of income have contributed to the evolution of inequality in monetary income in Mexico, we decompose the Gini coefficient in selected years using the method set forth by Lerman and Yitzhaki,[25] who showed that the Gini coefficient for total income inequality (G) with K income sources can be expressed as

$$G = \sum_{k=1}^{K} S_k G_k R_k$$

where S_k is the share of source k in total income, G_k is the Gini coefficient of the income source k, and R_k is the Gini correlation between the income source k and total income.[26] This decomposition of the Gini coefficient shows that the

24. See Esquivel (2008). Average household size fell from 5.68 members in 1996 to 5.16 in 2000 and 4.97 in 2006; the proportion of working adults in the household rose from 58 percent in 1996 to 59 percent in 2000 and 62 percent in 2006. These trends reflect two important changes in demographic patterns: the reduction in fertility rates overall, with more pronounced declines among the poorer sectors of the population, and the increase in female participation in the labor force, particularly among the poorer sectors. Between 1996 and 2006, the average number of children under 12 years of age per household fell from 2.3 to 1.7 in the lowest income quintile; in the top quintile, it fell from 1.5 to 1.3. See SEDLAC (Socio-Economic Database for Latin America and the Caribbean) (www.depeco.econo.unlp.edu.ar/sedlac/). The participation of adult (25- to 64-year-old) women in the labor force during this period rose from 45.3 to 57 percent. SEDLAC (www.depeco.econo.unlp.edu.ar/sedlac/.)

25. Lerman and Yitzhaki (1985).

26. Lerman and Yitzhaki's method allows you to see only by how much inequality would change if the share of a particular income source increases but its distribution remains unchanged. It is, therefore, a static decomposition and applies to very small changes. In contrast, the previous method is "dynamic"—that is, it is designed to analyze the impact of a change in the distribution of a particular income source.

contribution of income source k to inequality depends on the interaction of three elements: the relative importance of the particular income source in total income (S_k); the level of inequality of that income source (G_k); and the correlation between the distribution of that income source and that of total income (R_k). Therefore, an income source (k) that represents a relatively large share of total income (high S_k) could have a large effect on inequality as long as it is unequally distributed (that is, if it has a relatively high G_k). However, if G_k is low, it will cancel this effect. On the other hand, if an income source is very unequally distributed (high G_k) but is not highly correlated with total income (meaning that it has a low R_k, as in the case of well-targeted transfer programs), then it may actually reduce inequality.

Stark, Taylor, and Yitzhaki (1986) showed that with this type of decomposition one can estimate the effect of a small percentage change (π) in a given income source on total inequality (holding all other income sources constant) through the following expression:

$$\frac{\partial G}{\partial \pi} = S_k(G_k R_k - G)$$

or, alternatively,

$$\frac{\partial G / \partial \pi}{G} = \frac{S_k G_k R_k}{G} - S_k$$

This expression means that the percentage change in inequality resulting from a marginal percentage change in income source k is equal to the relative contribution of component k to overall inequality minus the initial share in total income of income source k.

We decompose the Gini coefficients for monetary income following the approach just described for the years 1994, 2000, and 2006.[27] The results are summarized in figure 7-4.[28]

At the national level there are three sources of income that increase inequality and three that reduce inequality. The inequality-increasing sources of income are income from "own" businesses (profits), income from property (rents), and pensions.[29] The impact of each income source on inequality increased between 1994 and 2006. In the case of pensions, the trend was due to an increase in the share

---

27. In the decomposition exercise Esquivel (2008) made use of the descogini Stata program in López-Feldman (2006). The "base" year used in this decomposition is 1994 and the income concept is current monetary income; in the previous decomposition the base year used is 1996 and the income concept is total income. The difference in the income concept used in the two decompositions does not affect the main conclusions from the results.

28. For more details (for example, actual numbers) see Esquivel (2008).

29. Pensions include both private and public pensions and pensions that are part of government welfare transfers. Pensions are gross—that is, contributions to social security are not subtracted.

Figure 7-4. *Decomposition of the Gini Coefficient by Income Source for the Nation, Urban Areas, and Rural Areas*

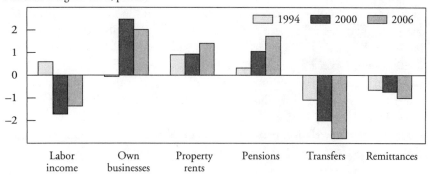

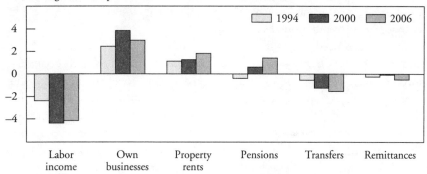

Rural Marginal Effect on Gini Coefficient

Rural: marginal effect, percent

Source: Esquivel (2008).

of pensions in total income and, above all, in the Gini correlation of pensions with total income. The (positive) Gini correlation of pensions rose from 0.64 in 1994 to 0.66 in 2000 to 0.70 in 2006; the cause is not clear.

The inequality-reducing sources of income at the national level are labor income (since 2000), remittances, and transfers.[30] However, their impact differs somewhat between urban and rural areas. For example, labor income is a very important inequality-reducing force in urban areas but not in rural areas. In fact, in 2006 labor income in rural areas is inequality-increasing.

Remittances had a significant impact on inequality at the national level in all three years, even though they did not seem to have a large marginal effect in either sector in 1994. This apparently paradoxical result is explained by the fact that while the Gini correlation between remittances and rural monetary income is close to 50 percent, the Gini correlation between remittances and monetary income at the national level is much lower. Thus, remittances had an effect at the national level because they were heavily concentrated in the bottom half of the *national* income distribution.[31] They reduced income inequality by reducing the rural-urban income gap, not by reducing inequality within each sector. That changed in 2000 and more decisively in 2006.

Transfers reduced inequality both at the national level and in urban and rural areas in all three years.[32] That effect grew over time. By 2006 transfers became the income source with the largest inequality-reducing effect of all the sources considered in this exercise: that is, a marginal increase in transfers would reduce inequality by more than the same marginal increase in labor income or remittances. Transfers became more inequality-reducing over time for three reasons: their share in total income rose; the inequality in the distribution of transfers fell; and their Gini correlation with total monetary income fell. Those changes were especially pronounced in rural areas, where the share of transfers in total income rose from 7 percent in 1994 to 10 percent in 2000 and 2006; the Gini coefficient of transfers fell from 0.93 in 1994 to 0.89 in 2000 and 0.78 in 2006; and the Gini correlation between transfers and total monetary income fell from 0.42 in 1994 and 2000 to 0.31 in 2006.[33]

The share of transfers in total income rose because there was a significant expansion in coverage of public transfers. In 1994, 23.8 percent of all households reported receiving part of their monetary income through a private or public transfer; in 1996, the figure was 29 percent; in 2000, 34 percent; and in 2006,

30. Transfers include public and private transfers (including gifts and donations) except for remittances and the pensions that are part of government welfare transfers (the latter are included under pensions).

31. See, for example, Esquivel and Huerta-Pineda (2007).

32. Transfers here include government transfers and private transfers excluding pensions and remittances. Private transfers (excluding remittances) are relatively small on average.

33. The Gini coefficient for transfers is very high because it is calculated for the entire population, including those who do not receive any transfers.

45.5 percent.[34] The lion's share of the increase was due to implementation of the conditional cash transfer program Progresa/Oportunidades in 1997. By 2006, Progresa/Oportunidades reached 14.8 percent of households in Mexico.[35]

Alejo and others estimates the combined marginal effect of the changes in coverage, average benefit, and distribution for *all* public transfers (pensions, Progresa/Oportunidades, Procampo, and so forth). Those results are not strictly comparable with the previous decomposition;[36] nevertheless, some of the findings are insightful. While the combined marginal effect of what the authors call public transfers increased inequality for 1996–2000, it reduced inequality for 2000–06. In the latter period, the inequality-reducing effect of the increase in coverage (percentage of households that receive public transfers) and the increase in the magnitude of the average benefit more than compensated for the inequality-increasing effect of a rise in the inequality in the distribution of public transfers.[37] Also, during 2000–06, the inequality-reducing marginal contribution of the changes in public transfers was large enough to compensate for the increase in inequality stemming from changes in the interaction term that measures the correlation between public transfers and total income. In contrast, during 1996–2000 the inequality-increasing effect of the interaction term dominated.

In sum, starting in the late 1990s, monetary government transfers became more generous, transfers became more equally distributed among recipients, and recipients of transfers increasingly belonged to the relatively poorer segments of the population. That undoubtedly reflects the implementation of Progresa/Oportunidades, analyzed below. However, government transfers are not as progressive as one would like them to be. The Gini correlation between transfers and total monetary income remains positive, although it fell quite significantly between 1994 and 2006.

Labor Income Inequality and the Skilled-Unskilled Wage Gap

The results of the decomposition exercises suggest that one of the most important inequality-reducing forces between 1996 and 2006 was the evolution of labor income inequality. Note that labor income is basically the result of multiplying hours worked by hourly wages (here defined as including remuneration to the self-employed). If we assume that hours worked did not change much from 1996

34. Esquivel (2008).

35. For more details about Progresa/Oportunidades see, for example, Levy (2006).

36. In this decomposition, pensions were treated as if the full amount corresponds to a public transfer. Strictly speaking, that is not the case, because pensions include private pensions and also because part of public pensions is personal savings (contributions by employees) and not transfers from the government. The public transfer of pensions tends to be regressive (see later discussion), so the inequality-reducing effect of government transfers in 2002–06 was probably quite strong given that the total (including pensions) was inequality-reducing too.

37. Alejo and others (2009), table 16.

Figure 7-5. *Skilled and Unskilled Industrial Wages, 1984–2007*

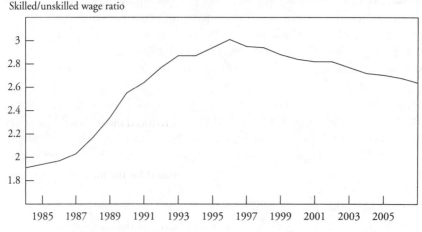

Skilled/unskilled wage ratio

Source: Esquivel (2008).

to 2006,[38] the change in labor income inequality must have been caused by changes in hourly wage inequality.

Here we focus on one key dimension of wage inequality: the gap between skilled and unskilled wages. Figure 7-5 shows the evolution of the ratio of nonproduction workers' wages to production workers' wages from 1984 to 2007.[39] This ratio is frequently used as a rough proxy for the skilled-unskilled wage ratio. (It is, of course, an oversimplification, since there are production workers who are highly skilled and nonproduction workers who are relatively unskilled.) The pattern of wage inequality is remarkably similar to the pattern of inequality in the various definitions of income shown in figure 7-1: figure 7-5 shows an increase in wage inequality between 1984 and the mid-1990s, followed by a steady decline since then.

As shown in Legovini, Bouillón and Lustig (2005), changes in the returns to skills (in particular, an increase in the premium for tertiary education) accounted for a significant share of the rise in household per capita income inequality between 1984 and 1994. During the 1994–2004 period, the opposite appears to have occurred.

38. Actually, between 1996 and 2006, weekly hours in all jobs fell very slightly, from 45.6 to 45.1, and the decline was concentrated in low education (poorer) workers, which would be an inequality-increasing change. That means that the inequality-reducing changes in the distribution of hourly earnings must have been large enough to compensate for the inequality-increasing effect of the changes in the distribution of hours worked. Data on weekly hours and hourly wages can be found at SEDLAC (www.depeco.econo. unlp.edu.ar/sedlac/).

39. The data for this graph came from the Industrial Survey in Mexico, which has monthly and annual data on total wages paid and total hours worked in the industry by both production and nonproduction workers. This figure is an updated version of similar figures published in Esquivel and Rodríguez-López (2003) and Chiquiar (2008).

The rapid increase in wage inequality that occurred in Mexico between 1984 and the mid-1990s has been the subject of a fairly large body of research.[40] The increase in the skilled-unskilled gap coincided with the unilateral trade liberalization of the Mexican economy that started in the mid-1980s. In that sense, the evolution of Mexico's wage inequality was unexpected; Mexico has an abundance of relatively unskilled labor (at least from the perspective of its main trade partner, the United States), and standard theories of trade would have predicted exactly the opposite pattern (that is, a reduction in the skilled-unskilled wage ratio).[41]

The explanations that have been proposed for this apparent paradox can be roughly divided into two groups: the first emphasizes factors affecting the bottom part of the income distribution (less-skilled and less-experienced workers); the second emphasizes factors affecting the upper part of the distribution. In the first group, there are theories emphasizing the reduction in real minimum wages (Fairris, Popli, and Zepeda 2008) as well as theories suggesting that the mid-1980s reduction in tariffs disproportionately affected low-skilled-labor-intensive industries (Hanson and Harrison 1999). In the second group, some theories have emphasized the increase in the demand for skilled workers associated with one or more of the following factors: exogenous skill-biased technological change (Cragg and Eppelbaum 1996 and Esquivel and Rodríguez-López 2003); foreign direct investment (Feenstra and Hanson 1997); and quality upgrading by exporting firms (Verhoogen 2008). Other explanations have suggested that education inequality also could have played a role (López-Acevedo 2006) or that these trends could be indicating only short-run effects (Cañonero and Werner 2002). Many of the proposed explanations are not mutually exclusive.

The post-1996 reduction in wage inequality in Mexico has been much less studied. Robertson (2007) suggests that Mexico's manufacturing workers are now complements to, rather than substitutes for, U.S. workers. He also posits that there has been a significant expansion of assembly-line plants in Mexico (*maquiladoras*), which has increased demand for less-skilled workers.[42] Campos (2008) emphasizes the supply-side explanations based on changes in the composition of the labor force.

40. See, for example, Esquivel and Rodríguez López (2003); Airola and Juhn (2005); Robertson (2007); Acosta and Montes-Rojas (2008); Chiquiar (2008); Verhoogen (2008), and the references cited therein.

41. For a review of the literature for Mexico and Latin America more broadly, see de Hoyos and Lustig (2009).

42. Robertson (2007) noticed that the pattern of wage inequality in Mexico is puzzling because no single theory could explain the evolution of wage inequality before and after NAFTA. There are, however, some tentative theoretical explanations for the pattern. For example, Atolia (2007) suggested that, under certain circumstances, even if the standard prediction from a Hecksher-Ohlin-Samuelson model works as predicted in the long run, there may be some short-run (or transitory) effects of trade liberalization that may lead to an outcome that differs from the long-run outcome. The difference between short-run and long-run effects on inequality results from two factors: first, an asymmetry in the contraction and expansion of some sectors; second, capital-skill complementarity in production.

Esquivel (2008) investigates the role of both demand- and supply-side factors by looking at male workers' mean-log wages in Mexico for selected years and for different combinations of education and years of experience.[43] Between 1989 and 1994, most of the changes in the wage distribution occurred in the upper tail of the distribution (workers with high wages and high levels of education and experience). The increase in wage inequality in those years was not caused by a (relative) decline in the wages of the low-skilled or less-experienced workers; it was the result of a rise in the wages of the high-skilled or more-experienced workers.[44] Average wages of workers with lower levels of education and/or fewer years of experience showed the largest increases, even though average real and legislated minimum wages over the period were practically flat. That suggests that any convincing story of the post-NAFTA reduction in wage inequality has to explain the relative increase in the wages of the low-skilled, less-experienced workers as opposed to the reduction of the wages of the high-skilled, more-experienced workers).[45]

This pattern suggests that at least two leading forces are at play. During 1984–94, the only explanations that seem to be compatible with the observed trend in inequality are those suggesting the introduction of skill-biased technological change, either exogenously or endogenously through multinational and/or quality-upgrading exporting firms.[46] For the post-NAFTA period, there are at least three possible explanations. Two, as previously mentioned, are an increase in the relative supply of skilled workers and an increase in the demand for unskilled labor resulting from the expansion of *maquiladoras* in Mexico's manufacturing sector.[47] The third explanation is based on the standard Hecksher-Ohlin model with a lag.[48] The predicted pattern of a lower skill premium may have manifested itself with a lag either because the impact of trade liberalization on wages took a few years or because it was previously masked by a stronger force, such as skill-biased technological change.[49]

Testing the alternative hypotheses is beyond the scope of this chapter. However, on the basis of the patterns of wage inequality reviewed here, we may be able

43. Esquivel (2008). The data were collected and organized by Campos (2008). Workers are classified according to the level of education achieved (less that lower-secondary, lower-secondary, upper-secondary, and college education) and the number of years of work experience (less or more than 20 years of experience).

44. This makes explanations based on changes in the lower tail of the wage distribution—such as those based on a falling real minimum wage or on a bias against unskilled-labor-intensive industries caused by trade liberalization—unconvincing. In contrast, between 1996 and 2006 the reduction in wage inequality was caused by changes in the lower tail of the income distribution.

45. It should be noted that this occurred within a context in which average real and legislated minimum wages had been practically flat since the mid-1990s.

46. Cragg and Eppelbaum (1996); Esquivel and Rodríguez-López (2003); Feenstra and Hanson (1997); Verhoogen (2008).

47. Campos (2008); Robertson (2007).

48. Chiquiar (2008).

49. Cañonero and Werner (2002); Esquivel and Rodríguez-López (2003).

Figure 7-6. *Workforce Composition by Level of Education and Experience, 1989–2006*

Values in percent

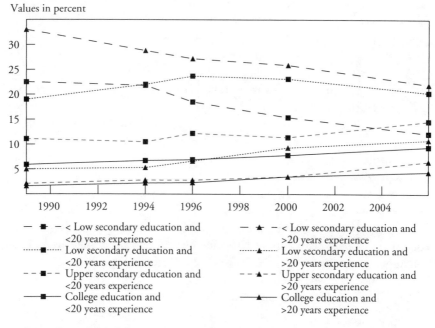

— ■ — < Low secondary education and
       <20 years experience
·····■····· Low secondary education and
       <20 years experience
– – ■ – – Upper secondary education and
       <20 years experience
———■——— College education and
       <20 years experience

— ▲ — < Low secondary education and
       >20 years experience
·····▲····· Low secondary education and
       >20 years experience
– – ▲ – – Upper secondary education and
       >20 years experience
———▲——— College education and
       >20 years experience

Source: Esquivel (2008).

to identify which hypothesis is more plausible. Figure 7-6 shows the composition of Mexico's workforce between 1989 and 2006 by level of education and experience. The observed pattern reflects the interaction of both supply and demand factors. In general, the figure shows that from 1989 to 2006 there was both a reduction in the share of the least-skilled workers (those with less than lower-secondary education) and less-experienced workers (those with less than 20 years of experience) and an increase in the share of the most-skilled workers (those with college education) and more-experienced workers (those with more than 20 years of experience). The most dramatic changes, however, took place in the share of workers with less than lower-secondary education. That group, which accounted for almost 55 percent of workforce in 1989, represented only about one-third of the workforce by 2006. That reduction was compensated by an increase in the shares of all other groups of workers. These trends, which had already been present between 1989 and 1994, accelerated in the post-NAFTA period.

These results suggest that most of the relative increase in the wages of low-skilled/less-experienced workers is associated with changes in the composition of the workforce in Mexico. In particular, the increase is associated with a reduction in the relative number of unskilled workers. That result is not incompatible with the hypothesis suggested in Robertson (2007) of an increase in the demand for unskilled workers. But Robertson's hypothesis by itself cannot explain the simultaneous increase in the relative wages of those workers and the reduction in their share in Mexico's labor force. That conclusion is reinforced by the fact that the relative wages of workers whose share in the supply of labor has diminished are those that have had the largest increase. The increases in the wages of these workers are close to 20 percent—and in some cases even close to 30 percent—for the ten-year period. In contrast, the categories of workers that have become relatively more abundant (more-educated/more-experienced workers) have had either stagnant or decreasing wages since 1996.[50]

The reduction in the relative supply of workers with low levels of skills (education) reflects a significant increase in average years of schooling for the bottom two quintiles, which reduced educational attainment inequality considerably between 1994 and 2006. Over that period, average schooling for the bottom quintile rose from 2.8 to 4.8 years, a 73 percent increase. Over the same period, average schooling in the top quintile rose only 22 percent, from 9.9 to 12.1 years. That pattern can be attributed to the substantial changes in public spending on education that took place in the 1990s and, more marginally, to the effects of the conditional cash transfer program Progresa/Oportunidades on individuals of beneficiary households who reached 15 years of age or more by 2006 (recall that one of the conditions of the program is that children must stay in school).

Rising Progressivity in Government Spending on Education

Public spending on education in the 1970s and 1980s was heavily biased toward higher education. In the 1970s, the share of educational spending allocated to upper-secondary and tertiary education grew from 20 percent to 42 percent while the share of spending on basic (primary and lower-secondary) education declined by an equivalent amount, despite the expansion in enrollment in public basic education from 9.7 to 16.5 million students. The impact on spending per student in basic education was aggravated in the 1983–88 adjustment period, when basic education absorbed a disproportionate share of budgetary cuts. That bias was reversed after 1988, with an increasing reallocation of educational spending toward basic education.[51] Between 1992 and 2002 spending per student on tertiary education expanded in real terms by only 7.5 percent. In contrast, spending per student on primary education increased by 63 percent. The relative ratio of spending per student on tertiary education to spending per student on primary education thus declined from a historical maximum of 12 in 1983–88 to less than 6 in 1994–2000.[52] One of the consequences

50. See Esquivel (2008) and chapter 1 in this volume.

51. Aspe and Beristáin (1984, p. 323) found that public spending in education was quite inequitable before the changes that began in 1988.

52. By comparison, the average ratio for high-income OECD countries is close to 2. See OECD (2008).

was an expansion of schools in areas where they did not exist before, addressing supply-side constraints.

At the same time, policymakers sought to address the demand-side constraints that limited use of post-primary public education services by the poor. For example, the high opportunity cost of sending children in poor rural households to school often led parents to withdraw them during the last years of primary education or after its completion. Through the conditional cash transfer program Progresa/Oportunidades, launched in 1997, the government tied monetary transfers for poor households to school attendance and participation in basic health services.[53] Altogether, changes in the supply of and demand for education resulted in a significant increase in average years of schooling and a reduction in school attainment inequality. Average years of schooling rose from 6.1 in 1994 to 8.3 in 2006, and the concentration coefficient for attainment declined from 0.345 in 1994 to 0.276 in 2006.[54]

The effect of the reforms are shown in figure 7-7, which presents the distribution of benefits from different levels of public education received by population deciles, ranked by per capita household income.[55] Figure 7-7 also shows the distribution of total education spending for 1992 and 2006. Over this period, the distribution of total public spending on education changed from mildly regressive to progressive in absolute terms,[56] with the poorest decile obtaining a share of educational spending (12 percent) that was twice as large as the richest decile's share (6 percent).[57] Spending on all levels has become more progressive (or, in some cases, less regressive), but the most important change is observed in the case of lower-secondary education. This change is explained by at least three factors: most important, the dynamics of educational expansion (as coverage of primary education expanded, larger numbers of poor students became at least formally

53. For a description of Progresa/Oportunidades see, for example, Levy (2006).

54. Scott (2009b).

55. For details on methodology and sources of information, see Scott (2009a).

56. Progressivity in *absolute* terms means that the poor receive a disproportional share of transfers—that is, the x percent poorest population receives more than x percent of transfers—while progressivity in *relative* terms means that the transfers received by the poor are higher as a share of their pretransfer income than those received by the rich. We follow the common, if somewhat confusing, practice below in using the term "progressive/regressive" without qualification to mean progressive in absolute terms in the case of spending and in relative terms in the case of taxes.

57. In order to estimate the effect of transfers in kind, such as public spending on education, Scott (2009b) applies a benefit incidence analysis based on the use of public services reported in ENIGH, valued at cost of provision. This imputed distribution of transfers received, valued in monetary terms, is then used to obtain an estimate of the monetary and in-kind post-transfer Gini coefficient, and thus—by comparing it to the pre-transfer Gini—of the total distributional impact of all transfers. These imputations augment the concept of nonmonetary income reported in ENIGH and differ from the nonmonetary concepts already included in the latter (notably imputed owner-occupied housing rent) because of the method of valuation used to obtain the relevant monetary values: cost of provision (in-kind public services) versus self-reported valuation (imputed rent). The present analysis reports the estimated effect of the transfers on the Gini coefficient in purely accounting terms, following common practice in benefit incidence analysis.

qualified to access the next level); the conditional transfers of Progresa/Oportu-
nidades, which provide increased payments for secondary education; and, less
encouraging, the tendency among higher-income groups to opt out of public primary and secondary schools because they are of lower quality that private schools.
In other words, public spending on basic education is progressive in part because
richer households opt out of public schools and because of that government
spending on basic education goes primarily to poorer households. An immediate
corollary is that efforts to improve the quality of public education would, if successful, necessarily be so at the cost of equity.

Access to tertiary education, on the other hand, is still highly regressive, having
improved only slightly since 1992. The participation of the poorest quintile is
insignificant and among the lowest in Latin America.[58] As in the case of secondary
education, participation is slowly improving and should increase in the future simply as a consequence of advancing coverage in the earlier educational levels. But
two important hurdles remain. First, the high opportunity cost of tertiary education will require a reform in university financing, such as by offering public subsidies to the poor through scholarships or student loans rather than simply offering
free tuition to middle- and upper-income groups. Second, if poor students are to
compete effectively with private high school graduates for scarce university spots,
the government must upgrade the quality of public secondary education.

It is also important to note that health might have also contributed to a change
in the relative returns to skills. Between the mid-1990s and the mid-2000s health
spending and spending on food subsidies and nutrition became considerably progressive.[59] Government policy focused on both expansion of the supply of health
services and demand for health services by the poor, the latter through Pro-
gresa/Oportunidades. More equitable access to health services might have contributed to improving the productivity of low-skilled workers; for example,
improved access to health services may have translated into fewer days of work
missed due to illness. Better access to health services might also have improved
the cognitive development of children in poor households, thereby improving
their educational achievement and productivity.[60]

Pro-Poor Government Spending:
The Distributional Impact of Progresa/Oportunidades

In addition to changes in the distribution of labor income, monetary transfers—in particular, government transfers—became an important inequality-
reducing force from 2000 to 2006. Monetary transfers' equalizing contribution
has been increasing over time, at the national level as well as in urban and rural

58. Scott (2002).
59. Scott (2009b).
60. See, for example, Lustig (2006, 2007).

Figure 7-7. *Distribution of Benefits of Public Spending on Education by Income Decile, 1992 and 2006*[a]

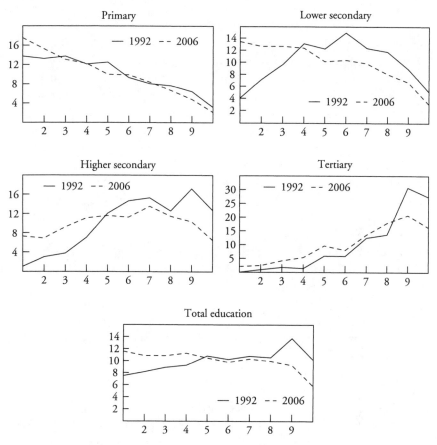

Source: Scott (2009b).

a. Population deciles are ordered by pre-transfer household income per capita.

areas.[61] According to the decomposition results presented in figure 7-4, government transfers became the income source with the largest equalizing effect of all the sources considered in this exercise: that is, a marginal increase in transfers would reduce inequality by more than a marginal increase in labor income or remittances. That development stemmed from a significant policy shift in 1997, when the government launched the conditional cash transfer program Progresa (renamed Oportunidades in 2000).[62]

61. Transfers here include government transfers and private transfers excluding pensions and remittances. Thus, it is not equivalent to government transfers only.

62. For a detailed analysis of Programa de Educación, Salud, y Alimentación (Progresa) see, for example, Levy (2006).

Progresa/Oportunidades is an innovative federal government program that targets rural and urban households in Mexico that fall within the extreme-poverty category.[63] It complements traditional supply-side spending on social services with demand-side subsidies. The program has three components: education, nutrition, and health. The education component grants cash transfers based on school attendance, high school completion, and the need for school supplies. The nutrition and health components offer cash and in-kind transfers (nutritional supplements, vaccinations, preventative treatments, and so forth), based on regular visits to a health clinic. The average monthly transfer is about US$35,[64] and estimated total transfers are equivalent to, on average, 25 percent of eligible rural households' average monthly income. The program's size is significant in terms of beneficiaries yet inexpensive in terms of cost. By the end of 2005, Progresa/Oportundiades granted benefits to 5 million families (about 24 percent of the Mexican population). Its budget in 2005 equaled 0.36 percent of GPD (compared with 0.02 percent in 1997), and it commanded 2.29 percent of the programmable public expenditure budget.[65]

Numerous studies have found that the program has had significant impacts on education and health.[66] Comparing post-primary enrollment before the program (1996–97) and after the program (2002–03), one study reported an average increase of 24 percent in rural areas.[67] Of note was enrollment in secondary education in rural areas, which rose by 11 percent for girls and 7.5 percent for boys two years after the program was launched.[68] Another study found that demand for health services among Progresa/Oportunidades beneficiaries was 67 percent higher than demand in communities not participating in the program,[69] and infant mortality was found to fall at a rate 11 percent higher among beneficiaries than among nonbeneficiaries.[70] Another study estimated that maternal mortality was 11 percent lower and infant mortality was 2 percent lower in rural communities that participated in the program than in those that did not.[71] Like improved access to education, these health gains may help explain recent changes in the relative returns to skills. Better access to health services may have improved the productivity of low-skilled workers; for example, improved

63. This section is based on Lustig (2007).

64. This figure can increase in families with school-age children. In 2005, Progresa/Oportunidades granted monetary benefits and benefits in kind equal to direct monetary monthly assistance of US$44.30 per family (Levy 2006).

65. Although the Social Development Secretariat is in charge of the program, most of the health budget of Progresa/Oportunidades is not included in its own line item in the budget; it is part of public spending on health.

66. See, for example, Parker (2005) and Schultz (2000).

67. Parker (2005).

68. Schultz (2000).

69. Bautista and others (2004).

70. Barham (2005).

71. Hernández and others (2003).

access to health services may have translated into fewer days of work missed due to illness. Better access to health services may have also improved the cognitive development of children in poor households, thereby improving their educational achievement and productivity.[72]

Similar gains may be associated with the change in the distribution of food subsidies brought about by Progresa/Oportunidades. The program transformed the broadly neutral distribution of government spending on food subsidies into a highly progressive one: the share benefiting the poorest decile increased from 8 to 33 percent between 1994 and 2000. Several factors may explain that shift. First, the "discovery" of a redistribution technology: in 1997 the Progresa pilot program showed that distributing food subsidies (and cash transfers) to poor families in remote rural localities was operationally feasible. Second, the empowerment of rural voters as a consequence of Mexico's democratization process gave them potentially more voice in the allocation of government resources. Third, unlike health and education, food subsidies are not under the purview of Mexico's powerful public sector unions, which have successfully blocked pending reforms in the case of education and health services. Finally, in contrast to education and health service provision, the reallocation of food subsidies is not constrained by labor shortages (lack of qualified doctors and teachers in poor rural areas) or physical infrastructure.[73]

Beyond its effects on education, health, and nutrition, Progresa/Oportunidades has had a positive impact on poor households' consumption, saving, and investment, thereby helping to reduce poverty and inequality in Mexico. In 2004, poverty incidence among program participants (the percentage of the population associated with the program that is below the poverty line) fell by 9.7 percent in rural areas and 2.6 percent in urban areas. The corresponding declines in urban areas were 4.9 and 1.7 percent.[74] In terms of its impact on the distribution of income, the direct effect of Progresa/Oportunidades transfers reduced the Gini coefficient from 0.502 to 0.494, which is the equivalent of close to one-fifth of the decline in the Gini coefficient between 1996 and 2006.[75]

Politically, Progresa/Oportunidades has set new standards for social policy in Mexico.[76] It is the first social program in Mexico to apply transparent targeting mechanisms, effectively identifying the poorest rural localities and households and using, at the household level, proxy-means tests to select beneficiaries based on a full census of socioeconomic characteristics and economic assets within these

---

72. See, for example, Lustig (2006, 2007).

73. For a discussion of the political economy of the reform, see Scott (2009a).

74. Cortes, Solís, and Banegas (2006).

75. Scott (2009b). The impact on the Gini coefficient takes account of only the direct effect. The effects on inequality of changes in behavior or of higher human capital among the poor are not contemplated in this calculation.

76. This section is based on Scott (2006).

localities. Progresa/Oportunidades is also the first social program in Mexico to be subject to rigorous impact evaluations.[77] The program is notable in having survived not only a change of administration (no other major antipoverty initiative over the past two decades has done so) but also in having survived the first change in 70 years of the political party in power. In fact, rather than discard the program, the new party's administration changed its name from Progresa to Oportundiades, and beginning in 2001 the new government increased coverage from 2.3 to 4.2 million households (mainly in rural areas) and added semi-urban and urban localities to the already established rural areas.

The political economy of Progresa/Oportunidades' survival through various administrations is the result of a "perfect combination" of factors that merit note here. In contrast to the intensive government media campaigns accompanying most flagship antipoverty programs in Mexico, the government refrained from such a campaign in the case of Progresa, facilitating its political survival beyond the administration and the PRI regime.[78] Second, the rapid expansion of the program (with 2.5 million direct beneficiary households by the end of the 2000) ensured its support by a large constituency. Third, just as important, the decision to make the program transparent and to invest in ambitious and highly credible external impact evaluations contributed significantly to the program's political survival. However, Progresa/Oportunidades was not completely immune to damaging political economy issues. In 2001, when it was rebranded as Oportunidades, the program was expanded to cover urban areas and upper-secondary education, inevitably reducing its targeting efficiency: while the poorest quintile benefited from 71 percent of program resources in 2000, that figure dropped to 55 percent in 2006.

In sum, Progresa/Oportunidades is an example of "redistributive efficiency." With as little as 0.36 percent of GDP and 4 percent of redistributive spending, the program accounts for 18 percent of the change in the post-transfer Gini and 81 percent of the change in the Gini after inclusion of programs targeting the poor.[79] If one compares the redistributive impact of this program only with the redistributive impact of all monetary transfers and subsidies combined (including Oportunidades), the impacts are equal.[80] That implies that the progressive incidence of the remaining transfers that target the poor and other spending categories is wiped out by the regressive effect of all other untargeted monetary transfers and subsidies.

Unfortunately the redistributive efficiency of Progressa/Opportunidades is an isolated case among redistributive instruments currently operating in Mexico. Even though government spending became undeniably more pro-poor during the

77. See, for example, International Food Policy Research Institute (www.ifpri.org) for the principal evaluation results. See also Parker (2005) and Schultz (2000).
78. The PRI (Partido Revolucionario Institucional [Institutional Revolutionary Party]) regime refers to the almost one-party regime that characterized Mexico for 70 years.
79. Scott (2009b).
80. Scott (2009b).

last decade, a lot still needs to be changed to make redistributive spending a powerful instrument for reducing inequality in Mexico.

The Distributional Impact of State Action:
Government Spending and Taxes

Since the early to mid-1990s, social spending, and particularly spending on programs targeting the poor, has expanded considerably (see figures 7-8 and 7-9). As
discussed above, spending on education, health, and nutrition became more progressive. In addition, with the introduction of Progresa/Oportunidades, the Mexican government found ways to redistribute income through transfers in an efficient and cost-effective way. Despite the progress, 58 percent of government
redistributive spending in 2006 was regressive (and of that 58 percent, 11 percent
increased income inequality). In advanced countries, government transfers are
able to reduce primary (that is, market) income inequality by 30 to 50 percent.
In contrast, in Mexico the post-transfer Gini coefficient in 2006 was only 9.3 percent—and a meager 1.7 percent if transfers in kind are excluded—lower than the
primary income pre-transfer Gini.

Estimating the redistributive impact of government spending entails considerable methodological challenges. Most income and expenditure surveys report government monetary transfers as a component of household income. The contribution of those transfers to overall income inequality can then be estimated by
applying standard decomposition techniques on inequality measures by income
source. That is the path followed above. However, while in mature welfare states
monetary transfers represent between a third and a half of total social spending
and account for reductions in inequality on the order of 20 to 50 percent,[81] in
developing countries monetary transfers are a small part of total government
transfers and in the case of Latin America account for reductions in inequality of
around 2 percent. The largest share of redistributive spending in Latin America
occurs through government transfers in kind, which in general are not included
in the income concept measured in household surveys.

In Mexico, the two cash transfer programs reported in the ENIGH survey
(Oportunidades and Procampo) represent a mere 5 percent of the portion of public spending devoted to "redistributive" objectives (see table 7-2).[82] The remaining 95 percent of government transfers is not covered by the Gini decomposition
nalysis presented above. That means that standard analysis of inequality dynamics excludes a significant portion of a "true" measure of income, which, if measured correctly, would have to include all government transfers. To illustrate, in

81. These reductions are measured in purely accounting terms—that is, as the difference between the
pre-transfer Gini and post-transfer Gini, without taking into account any behavioral responses. Ervik
(1998); Smeeding and Phillips (1999).
82. We put *redistributive* in quotations because not all these transfers are progressive.

Figure 7-8. *Evolution of Social Spending, 1925–2006*[a]

Social spending/public spending (programmable)   Social spending/GDP

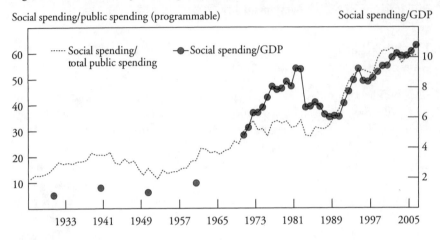

Source: Scott (2009b).
a. Programmable spending excludes debt servicing.

Figure 7-9. *Evolution of Extreme Poverty, Anti-Poverty Spending, GDP, and Gini Coefficient*[a]

Average annual change, percent

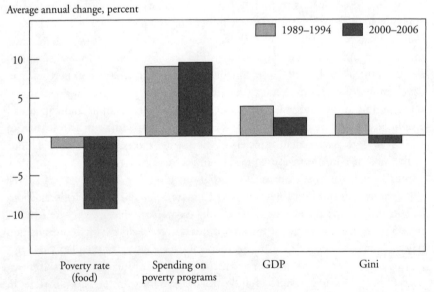

Source: Scott (2009b).
a. Poverty is measured using the official extreme poverty line (pobreza alimentaria, or "food poverty"). Poverty programs for 2000–06 are those listed under Programs Targeting the Poor in table 7-2. For 1989–94, the list was different; among other differences, it included Pronasol and excluded Progresa/Oportunidades (launched in 1997).

Table 7-2. *Government Redistributive Spending by Category and Program, 2006*

Concept	Current Mexican pesos (millions)	Total transfers (percent)	Household income before taxes and transfers (percent)
Household income before taxes and transfers	7,521,608		100
Taxes (including social security contributions)	1,038,283		13.8
Social spending (official classification)	988,369		13.1
Total transfers analyzed	964,567	100	12.8
Transfers in kind (lines A+B)	654,675	68	8.7
Other transfers[a] (lines C+D)	309,892	32	4.1
Memo item: Total not targeting the poor	916,696	95	12.1
Total targeting the poor	47,871	5	0.6
A. Education	402,385	42	5.3
Preschool	44,583	5	
Primary	135,352	14	
Lower secondary	86,817	9	
Upper secondary	52,932	5	
Tertiary	82,701	9	
B. Health	252,290	26	3.4
Services for the insured	159,986	16	
Services for uninsured (SSA)	92,304	10	
Seguro Popular	11,700	1	
IMSS-Oportunidades	5,716	1	

(continued)

2006 average household income, which increased by 4.1 percent when all monetary transfers and subsidies were included, increased by 12.8 percent when in-kind transfers (education and health) were added to the latter.

Table 7-2 presents the 2006 totals of government transfers in cash and in kind as well as in the form of subsidies, including value-added tax (VAT) exemptions or fiscal spending, for the main redistributive categories and programs.[83] The programs are described in table 7-3. The categories and programs covered here include all public education and health spending (at the federal and state levels) as well as all federal public spending on pensions (the subsidized component),

83. In-kind transfers, which include mainly education and health services, may be highly valued by some (though not all) beneficiaries. They are nontradable, highly labor-intensive services that depend on locally available infrastructure for access and are therefore highly variable in quality. One relevant implication for the present analysis is that the gap between the public cost of the transfer and the monetary benefit to recipients is likely to be larger for in-kind transfers than for monetary transfers or direct subsidies. Another is that the low quality of services may act as an implicit, but effective, targeting mechanism because the nonpoor will opt out on their own.

Table 7-2. *Government Redistributive Spending by Category and Program, 2006 (Continued)*

Concept	Current Mexican pesos (millions)	Total transfers (percent)	Household income before taxes and transfers (percent)
C. Subsidies[a]	262,021	27	3.5
Pensions[b]	85,230	9	1.1
IMSS	50,004	5	
ISSSTE	35,226	4	
Consumption subsidies	107,153	11	1.4
Residential areas electricity subsidy	64,935	7	
Gasoline and other fuel subsidies	42,218	4	
Memo item: Consumption subsidies[c]	270,102		3.6
VAT exemptions on food and prescription drugs	162,949		
Agricultural subsidies	69,638	7	0.9
Procampo	15,025	2	
D. Programs targeting the poor	47,871	5	0.6
Targeted monetary (mainly)	45,179	4	
Oportunidades	33,526	3	
Vivienda (Tu Casa)	4,234	0.4	
DIF/feeding programs	2,806	0.3	
Liconsa	1,300	0.1	
Programa de Empleo Temporal (PET)	1,090	0.1	
Opciones Productivas	401	0	
Other scholarships (excluding Oportunidades)	1,571	0.2	
Piso Firme	251	0	
Hábitat	1,992	0.2	
Microrregiones	700	0.1	

Sources: Scott (2009a). See description of programs in table 7-3.

a. Excludes VAT (value-added tax) exemptions (also known as fiscal spending) and includes subsidies and monetary transfers to agriculture such as Procampo and Ingreso Objetivo.

b. Government subsidy—that is, pensions net of contributions from workers and employers.

c. Includes VAT exemptions (also known as fiscal spending).

energy and agricultural subsidies, and the main programs targeting the poor. Altogether, those items comprise a total of twenty-five programs or specific spending categories, which, in 2006, amounted to close to US$100 billion (10 percent of Mexico's GDP), 12.8 percent of primary household income (income before taxes and transfers, also called pre-fiscal income), 60 percent of total public spending,[84]

84. The remainder includes spending on administration, defense, and so forth.

Table 7-3. *Description of Main Categories and Programs*

Program	Description
Health and pensions (social security)	
IMSS	The principal social security institution providing health services and other benefits to private sector workers, created in 1943. Its pension system was reformed in 1997 to a "fully funded," defined contribution scheme administered by private entities.
ISSSTE	The principal social security system covering federal and state government bureaucracy and workers.
Health Services SSA	Health services for the uninsured provided by the state and federal government ministries of health.
Seguro Popular	Health program created in 2004 to provide basic health insurance to the formally uninsured, with a projected coverage of 12 million households by 2010.
IMSS-Oportunidades	System of rural health clinics for the uninsured targeting poorer localities, administered by IMSS but funded by the Health Ministry; created in 1970s as IMSS-Coplamar.
Consumption subsidies	
Gasoline and other fuels subsidy	Special tax on gasoline (IEPS) that has become a negative tax, or a subsidy, since 2006, as price adjustments lagged the increase.
VAT exemptions on food and prescription drugs	Fiscal spending associated with VAT exemptions on food and prescription drugs, principally.
Agricultural subsidies	
Procampo	Agricultural subsidy created in 1994 to compensate producers of basic crops for the opening up of agricultural markets under the North American Free Trade Agreement; provides a direct transfer per hectare instead of per output as before. Agricultural Ministry.
Ingreso Objectivo	Agricultural subsidy based on a target price. Agricultural Ministry.

(continued)

and 97 percent of total social spending. Using ENIGH 2006, we analyze their distributive impact using standard benefit incidence analysis.[85]

It is important to note that social spending as defined in official government budgetary classifications and the concept of redistributive spending used this incidence analysis are not the same. The fact that in 2006 they are so close in actual

85. Public spending data on all programs reported in table 7-2 are obtained from the Public Accounts of the Federation for the relevant years. For health spending at the state level, we use the National and State Health Accounts published by the Health Ministry. Education spending at the state level is estimated from federal per-student spending rates and the total number of students in schools financed by states as reported by the Education Ministry. Spending on education and health at the state level includes spending on education and health financed through earmarked federal transfers, revenues from federal revenue-sharing programs, and fiscal revenues collected by the states themselves.

Table 7-3. *Description of Main Categories and Programs (Continued)*

Program	Description
Programs targeting the poor	
Oportunidades	CCT program created in 1997, currently covering 5 million households, providing direct monetary transfers conditional on school attendance and health visits. Originally targeting at poor rural communities and basic education, in 2001 it was gradually extended to urban localities and higher education services. Social Development Ministry.
Vivienda (Tu Casa)	Housing credit program targeting the uninsured. Social Development Ministry.
DIF feeding programs	School breakfast and kitchen program.
Liconsa	Target milk subsidy program, providing rations of milk at half price in urban localities. Social Development Ministry.
Programa de Empleo Temporal (PET)	Workfare program created in 1995, providing a maximum of 88 days of work for a low wage (originally 90 percent of the minimum wage, at present 99 percent).
Opciones Productivas	Support for productive projects including technical assistance and credit. Social DevelopmentMinistry.
Rural old age pension	Universalrural noncontributory basic pension for the population 70 years or older created in 2007, offering $500 pesos (US$37) per month.
Other scholarships (excluding Oportunidades)	Scholarship income reported by households in the ENIGH income and expenditure survey, excluding Oportunidades scholarships.
Piso Firme	Provides financing to purchase material inputs to built cement floors for houses with dirt floors in poor rural localities.
Hábitat	Urban development, infrastructure, and participation program. Social Development Minsitry.
Microrregiones	Rural development program providing infrastructure and productive inputs to jump-start local economic development. Social Development Ministry.

Source: Scott (2009b).

amounts is a coincidence. In addition to spending on education, health, and programs targeting the poor, redistributive spending includes spending on agricultural and consumption subsidies, which are excluded from social spending. In the case of pensions for social security beneficiaries, redistributive spending includes just the subsidy component (that is, it excludes the contributions made by workers and employers) whereas social spending includes all spending on social security pensions regardless of how they are financed. Finally, redistributive spending excludes some of the spending items included in social spending because they cannot be "mapped" to specific households. That includes social spending on public goods such as rural roads, for example.

If we disaggregate the total redistributive spending presented in table 7-2 by category, in-kind transfers of education and health represent 42 and 26 percent of the total respectively and together they represent 68 percent of the total. The distribution of the remaining 32 percent[86] is as follows: 11 percent is general subsidies for electricity for residential areas and for gasoline and other fuels; 9 percent is pensions (the subsidized component),[87] 7 percent is agricultural subsidies, and 5 percent is monetary transfers to the poor.[88]

In order to estimate the incidence of redistributive spending, first we record the distribution of total spending on each program or category by population deciles ordered by total current income per capita before taxes and transfers (primary or pre-fiscal income); then we measure the degree of progressivity using concentration coefficients (CC).[89,90] The CCs are a Gini coefficient of the distribution of

86. The benefit incidence analysis does not include VAT exemptions on the spending side. They are included in the analysis of tax incidence.

87. Although pensions are reported in the ENIGH survey, the totals cannot be treated as government transfers because the ENIGH data do not allow one to disaggregate public from private pensions or the subsidy from the saving component in public pensions. Pension income must therefore be decomposed as a separate income component, and, as shown in the decomposition of inequality by income source above, it is inequality-increasing. The incidence analysis presented below includes only the tax-financed subsidies to the public pension systems and uses information on social security affiliation reported in the ENIGH (for active workers only) to impute them.

88. Line D in table 7-2. Although some of the transfers (Vivienda, DIF desayunos, Liconsa, Programa de Empleo Temporal, Opciones Productivas, Piso Firme, Hábitat, Microrregiones) are not reported in the ENIGH's published database, they were included in a special module of social programs commissioned with the ENIGH (2002, 2004, 2006) by Sedesol. Thus we were able to include them in the incidence analysis presented below.

89. For details, see Scott (2009b, 2005). The main data source for the analysis is the 2006 ENIGH household income and expenditure survey. In addition to being the most detailed source available for household income, the ENIGH survey reports the main public monetary transfers (Progresa/Oportunidades and Procampo); the use of public education and health services by household members; whether household members contribute to the social security systems; and spending on electricity, gasoline, and other fuels and on consumption goods that are subject to or exempted from VAT. As is common in household surveys, total household income in ENIGH tends to be underreported by a large margin when compared with the closest equivalent concept of total household income in Mexico's National Accounts (the ratio of total household income in National Accounts to total household income in the survey was equal to 1.87 in 2006). To estimate the incidence and redistributive effect of public transfers it is necessary to ensure comparability between public transfers obtained from the National Accounts and private income reported in ENIGH. To do that, the data in the National Accounts is adjusted proportionately by the ratio described above to ensure consistency with household income estimated from ENIGH surveys and the totals in the National Accounts.

90. With the exception of Oportunidades, which is reported in the ENIGH survey, the information for the targeted programs included in the analysis was obtained from a special module on social programs commissioned by the Social Development Ministry as part of the 2006 ENIGH. The distribution of agricultural public expenditures, in particular Procampo and Ingreso Objetivo, is obtained from the administrative beneficiary database and reported as producer deciles ordered by the size of land holdings. The inclusion of the latter results with the ENIGH-based estimates is justified by the assumption that the size of land holdings is positively correlated with income. The only agricultural subsidy reported in ENIGH is

transfers (or taxes, depending on the case) with the population ranked according to total pre-transfer current income per capita.[91] A negative CC means that the category or program is progressive in absolute terms—that is, the poor receive more than the rich in per capita terms. A positive CC, which is lower than the Gini of primary (pre-fiscal) income, means that the category or program is regressive in absolute terms—that is, the poor receive more than the rich in *proportion* to their respective incomes but less in per capita terms (this is sometimes called progressive in relative terms). A positive CC that is higher than the Gini of primary (pre-fiscal) income means that the category or program is regressive in relative (and thus, absolute) terms—that is, the post-program distribution is more unequal than the distribution of primary income. By definition, if a program is regressive in relative terms, it must be regressive in absolute terms, but the converse is not true.

The concentration coefficients of redistributive spending by program or spending category are shown in figure 7-10. The CCs range from the most progressive program (in absolute terms), Oportunidades (-0.53), to the most regressive program (in relative terms), Ingreso Objetivo (0.81).[92] Most of the programs targeting the poor (line D in table 7-2), the pro-poor health "insurance" program Seguro Popular,[93] health services provided by the Ministry of Health for the uninsured, and basic education (pre-school, primary, and lower-secondary) are progressive (pro-poor) in absolute terms. The programs that make the post-transfer distribution worse than the pre-fiscal distribution are primarily the cash transfer programs to agricultural producers (for example, Ingreso Objetivo) and subsidized pensions to employees of some state-owned companies. In between is a large number of programs and categories that are regressive in absolute terms but progressive in relative terms: for example, energy subsidies (for gasoline, LP gas, and residential electricity) and other generalized consumption subsidies (including VAT exemptions), social security benefits, and tertiary education.

Concentration coefficients, by definition, do not capture nuances in the actual distribution of benefits. A more complete picture can be obtained by looking at the benefit incidence by deciles or quintiles. Scott (2009b) finds that sixteen programs transfer an amount at least equal to their population share to the bottom quintile—that is, they are progressive in absolute terms (figure 7-10). On the

---

Procampo, but the survey is not designed to report the distribution of this program accurately. A large fraction of Procampo's benefits are concentrated on a small group of producers at the top end of the land and income distribution. As are other household surveys in Latin America, the ENIGH survey is especially limited in capturing income at the top end of the distribution, for well-known reasons of small sample size and underreporting (see discussion in chapter 1). Therefore, it significantly underestimates the concentration of Procampo transfers.

91. Concentration coefficients are also sometimes called "quasi-Ginis." They were calculated on the basis of transfers received by population decile. Concentration coefficents are also calculated for taxes.

92. Concentration coefficients can range from −1 to 1. The closer they are to −1 (1) means that the fiscal resources are allocated in a pro-poor (pro-rich) way.

93. Scott (2009b).

Figure 7-10. *Concentration Coefficients for Redistributive Public Expenditures, 2006*[a]

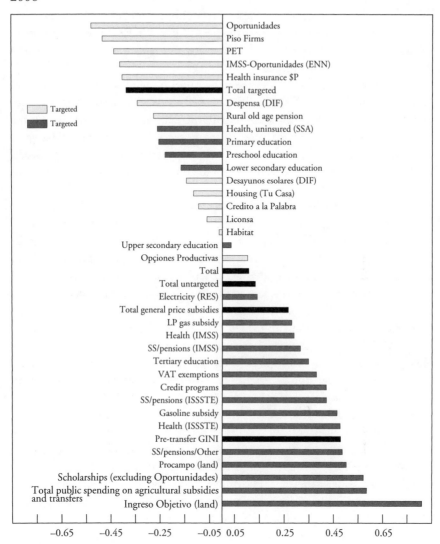

Source: Scott (2009b).

a. Estimates based on the Module on Social Programs (ENIGH 2006), except in the case of Procampo and other agricultural transfers and subsidies. For a definition of concentration coefficient (CC) see text. The CCs for Procampo and other agricultural subsidies are based on administrative data and producer deciles ordered by size of land holdings; the latter is taken as a proxy for income. These CCs overestimate how regressive these programs are. In spite of the fact that Procampo's CC is below the pre-transfer Gini, it is safe to assume that Procampo is actually not more regressive than the pre-fiscal distribution. That assumption is further supported by the fact that the design of the program does not link benefits to output. It is also supported by the fact that the ENIGH-based CC for Procampo is actually only mildly regressive, although ENIGH underestimates the regressivity of the program. Finally, it is supported by orderings using the (estimated) value (instead of size) of land, which reveal Procampo to be less regressive than simple orderings based on land size. For more details see Scott (2009c). The share in government redistributive spending of items in this figure can be found in table 7-2. For a description of the programs, see table 7-3.

other end, twelve programs are regressive in absolute terms and five are regressive in relative terms—that is, they make the post-program income distribution more unequal.[94] Programs that are regressive in relative terms do not reach the poor and in effect worsen income inequality.

In 2006 only 42 percent of all the redistributive spending categories (monetary transfers, subsidies,[95] and in-kind transfers) were progressive in absolute terms (that is, the poor received more than the rich in per capita terms). Of the remaining 58 percent of redistributive spending, 47 percent was regressive in absolute terms and 11 percent was allocated to programs that were regressive in relative terms—that is, the distribution of income worsened as a result of those programs.

The overall impact of total redistributive spending can be seen in table 7-4. Given that regressive programs use a larger share of fiscal resources, they effectively cancel the pro-poor impact of the progressive ones, producing a slightly regressive (in absolute terms) global distribution of public spending. In-kind transfers are generally neutral (in absolute terms), monetary transfers that target the poor are progressive in absolute terms, and the rest of the transfers are either regressive in absolute or relative terms.[96] However, because the bulk of government redistributive spending (89 percent) is allocated to programs that are either progressive in absolute terms (42 percent) or to programs that—even though they are regressive in absolute terms—make the post-transfer distribution less unequal than the pre-transfer one (47 percent), government redistributive spending reduced the pre-fiscal Gini coefficient by 9.3 percent in 2006.[97] If we exclude the impact of transfers in kind, the reduction in the Gini coefficient becomes much smaller, a mere 1.7 percent.

Let us now turn to the redistributive impact of taxes, including social security contributions. Table 7-4 presents the estimates of tax incidence for 2006 calculated by the Finance Ministry (SHCP 2008).[98] The incidence of taxes is progressive but only mildly so: taxes paid by the poorest decile are equal to 6.7 percent of their pre-fiscal income while the figure for the top decile is 13.9 percent. Taxes reduce the pre-fiscal Gini by 2.8 percent. The combined effect of all government redistributive spending and taxes reduces the Gini from 0.5024 to 0.4387, or

94. Although Procampo, strictly speaking, is probably not regressive in relative terms, as discussed later. That would bring the total number of programs that are regressive in relative terms to three instead of four.

95. This category includes general subsidies to gasoline and other fuels, subsidies and monetary transfers to agricultural producers, and the subsidized part of social security pensions.

95. Scott (2009b).

97. Since this estimate includes the valuation of social services based on government spending (transfers in kind in education and health), the redistributive impact must be viewed as an upper bound that would have to be adjusted downward to the extent that the value of services received is less than the budgetary cost of provision.

98. The tax incidence analysis uses the same database (ENIGH 2006) and applies the same methodology as the spending incidence analysis reported here, so the tax and transfer incidence estimates are comparable.

Table 7-4. Incidence and Redistributive Impact of Transfers and Taxes, 2006ᵃ

Percent

| | Distribution (as a proportion of category's total) | | | | | | | | Incidence (as a proportion of pre-fiscal household income) | | |
| | Transfers (1) | Taxes (2) | Household income | | | | | | Transfers (9) | Tax (10) | Net (after taxes and transfers) (11) |
Decile			Pre-transfers and taxes (3)	Post-monetary transfers and subsidies (4)	Post-monetary transfers, subsidies and transfers in kind (5)	Post-tax (6)	Post monetary transfers and subsidies and taxes (7)	Post all transfers (column 5) and taxes (8)			
Adjusted											
1	8.2	0.9	1.5	1.6	2.3	1.5	1.7	2.4	74.7	–6.7	68
2	8.4	1.3	2.5	2.7	3.2	2.7	2.8	3.4	43.7	–5.9	37.8
3	8.4	2.1	3.4	3.5	4	3.6	3.7	4.2	32.5	–6.9	25.6
4	8.7	3	4.3	4.4	4.9	4.5	4.6	5.1	26.6	–7.6	19
5	8.7	3.5	5.3	5.4	5.7	5.5	5.6	5.9	21.9	–7.5	14.4
6	9.3	5.2	6.7	6.7	7	6.8	6.9	7.2	18.5	–8.7	9.8
7	10.1	6.2	8.2	8.2	8.4	8.4	8.5	8.7	16.4	–8.5	7.9
8	11.1	9.9	10.8	10.8	10.8	10.9	10.9	11	13.6	–10.2	3.4
9	11.9	16.4	15.8	15.8	15.4	15.8	15.7	15.3	10	–11.5	–1.6
10	15.1	51.6	41.4	40.8	38.3	40.1	39.5	36.9	4.8	–13.9	–9
Total	100	100	100	100	100	100	100	100	13.3	–11.1	
CC/G*	0.1047	0.6132	0.5024	0.4937	0.4558	0.4885	0.4794	0.4387			
Percent change in G				–1.7	–9.3	–2.8	–4.6	–12.6			

Source: Based on Scott (2009b).

a. Transfers include all the categories described in table 7-2; in the case of pensions, they include the subsidized component only. Taxes include all taxes and contributions to social security. Transfers in kind correspond to Education and Health categories in table 7-2. Monetary transfers and subsidies correspond to Subsidies and Programs Targeting the Poor categories in table 7-2. Asterisk = not in percent. CC = concentration coefficient; G = Gini coefficient.

12.6 percent. If we exclude the impact of in-kind transfers and consider the effect of monetary transfers and subsidies only plus the effect of taxes, the Gini falls from 0.5024 to 0.4794 or 4.6 percent.

In sum, although government redistributive spending has become more progressive over the last decade and although both spending and taxes reduce pre-fiscal inequality, there still is a lot of room for improvement in making state action more progressive on the fiscal front.

Summary and Conclusions

After more than a decade of rising income inequality between the early 1980s and early 1990s, Mexico's inequality finally began to decline in the post-NAFTA years. Between 1996 and 2006, the Gini coefficient for total income fell from 0.543 to 0.498, or 0.8 percent a year; the decline was higher, 1 percent a year, in the more recent period between 2000 and 2006. A more detailed analysis of income patterns reveals that during the past decade the bottom quintile experienced an above-average increase in its income while the top decile grew at below-average rates. The results of the decomposition exercises discussed in this chapter suggest that the improvement in incomes at the bottom of the distribution is linked to the higher relative wages of low-skilled workers, a rise in the share of remittances in rural areas, and the expansion of government monetary transfers to the poor.[99]

The reduction in the skill premium appears to explain the loss in the relative position of the upper deciles, particularly in urban areas. The reduction in the premium occurred because wages (or labor earnings, more precisely) increased more for low-wage workers than for the rest. A preliminary exploration of the causes indicates that this flattening of the wage distribution coincided with a significant change in the composition of the labor force in terms of education. Between 1989 and 2006, the share of workers with less than lower-secondary education fell from 55 percent to around 33 percent.

That educational upgrading of the labor force is associated with important changes in government spending on education.[100] In addition to the budgetary

99. The decomposition of inequality by income source clearly shows that, at the national level, there were three inequality-increasing income sources (pensions, income from own businesses, and income from property) and three inequality-reducing income sources (labor income since 2000, remittances, and transfers). Labor income became a very important inequality-reducing force in urban areas, as summarized earlier, but not in the rural sector, where in 2006 it was even inequality-increasing. In contrast, transfers became a very important inequality-reducing income source in rural areas and to a lesser extent in urban areas. The inequality-reducing contribution of transfers increased over time, both at the national level and for urban and, especially, rural households. By 2006 transfers became the income source with the largest inequality-reducing effect of all the income sources considered here; notably, a marginal increase in transfers would reduce inequality by more than a marginal increase in labor income or remittances.

100. To what extent can the relative decline in the supply of workers with low skills be attributed to outmigration? There is no study that directly addresses this question for the period covered in this chapter.

allocation between educational levels, progressivity in educational spending was improved by addressing two important constraints to access through implementation of the conditional cash transfer program Progresa in 1997: the limited availability of secondary schools in rural areas and constraints on demand for education, such as the high opportunity cost of attending school for children of lower-secondary and secondary school age in poor rural households.

The persuasiveness of the labor-supply side of the story is strengthened by the fact that for workers whose share in the labor force declined (rose), wages tended to increase (decline) or increase more rapidly (slowly). Of course, an increase in demand for low-skilled workers could have reinforced the supply-side changes in labor force composition. As mentioned, there are indications that the greater integration of Mexican and U.S. production turned Mexico's manufacturing workers into complements rather than substitutes for U.S. workers. That integration also contributed to expanding assembly-line production in Mexico, which increased the demand for low-skilled workers. In addition, it is possible that remittances and government transfers also increased demand for low-skilled workers, as recipients used the resources for home improvements or demanded more goods and services in local communities—something that could have had a local multiplier effect.[101]

The sharp rise in the role and inequality-reducing impact of public transfers was a consequence of a significant policy shift in the mid-1990s, in particular when the government launched Progresa. During 1996–2006 the size of public transfers increased and became more equally distributed among recipients; in addition, the recipients of transfers increasingly belonged to relatively poorer segments of the population. Moreover, government spending on education, health, and nutrition became more progressive. With the introduction of Progresa/Oportunidades, the Mexican government found ways to redistribute income in an efficient and cost-effective way through transfers.

However, despite this undeniable progress, when all government redistributive spending is considered,[102] benefits incidence analysis shows that 58 percent was

---

However, available evidence suggests that people with moderate to high levels of education are more likely to migrate than those with low levels of education (Hanson, 2006) so that, if anything, the relative scarcity of low-skilled workers should be affected less by outmigration than the relative scarcity of skilled workers.

101. The actual picture may not be as positive. Income inequality in Mexico has been falling during a period of low growth. If low growth is a consequence of the fact that not many jobs are being generated in the high-productivity sectors and that in turn is a consequence of the high costs faced by firms in the formal sector, then both low growth and the fall in wage inequality might be a result of the same undesirable process. Levy (2008) argues that that is in fact what has happened in Mexico and that the main culprit is, in some aspects, Mexico's social policy, which has created disincentives for employment generation in the formal sector. Pages, Pierr, and Scarpetta (2009) finds evidence that job creation in Mexico—and other Latin American countries—occurred disproportionately in low-productivity and low-wage sectors. They call this "growthless jobs."

102. And not just the portion of redistributive transfers captured by the income concept in household surveys, which is, as mentioned earlier, a mere 5 percent of total redistributive government spending.

still regressive in absolute terms (of which 11 percent increased income inequality). In advanced countries, government transfers are able to reduce primary or market income inequality between 30 and 50 percent. In Mexico, in contrast, the post-transfer Gini coefficient in 2006 was only 9.3 percent—and a meager 1.7 percent if we exclude transfers in kind—smaller than the pre-transfer Gini.

Unfortunately, the redistributive efficiency of Progresa/Opportunidades is an isolated case among the redistributive instruments currently in use in Mexico. The most regressive programs—those that worsen the distribution of income— are primarily those associated with agricultural subsidies and transfers as well as the subsidized component of pensions for employees of state-owned enterprises. Other programs and spending categories are regressive, but only in absolute terms. One of them is government spending on tertiary education, which, although it has been improving, is regressive because tertiary school enrollment among the poorest quintile is insignificant (and among the lowest in Latin America). In order to change that in a fundamental way, the government must compensate the poor for their high opportunity cost of pursuing tertiary education. Perhaps, in partnership with the private sector, the government should implement large-scale scholarship or student loan programs that target the poor. In addition, the availability of tertiary-level facilities must be expanded, given that at present not all students who wish to pursue a tertiary education are admitted because of supply-side constraints. A more important issue, and perhaps the most difficult to tackle, is the quality of public education, which will have to be improved at all levels and at the upper-secondary level in particular.

Today Mexico's poor are not able to attend public universities because of the low quality of their pre-university education. Poor children who graduate from low-quality public high schools lose out when they compete for scarce university places with students who graduate from high-quality private high schools. However, even if the competition to attend public universities were to be eliminated, students who attended poor-quality public schools would either fail or become second- or third-rate professionals. Substantially improving the quality of public education is essential to making state action more progressive. To a large extent, public spending on basic public education is progressive in absolute terms because higher-income groups opt out of public schools because of their lower quality. An immediate corollary is that efforts to improve the quality of public education, if successful, would necessarily come at the cost of equity in the use of public resources. However, in this case, that would be a welcome "cost."

What are the chances that such reforms might occur? Between the mid-1990s and mid-2000s, the state became more redistributionist, although not by strengthening the power of labor and peasant organizations. Large chunks of the traditional corporatist labor unions and agrarian organizations lost power—and access to economic resources—during the period of structural reforms and as part of the democratization process. That meant that such corporate organizations were unable to capture part of the economic rents as they did before the reforms; however, other institutions representing the interests of the poor and disenfranchised did not replace them.

Thus, state-led redistribution took place mainly through straightforward fiscal policy. In particular, in the areas of education and health and through targeted programs such as Progresa/Oportunidades, fiscal policy expanded and directed resources away from the top and the middle ranges of the distribution toward the poor. State-led redistribution was a top-down process led by enlightened technocrats that was made possible by the weakening of the power of corporatist organizations; it had less to do with the empowerment of the poor and disenfranchised.[103] However, not all corporatist organizations were weakened. One of the remaining diehards is the powerful teachers' union, which has succeeded in blocking most attempts to improve the quality and accountability of the public school system. In addition, the democratization process itself has weakened the ability of the state to implement top-down reforms because the ruling party does not have a congressional majority; therefore, in order to create viable coalitions, the chief executive has to make concessions that inevitably block reforms designed to eliminate the entitlements of some politically powerful groups, such as agricultural producers, rent-seeking, monopolistic entrepreneurs, workers in state-owned oil and electricity companies, and the teachers' unions.

Although the political economy outlook is not encouraging, it does not mean that the government should not try to push for reforms. However, one aspect of reform is usually overlooked in the discussion of equity and state action. Policy recommendations often emphasize the elimination or reduction of spending categories or programs that are regressive in absolute terms (that is, the poor receive less than the rich in per capita terms). The problem with that is twofold. First, even though regressive in absolute terms, the incidence of those spending categories is progressive in relative terms, and, in the absence of compensatory mechanisms, eliminating them would make the poor worse off. That is the case, for example, of the VAT exemptions on food and prescription drugs. Second, the portion of distribution that receives higher per capita benefits includes large chunks of the middle and lower-middle classes, which may be right in resisting a reform that could affect their or their children's social mobility or welfare. In addition, progressive leadership may want to financially support a burgeoning middle class because of the role it plays in fostering stable and democratic institutions.

References

Acosta, Pablo, and Gabriel V. Montes-Rojas. 2008. "Trade Reform and Inequality: The Case of Mexico and Argentina in the 1990s." *World Economy* 31, no. 6: 763–80.

103. For a discussion of the political economy of redistribution, see chapter 3 in this volume.

Airola, Jim, and Chinhui Juhn. 2005. "Wage Inequality in Post-Reform Mexico." IZA Discussion Paper 1525 (March). Bonn, Germany: Institute for the Study of Labor (IZA).

Alejo, Javier, and others. 2009. "Cambios en la desigualdad del ingreso en América Latina. Contribución de sus principales determinantes (1995–2006). Informe Final." Paper prepared for the UNDP project "Markets, the State, and the Dynamics of Inequality in Latin America," coordinated by Luis Felipe López-Calva and Nora Lustig (http://undp.economiccluster-lac.org/).

Aspe, Pedro, and Javier Beristáin. 1984. "Distribution of Educative and Health Services." In *The Political Economy of Income Distribution in Mexico,* edited by Pedro Aspe and Paul. E. Sigmund. New Jersey: Holmes and Meier.

Atolia, Manoj. 2007. "Trade Liberalization and Rising Wage Inequality in Latin America: Reconciliation with HOS Theory." *Journal of International Economics* 71, no. 2 (April): 467–94.

Barham, Tania. 2005. "Providing a Healthier Start to Life: The Impact of Conditional Cash Transfers on Infant Mortality." Ph.D. dissertation/working paper, Department of Agriculture and Resource Economics, University of California Berkeley.

Barros, Ricardo Paes de, and others. 2009. "Markets, the State, and the Dynamics of Inequality: Brazil's Case Study." Paper prepared for the UNDP project "Markets, the State, and the Dynamics of Inequality: How to Advance Inclusive Growth," coordinated by Luis Felipe López -Calva and Nora Lustig (http://undp.economiccluster-lac.org/).

———. 2006. "Uma análise das principias causas da queda recente na desigualdade de renda brasileira." *Econômica* (Brasília) UFF 8, no. 1: 117–47.

Bautista, Sergio, and others. 2004. "Impacto de Oportunidades en la Morbilidad y el Estado de Salud de la Población Beneficiaria y en la Utilización de Servicios de Salud: Resultados de Corto Plazo en Zonas Urbanas y de Mediano Plazo en Zonas Rurales." In *Evaluación externa de impacto del programa Oportunidades 2004*, Tomo II, *Salud,* edited by Bernardo Hernández and Mauricio Hernández. México D.F.: CIESAS/INSP.

Campos, Raymundo. 2008. "Why Did Wage Inequality Decrease in Mexico after NAFTA?" Unpublished paper. UC-Berkeley (October).

Cañonero, Gustavo, and Alejandro Werner. 2002. "Salarios Relativos y Liberalización del Comercio en México." *El Trimestre Económico* 69, no. 273: 123–42.

Chiquiar, Daniel. 2008. "Globalization, Regional Wage Differentials, and the Stolper-Samuelson Theorem: Evidence from Mexico." *Journal of International Economics* 74, no. 1: 70–93.

CIDE-ITAM. 2004. *Análisis de las Finanzas Públicas en México.* CONACYT-CIDE-ITAM-Foro Consultivo Científico y Tecnológico.

Coady, David. 2000. "The application of social cost-benefit analysis to the evaluation of PROGRESA." Working Paper, International Food Policy Research Institute.

Corbacho, Ana, and Gerd Schwartz. 2002. "Mexico: Experience with Expenditure Pro-poor Policies." Working Paper WP/02/12. IMF (International Monetary Fund).

Cortes, Fernando, Patricio Solís, and Israel Banegas. 2006. *Oportunidades y pobreza en México: 2002-2004.* Ciudad México: El Colegio de México.

Cragg, Michael, and Mario Epelbaum. 1996. "Why has Wage Dispersion Grown in Mexico? Is it the Incidence of Reforms or the Growing Demand for Skills?" *Journal of Development Economics* 51, no. 1: 99–116.

Eberhard, Juan, and Eduardo Engel. 2008. "Decreasing Wage Inequality in Chile." Mimeo.

Ervik, Rune. 1998. "The Redistributive Aim of Social Policy: A Comparative Analysis of Taxes, Tax Expenditure Transfers and Direct Transfers in Eight Countries." Luxembourg Income Study Working Paper 184. Luxembourg.

Esquivel, Gerardo. 2008. "The Dynamics of Income Inequality in Mexico since NAFTA." Paper prepared for the UNDP project "Markets, the State, and the Dynamics of Inequality:

How to Advance Inclusive Growth," coordinated by Luis Felipe López-Calva and Nora Lustig (http://undp.economiccluster-lac.org/).

Esquivel, Gerardo, and Alejandra Huerta-Pineda. 2007. "Remittances and Poverty in Mexico: A Propensity Score Matching Approach." *Integration and Trade Journal*, no. 27 (July–December): 47–74.

Esquivel, Gerardo, and José Antonio Rodríguez-López. 2003. "Technology, Trade and Wage Inequality in Mexico before and after NAFTA." *Journal of Development Economics* 72, no. 2: 543–65.

Fairris, David, Gurleen Popli, and Eduardo Zepeda. 2008. "Minimum Wage and Wage Structure in Mexico." *Review of Social Economy* 66, no. 2 (June): 181–08.

FAO (Food and Agriculture Organization of the United Nations). 2005. *Evaluación de la Alianza para el Campo 2004.* Mexico.

Feenstra, Robert, and Gordon Hanson. 1997. "Foreign Direct Investment and Relative Wages: Evidence from Mexico's Maquiladoras." *Journal of International Economics* 42, no. 3-4: 371–93.

Hanson, Gordon. 2006. "Illegal Migration from Mexico to the United States." *Journal of Economic Literature* 44, no. 4 (December): 869–924.

Hanson, Gordon, and Ann Harrison. 1999. "Trade Liberalization and Wage Inequality." *Industrial and Labor Relations Review* 52 , no.2 : 271–88.

Hernández, Bernardo, and others. 2003. "Evaluación del Impacto de Oportunidades en la Mortalidad Materna e Infantil." In *Evaluación Externa del Impacto del Programa Oportunidades 2003*, vol. 2, edited by Bernardo Hernández Prado and Mauricio Hernández Ávila. Cuernacava, México: Instituto Nacional de Salud Pública.

de Hoyos, Rafael, and Nora Lustig. 2009. "Apertura comercial, desigualdad, y pobreza. Reseña de los enfoques metodológicos, el estado del conocimiento, y la asignatura pendiente." *El Trimestre Económico* (Fondo de Cultura Económica) (April–June) no. 302: 283–28.

INEGI (Instituto Nacional de Estadistica y Geografia). Various years. ENIGH (Encuesta Nacional de Ingresos y Gastos de los Hogares. México (http://www.inegi.org.mx/inegi/default.aspx?s=est&c=10205).

Legovini, Arianna, César Bouillón and Nora Lustig. 2005. "Can Education Explain Changes in Income Inequality in Mexico." In *The Microeconomics of Income Distribution Dynamics*, edited by François Bourguignon, Francisco H. G. Ferreira and Nora Lustig, pp. 275–312. World Bank/Oxford University Press.

Lerman, Robert, and Shlomo Yitzhaki. 1985. "Income Inequality Effects by Income Source: A New Approach and Application to the U.S." *Review of Economics and Statistics* 67, no. 1 (February): 151–56.

Levy, Santiago. 2006. *Progress against Poverty: Sustaining Mexico's Progresa-Oportunidades Program.* Brookings.

———. 2008. *Good Intentions, Bad Outcomes: Social Policy, Informality, and Economic Growth in Mexico.* Brookings.

López-Acevedo, Gladys. 2006. "Mexico: Two Decades of the Evolution of Education and Inequality." Policy Research Working Paper 3919. Washington: World Bank

López-Feldman, Alejandro. 2006. "Decomposing Inequality and Obtaining Marginal Effects." *Stata Journal* 6, no. 1: 106–11.

Lustig, Nora. 1998. *Mexico: The Remaking of an Economy.* 2nd. ed. Brookings.

———. 2006. *Invertir en salud para el desarrollo económico.* México D.F.: Comisión Mexicana de Macroeconomía y Salud (Fondo de Cultura Económica).

———. 2007. "A Note on Markets, the State, and the Dynamics of Inequality." Concept note for the UNDP project "Markets, the State, and the Dynamics of Inequality in Latin America," coordinated by Luis Felipe López-Calva and Nora Lustig (http://undp.economic cluster-lac.org/).

Mancera, C. 2008. "Resultados preliminares de los estudios de calidad de los servicios educativos que atienden a la población beneficiaria de Oportunidades en áreas rurales." Cuarta Sesión del Comité Académico de Expertos en Política Social. Mexico: Sedesol (Secretaria de Desarrollo Social).

————. 2008. *Education at a Glance 2008: OECD Indicators.* OECD (www.oecd.org/edu/eag2008).

Pages, Carmen, Gaella Pierr, and Stefano Scarpetta. 2009. *Job Creation in Latin America and the Caribbean: Recent Trends and Policy Challenges.* Washington: World Bank and Palgrave Macmillan.

Parker, Susan. 2005. "Evaluación del Impacto de Oportunidades sobre la Inscripción, Reprobación, y Abandono Escolar." In *Evaluación Externa del Impacto del Programa Oportunidades 2004,* edited by Bernardo Hernández Prado and Mauricio Hernández Ávila. Mexico: Instituto Nacional de Salud Pública.

Ravallion, Martin, and Shaohua Chen. 2003. "Measuring Pro-Poor Growth." *Economics Letters* 78, no. 1: 93–99.

Robertson, Raymond. 2007. "Trade and Wages: Two Puzzles from Mexico." *World Economy* 30, no. 9: 1378–98.

Robinson, James A. 2008. "The Political Economy of Redistributive Policies." This volume.

Schultz, Paul. 2000. *The Impact of Progresa on School Enrollments: Final Report.* Washington: International Food Policy Research Institute.

Scott, John. 2002. "High Inequality, Low Revenue: Redistributive Efficiency of Latin American Fiscal Policy in Comparative Perspective." Paper prepared for the conference "Fiscal Aspects of Social Programs: Studies on Poverty and Social Protection, Regional Policy Dialogue, Poverty Reduction, and Social Protection Network." Inter-American Development Bank (http://idbdocs.iadb.org/wsdocs/getdocument.aspx?docnum=616098).

————.2005. "Social Security and Inequality in Mexico: From Polarization to Universality." *Well-Being and Social Policy* 1: 59–82.

————. 2006. "Poverty and Inequality in Mexico under NAFTA: Trade Liberalization and Policy Failures." Unpublished paper. Mexico: CIDE.

————. 2009a. "Gasto Público y Desarrollo Humano en México: Análisis de Incidencia y Equidad." Working paper for *Informe de Desarrollo Humano de México 2008–2009.* México: PNUD.

————. 2009b. "Redistributive Constraints under High Inequality: The Case of Mexico." Paper prepared for the UNDP project "Markets, the State, and the Dynamics of Inequality: How to Advance Inclusive Growth", coordinated by Luis Felipe López-Calva and Nora Lustig (http://undp.economiccluster-lac.org/).

————. 2009c. "The Incidence of Agricultural Subsidies in Mexico." Paper for the project "Agricultural Trade Adjustment and Rural Poverty: Transparency, Accountability, and Compensatory Programs in Mexico." Washington: Mexico Institute, Woodrow Wilson International Center for Scholars (www.wilsoncenter.org/index.cfm?fuseaction=topics.home&topic_id=5949).

Sen, Amartya, and James E. Foster. 1973. *On Economics and Inequality.* 1997 reprint. Oxford University Press.

SHCP (Secretaria de Hacienda y Crédito Público). 2008. Distribución del pago de impuestos y recepción del gasto público por deciles de hogares y personas. Resultados para el año de 2006. SHCP.

Smeeding, Timothy M. and Katherin Ross Phillips. 1999. "Social protection for the poor in the developed world: the evidence from LIS." Working Paper no. 204. LIS.

Stark, Oded, J. Edward Taylor and Shlomo Yitzhaki. 1986. "Remittances and Inequality." *Economic Journal* 96, no. 383 (September): 722–40.

Pages, Carmen, Gaelle Pierr and Stefano Scarpetta. 2009. *Job Creation in Latin America and the Caribbean: Recent Trends and Policy Challenges.* Palgrave Macmillan and World Bank.

Székely, Miguel. 2003. "Es posible un México con menor pobreza y desigualdad." Research Papers 3. México: Sedesol (Secretaría de Desarrollo Social).

———. 2005. "Pobreza y Desigualdad en México entre 1950 y 2004." *El Trimestre Económico* 72, no. 288 (October-December).

Taylor, J Edward, George A. Dyer and Antonio Yunez-Naude. 2005. "Dissagregated Rural Economywide Models for Policy Analysis." *World Development* 33, no. 10: 1671–88.

Thomas, Vinod, Yan Wang, and Xibo Fan. 2000. *Measuring Education Inequality: Gini Coefficients of Education.* World Bank.

Tornell, Aaron, and Gerardo Esquivel. 1997. "The Political Economy of Mexico's Entry into NAFTA". In *Regionalism versus Multilateral Trade Arrangements,* edited by Takatoshi Ito and Anne O. Krueger. Chicago: University of Chicago Press.

van Doorslaer, Eddy, and Owen O'Donnell. 2008. "Measurement and Explanation of Inequality in Health and Health Care in Low-Income Settings." Discussion Paper No. 2008/04. UNU-WIDER (World Institute for Development Economics Research of the United Nations University).

Verhoogen, Eric. 2008. "Trade, Quality Upgrading, and Wage Inequality in the Mexican Manufacturing Sector." *Quarterly Journal of Economics* 123, no. 2 (May): 489–530.

World Bank. 2004. "Reforma del financiamiento para pensiones y actividades de asistencia social: evaluación del pasivo fiscal global de los sistemas públicos de pensiones en México." Mimeo.

———. 2006. "Decentralization, Poverty, and Development in Mexico." In Working Paper 35692, *Decentralized Service Delivery for the Poor,* vol. 1. Mexico: World Bank.

8

Inequality in Post–Structural Reform Peru: The Role of Market Forces and Public Policy

MIGUEL JARAMILLO AND JAIME SAAVEDRA

In 1940, according to census data, 57 percent of Peruvians more than 15 years of age had never gone to school at all and less than 5 percent had gone beyond primary school (Peru 1944). In 1961, prior to the agrarian reform of the late 1960s, the Gini coefficient for land concentration was 0.94 (Escobal, Saavedra, and Torero 1998). Participation in electoral processes was below 10 percent of the total population in 1939 (Jaramillo and Saavedra 2005). With those figures in mind, we can characterize the changes that came in the last half of the twentieth century as no less than dramatic. Access to primary school is now almost universal, and about 80 percent of children are enrolled in secondary school at the appropriate age. Moreover, land is much more equally distributed; the related Gini coefficient dropped dramatically, to 0.61 by 1994. Change in the sociopolitical realm also has been enormous. Fully 57 percent of Peru's total population participated in the 2000 presidential election. However, Peru is still among the more unequal countries in the world. Thus, it is clear that despite the progress that has been made, important challenges remain in advancing social equity in Peru.

The authors are grateful to Veronica Montalva and Martín Sotelo for excellent research assistance and to Michael Lisman for his very valuable editorial recommendations. They also would like to thank Nora Lustig and an anonymous referee for their useful comments and suggestions. The authors are solely responsible for any errors of fact or judgment.

In this chapter we analyze inequality trends in Peru, focusing in particular on the post–structural reform period of 1997 through 2006. Between 1997 and 2006—the post–structural reform period in Peru—the Gini coefficient for household per capita income declined from .54 to .49. We identify the proximate factors influencing those trends and link them to underlying forces associated with the market and with state policies. This strategy allows us to pinpoint both market mechanisms and state interventions that may play an important role in furthering inclusive growth. The analysis reveals that a decline in nonlabor income inequality contributed more than labor earnings to the fall in household per capita income inequality.[1] In fact, overall labor earnings inequality remained unchanged through 2006. The decline in nonlabor income inequality can be linked to the expansion of both monetary and in-kind government transfers targeting the poor as well as private transfers such as remittances, although further research is needed to understand the dynamics.

Underneath the unchanged labor income inequality, however, some interesting processes were taking place. First, the returns to education for individual workers (the skill-premium) fell. Second, the distribution of educational attainment became more equal.[2] Thus, both price and quantity effects were present for education, and both were equalizing in terms of individual labor earnings. When we move to the household level, however, the returns to education became unequalizing (probably signaling that a change has taken place in assortative matching and/or the participation of married educated women in the labor force). At the household level, changes in hours worked, urban-rural differences, and returns to education also were unequalizing; among the equalizing forces were returns to experience as well as changes in the structure of educational attainment (years of formal education). Also, unobserved factors played an equalizing role. Changes in the gender gap did not play a role.

Our analysis suggests that both market forces and government policies have influenced these processes. Market forces, with the help of demographics, caused a decline in returns to experience. On the other hand, since the early 1970s government policies have played a key role in the expansion of basic education and the consequent rise in educational attainment of the labor force. Thus, the supply of

1. This decline is statistically significant, and there is Lorenz dominance. The income concept used in this chapter is total (monetary plus nonmonetary) current (excluding capital gains) household income per capita after monetary and in-kind transfers, direct taxes, and social security contributions. Nonmonetary income includes imputed value of private payments in kind, owner-occupied housing, and auto-consumption. In-kind transfers (public and private) include imputed values for the following items: food, apparel, housing rent, fuel and electricity, furniture and other household items, health care, transportation and communication services, leisure and cultural activities, educational services, and other goods and services.

2. These results are similar to those found for Brazil; see Barros and others, chapter 6 in this volume. In chapter 2, Jaime Kahhat presents a theoretical discussion of the relationship between skill upgrading and earnings inequality.

semi-skilled and skilled workers rose relatively more than demand for them, with the consequent reduction in the skill premium for more educated workers. Transfers from public assistance programs as well as private transfers, mainly remittances, also have contributed to greater equality. Finally, government policies have contributed to reducing the urban-rural gap in access to basic infrastructure services, and there is evidence of an increase in equality of opportunity regarding access to education and basic infrastructure, though much more work remains to be done. Our results suggest three areas of focus for policies to promote inclusive growth: education, promotion of small businesses, and closing the gap between urban and rural areas in access to basic infrastructure services—and more generally, reducing inequality in opportunities to access good basic services (in education, health, justice, and so forth).

The chapter first presents an overview of the evolution of inequality in Peru during the last half of the twentieth century and analyzes in detail the trends in inequality in the post-reform period (1997–2006). It then identifies proximate factors explaining inequality changes through a parametric decomposition methodology and analyzes the incidence of public spending in Peru. It next compares the roles played by market forces and social policies behind the noted changes in inequality and finally presents conclusions and suggested policy options.

The Evolution of Inequality in Peru in the Last Half-Century

Because of problems with data comparability it is difficult to draw a clear conclusion regarding long-term trends in Peru's welfare distribution. Studies since the seminal work of Webb and Figueroa (1975) can be divided in two groups that differ from each other in terms of the data sources that they use, the resulting distribution trends, and the consequent interpretations of results.[3] The first group of studies, by Webb and Figueroa (as both individuals and coauthors), used national accounts and other diverse sources of information to analyze the evolution of the functional income distribution. Taken as a whole, this group of studies finds that income distribution began at a very high level of concentration and concentrated even more from 1950 to 1990 and that, even in the most optimistic of scenarios, it did not undergo significant changes during the 1990s. The studies, however, overlook inequality within occupational groups (wage laborers, urban independent workers, rural workers, and capitalists) since all of their attention is focused on the differences between those groups.

Studies in the second group are based on analyses of survey data. Those studies adequately collected household and personal income/expenditure data, thus

---

3. Studies in the first group include Webb (1977) and Figueroa (1982, 1990), in addition to Webb and Figueroa (1975). Those in the second group include Rodríguez (1991), Escobal and Agüero (1996), Escobal, Saavedra, and Torero (1998), Saavedra and Diaz (1999), and Glewwe and Hall (1994). For a detailed discussion of this literature and further references, see Jaramillo and Saavedra (2009).

Table 8-1. *Distribution of Household Income, Peru*

	1961	1971–72	1985–86	1991	1994	1996
50 percent poorest	12.3	10.7	18.8	21.0	22.9	24.5
20 percent richest	77.3	60.9	51.4	46.6	45.4	42.9
Gini coefficient	0.58	0.55	0.48	0.43	0.41	0.38

Sources: Escobal, Saavedra, and Torero (1998). Data for 1961 are from Webb (1977); data for 1971–72 are from Amat y León (1981); data for all other years are authors' estimates based on data from ENNIV.

allowing for estimation of inequality both between and within occupational groups. This group of studies, taken as a whole, suggests a trend of declining inequality from the early 1960s to the mid-1980s (see table 8-1). There are, however, comparability problems between the data from the early 1960s and the rest of the data, since they come from different sources, as Escobal, Saavedra, and Torero (1998) acknowledge. Moreover, there are comparability problems between the household surveys themselves, as they used different geographic domains of study as well as different data collection instruments. Consequently, it is not possible to draw a clear-cut conclusion based on these data.

Nevertheless, data on changes in the distribution of two key individual assets, land and education, tend to support the hypothesis of a long-term decline in inequality.[4] The Gini coefficient of land distribution declined dramatically in the three decades after 1961, from 0.94 that year to 0.61 by 1994.[5] Education also has expanded dramatically: since the early 1960s, the proportion of the population without any formal schooling dropped from 39 percent to 14 percent by the mid-1980s, while the share of those with secondary education grew from 11 percent to 36 percent. One would expect that such significant changes would have some bearing on the dynamics of inequality. Finally, as we find no systematic empirical evidence suggesting a declining trend in income distribution for the three decades after 1960, our analysis favors the conclusion that there was a reduction in inequality from the early 1960s to the early 1990s.

We have estimates starting from the mid-1980s of the distribution of both income and expenditures from household surveys: the Living Standards Measurement Study (Encuesta Nacional de Niveles de Vida [ENNIV]) for 1985 through 1996 and the National Household Survey (Encuesta Nacional de Hogares [ENAHO] for 1997 through 2006. Before analyzing them, however, it is useful to examine the data presented in figure 8-1, which depicts trends in GDP and poverty (for years with available data) since 1980. With that in mind, we can distinguish four periods (see table 8-2). The first period, which spans 1985 to 1990, is characterized by hyperinflation, macroeconomic crisis, and the spread of the

4. For an interesting discussion on the relationship between type of regime (democratic or authoritarian) and inequality trends in Peru, see Robinson, chapter 3 in this volume.

5. Escobal, Saavedra, and Torero (1998).

Figure 8-1. *Per Capita GDP and Poverty Rates, Peru, 1980–2007*

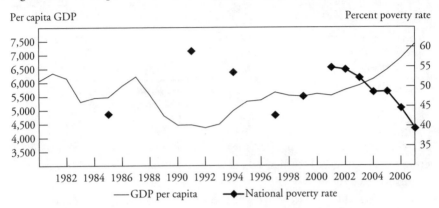

Per capita GDP   Percent poverty rate

——GDP per capita   ——National poverty rate

Sources: GDP in 2005 U.S. dollars (purchasing power parity) from the National Institute of Statistics (INEI); 1985–96 poverty rates from the Living Standards Measurement Study (ENNIV); 1999–2007 poverty rates from the National Household Survey (ENAHO). Authors' calculations.

terrorist activities of the Shining Path (Sendero Luminoso) and the Tupac Amaru Revolutionary Movement (Movimiento Revolucionario Tupac Amaru). The second period, which spans 1991 to 1996, features the implementation of a drastic economic stabilization plan simultaneously with profound structural reforms. Together, the third and fourth periods comprise what we call the post-reform period, when the reforms of the 1990s had already been implemented and the initial disruptions had settled. The third period, 1997 to 2001, is marked by recession and a slowing of the reform drive. The fourth period, 2001 to 2006, is one of continuous growth at rates that are above average for Latin America. Here we explore the connections between macroeconomic performance, the policy environment, sociopolitical events, and inequality outcomes in the first two of the four periods; we discuss the two latter periods later in the chapter.

The first period (1985–90) covers President Alan Garcia's first term in office. Heterodox policies to curb inflation and promote economic growth, including price controls, high tariffs on imports, increased public expenditures, and external debt repudiation initially managed some measure of success on both fronts. That success proved short-lived, however. In effect, after two years of high growth with lower inflation rates than in previous years, inflation again rose out of control while GDP quickly declined. Between 1988 and 1990, Peru's economy withstood a steep GDP decline of some 25 percent while hyperinflation became entrenched. Around the same time, the Shining Path and the Tupac Amaru Revolutionary Movement had gained ground not only in remote areas of Peru but in the capital city of Lima as well. Most international experience would suggest that this convergence of sociopolitical and macroeconomic crises would have unequal-

Table 8-2. *Economic Periods of Peru, 1985–2006*

Period	Years	Description
Period 1	1985–1990	Economic and sociopolitical crisis
Period 2	1991–1996	Stabilization and structural reform
Period 3	1997–2001	Post-reform recession
Period 4	2001–2006	Post-reform growth

Source: Authors' illustration.

izing effects.[6] The Peruvian experience in this period suggests the opposite, however. The Gini coefficients reported later in this chapter illustrate the decline in inequality during the first period. That decline was associated with a reduction in the concentration of income in the top quintile, which dropped by 5 percentage points, and compression in the salary structure as returns to education and experience declined (Saavedra and Díaz 1999). Thus, the crisis that stemmed from the populist policies of Garcia's presidency may have had some equalizing effect. There was a trade-off, however, as the poverty rate jumped 16 percentage points, from 43 percent in 1985 to 59 percent in 1990.

The second period (1990–96) began with Peru in the midst of its deepest economic and political crisis of the last hundred years. In August 1990, President Alberto Fujimori's administration began to implement an economic stabilization program. The four initial objectives of the program were to eliminate hyperinflation, reintegrate Peru into the international finance system, reestablish macroeconomic order, and resolve the balance of payments crisis. An especially important feature of the stabilization package was that it included a concurrent structural reform component. The structural reform involved a broad set of policies that went beyond restoring basic macroeconomic balance toward allowing the market more freedom to allocate resources, redefining the role of the state in economic activities, and promoting private initiatives (Jaramillo and Saavedra 2005; Abusada and others 2000). Specific policies were aimed at reducing barriers to foreign trade, making the labor market more flexible, deregulating the financial system, and opening up the capital account of the balance of payments. At the same time, aggressive privatizing of public firms began.

The stabilization program had strong recessive effects on the economy between 1990 and 1992 and lacked a coherent plan to ameliorate its social costs. It was not until 1994 that social expenditures began to increase as the country regained its international creditworthiness and structural adjustment loans began flowing into Peru. By 1993, inflation was declining and a period of sustained growth had begun; GDP registered an average annual growth rate of 6.4 percent from 1993 to

6. See, for example, the case of Argentina, analyzed in chapter 5 of this volume.

1997. At the same time, the performance of the labor market was positive, with the annual growth rate of salaried employment averaging 4.2 percent. By 1998 the employment rate reached 60 percent after having hit a low of 52 percent in 1992. Wages remained stagnant for unskilled workers but rose for skilled workers. Saavedra and Diaz (1999) associates increasing returns to education with higher demand for skilled workers across industries, which, in turn, seems to have been associated with trade openness and increases in investment. This economic climate brought new technologies and organizational requirements, which tend to be complementary factors associated with skilled labor. Inequality increased during the recession period (1991–94) and then declined in the upswing (1994–96).

Summarizing, two important trends in inequality can be detected in the analysis of the period from 1960 through 1996. First, although problems of comparability plague analyses of the period before the mid-1980s, a review of the relevant literature provides evidence to suggest a declining trend in inequality from the early 1960s to the mid-1980s. At the same time, indirect evidence, such as the expansion of basic education and the equalizing redistribution of land, also points toward the conclusion that by the year 2000, Peru was less unequal than it had been four decades earlier. Second, there is evidence in comparable data from the mid-1980s through the mid-1990s suggesting that inequality declined through the crisis-ridden Garcia administration (1985–90) and through the first half of Fujimori's subsequent administration, in spite of an increase during the early stabilization period (1991–94).

Trends in Inequality in Post–Structural Reform Peru, 1997–2006

Figure 8-2 shows trends in Gini coefficients of both household per capita income and expenditure at the national level. For the period from 1985 to 1994 we report data from Escobal, Saavedra, and Torero (1998), which used the now-discontinued ENNIV; for the period from 1997 to 2006 we present our own estimations from Peru's national household surveys (ENAHO). There are a number of technical differences between the two sources. Most important, the two sources' sampling frames differ. The geographical domains of study, the smallest sampling unit for which the sources have statistical inference, are diverse and thus are not strictly comparable. As presented above, inequality decreased during the period from 1985 to 1996. In the post-reform period of 1997 to 2006, we find year-to-year fluctuations around a declining trend in inequality. While the 1.3-point decline during the recession from 1997 through 2001 is not statistically significant, both the 3.6-point decline during the growth period of 2001 to 2006 and the 5-point decline over the entire period are statistically significant.

Labor earnings inequality does not show a declining trend as is observed in total income per capita. Instead, we observe an increase during the recessionary period from 1997 to 2001 (not statistically significant) and a reduction during

Figure 8-2. *Gini Coefficients of Per Capita Household Income and Expenditures,*
Peru

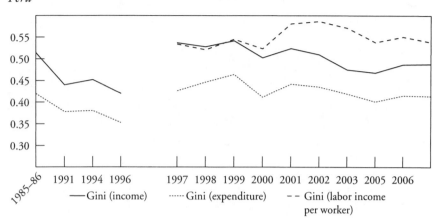

Sources: ENNIV (1985–86, 1991, 1994 and 1996); ENAHO (1997–2006, fourth quarter of each year). Calculations for 1985–94 are from Saavedra, Escobal, and Torero (1998); calculations for 1997–2006 are by the authors.

the growth period from 2001 to 2006 (statistically significant) that take inequality back to its 1997 level (not statistically significant). That suggests that trends in nonlabor income must have contributed decisively to the reduction in total income inequality.

Nonlabor income is made up of several elements: private money transfers from local sources, remittances from abroad, public monetary and in-kind transfers, unpaid expenditures, property rents (including homeownership), and returns to capital.[7] Overall, nonlabor income represents one-quarter of total income among Peruvian households. However, it varies widely across deciles, comprising about a fifth of total income in the richer deciles to about half in the poorest decile. The low share of labor income in the poorest deciles can be explained by lower earnings per worker, but it also is due to a much lower percentage of both adults and working adults.

Figure 8-3 shows annualized changes in total income, labor income, and non-labor income during the growth period (2001–06). The graph depicts a clear pattern of nonlabor income increasing much faster across the income distribution but with sharper increases in the lower deciles. Considering its share of total income, nonlabor income explains a larger part of the increase in total income of the poorest deciles and consequently of the reduction in income inequality.[8] Analysis of

7. Money transfers, remittances, rents of capital, and expenditures not paid for are self-reported. The value of in-kind transfers and rent of homeownership are imputed.

8. It should be noted that the same pattern emerges when different pairs of years, 1997 to 2006, are used for comparison.

Figure 8-3. *Growth in Labor and Nonlabor Income by Decile, Peru, 2001–06*

Percent change

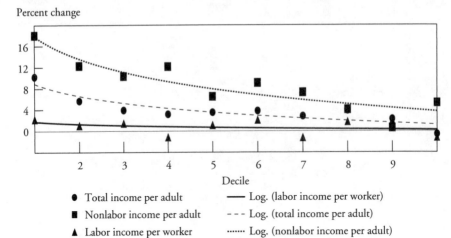

● Total income per adult   —— Log. (labor income per worker)

■ Nonlabor income per adult   - - - Log. (total income per adult)

▲ Labor income per worker   ······· Log. (nonlabor income per adult)

Source: ENAHO (2001–06, fourth quarter of each year). Authors' calculations.

which components of nonlabor income underlie these patterns cannot be done in detail because of data comparability problems. However, the available data, which we discuss later, suggest that nonmonetary public sector transfers are one factor in the larger increase in nonlabor income for the poor and hence in the reduction in total income inequality observed.

The data on the distribution of household per capita income and expenditures by quintiles reported in table 8-3 confirm the evidence on trends in inequality from Gini coefficients and suggest a reduction in concentration for the whole period from 1997 until 2006, accentuated after 2001. In addition, the data confirm the unequal nature of the distribution of welfare in Peru. Slightly more than half of total income and just less than half of total expenditures are concentrated in the top quintile. The differences for the whole period between the top and bottom quintiles for both incomes and expenditures also are pronounced, with the top quintile averaging 16 times more and 9 times more, respectively, than the bottom quintile.

Given Peru's geographic and cultural heterogeneity, it is interesting to explore potential differences in the evolution of inequality according to geographic domain. Therefore we have disaggregated the data to analyze the following three domains: rural areas, urban areas excluding metropolitan Lima (Resto Urbano), and metropolitan Lima.[9] Figure 8-4 shows the evolution of per capita income Gini

9. ENAHO has inference levels for these geographic domains. In fact, ENAHO has inference levels for more disaggregated geographic domains: urban and rural coast, urban and rural highlands region, and urban and rural rainforest region. It has them even for Peru's twenty-four political regions.

Table 8-3. *Distribution of Real Household Per Capita Income and Expenditure, Peru, 1997, 2001, and 2006*

	Distribution of monthly per capita expenditure (percent)			Distribution of monthly per capita income (percent)		
	1997	2001	2006	1997	2001	2006
Gini coefficient	0.45	0.44	0.41	0.54	0.52	0.49
Quintile 1	4.9	5.0	5.9	3.2	3.5	4.2
Quintile 2	9.2	9.5	10.3	7.3	7.6	8.2
Quintile 3	14.1	14.4	15.0	12.1	12.3	13.1
Quintile 4	21.2	21.8	21.9	19.6	19.9	20.8
Quintile 4	50.6	49.4	46.9	57.8	56.7	53.7
Ratio						
Quintile 5/Quintile 1	10.4	9.9	8.0	17.8	16.1	12.8
Quintile 5/Quintile 2	5.5	5.2	4.6	7.9	7.5	6.6
Quintile 5/Quintile 3	3.6	3.4	3.1	4.8	4.6	4.1
Quintile 5/Quintile 4	2.4	2.3	2.1	3.0	2.8	2.6

Source: Authors' calculations based on data from ENAHO (1997, 2001, and 2006, fourth quarter of each year).

coefficients for each geographic domain during the period from 1997 to 2006. First, we note that throughout most of that period, metropolitan Lima exhibited greater inequality but also larger fluctuations than Resto Urbano and the rural areas. However, inequality indicators in all three areas tended to converge in the last three years (2004 through 2006). Second, during the recessionary period between 1997 and 2001, we find that the decline in overall inequality was driven

Figure 8-4. *Gini Coefficients of Monthly Household Per Capita Income, Peru, 1997–2006*

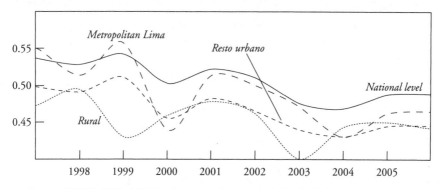

Source: ENAHO (1997–2006, fourth quarter of each year). Authors' calculations.

mostly by the decline in urban inequality, while in rural areas it fluctuated around a slightly declining trend. In the growth period of 2001 to 2006, there is a clear downward trend in both rural and urban areas, including metro Lima.

In sum, analysis of post-reform trends suggests that inequality decreased in the post-reform period through both a recession (though that result is not statistically significant) and a growth phase. Labor income inequality, however, did not decline, showing contrasting trends in the two post-reform subperiods: it rose during the recession of 1997 through 2001 (though that result is not statistically significant) and then declined through the growth period from 2001 to 2006. We confirm the role of nonlabor income in the decline of inequality by looking at changes in labor and nonlabor income by decile: changes in nonlabor income are greater throughout the distribution and much greater for those households in the lower part of the distribution. For the same households, the relative importance of nonlabor income also is greater. Finally, after disaggregating the data by geographical domain, we find that inequality levels are greater in urban than in rural areas and that the decline in inequality in the period from 1997 through 2006 also was larger in urban areas (including metro Lima) than in rural ones.

Proximate Factors behind Inequality: A Decomposition Analysis

It is reasonable to expect that structural reforms implemented during the early 1990s considerably modified relative prices. As a consequence, the relative contribution of factors explaining inequality also could have changed according to their importance to different economic sectors after the reforms. Therefore, for example, Saavedra and Diaz (1999) argues that the increasing role of education returns in income dispersion from 1992 to 1996 is associated with a greater demand for skilled workers. In light of the authors' data, that increase in returns to education would be a short-term effect of structural reforms concerning trade openness and the increase in foreign investment, which itself brought new technologies and greater investment in physical capital. Since we focus on a period following the implementation of structural reforms, we are able to evaluate their medium-term effects on inequality.

Following Bourguignon, Ferreira, and Lustig (2005), we used a microsimulation methodology, which consists of simulating counterfactual distributions by changing one factor at a time and holding other aspects constant. One of the advantages of this methodology is that it easily allows for assessing the partial contribution of a particular factor to changes in inequality while controlling for other factors. Furthermore, it allows for distinguishing the contribution of a factor to inequality due to changes in its distribution from its contribution due to changes in its market returns.

The counterfactual simulation methodology, following its parametric implementation, comprises the estimation of a household income-generation model in reduced form. Our analysis is restricted to labor income (specifically wage earnings and self-employment earnings) since that is the share of income most suitable for modeling information available in household surveys. The econometric specification of our model is similar to that used in Gasparini, Marchionni, and Sosa Escudero (2005) and Bourguignon, Fournier, and Gurgand (2001), which followed the reduced-form model of labor decisions introduced by Heckman (1974). This model consists of two equations, one for hourly earnings and the other for hours of work:

(7-1) $$w_i^* = X_{1i}\beta + \varepsilon_{1i}, i = 1, \dots, N \ \dots$$

(7-2) $$L_i^* = X_{2i}\lambda + \varepsilon_{2i}, i = 1, \dots, N \ \dots$$

$$\text{with:} \begin{cases} w_i = w_i^*, L_i^* > 0 \\ w_i = 0, L_i^* \le 0 \end{cases} \text{and} \begin{cases} L_i = L_i^*, L_i^* > 0 \\ L_i = 0, L_i^* \le 0 \end{cases}$$

where w_i and L_i correspond to observed earnings and hours of work, respectively; w_i^* is the reserve wage (reserve earning) for which an individual will agree to work for a determined number of hours; and L_i^* is the optimal choice of the number of hours of work given preferences and market conditions. We observe positive values of w_i^* and L_i^* if and only if a given individual works. The hourly earnings equation is estimated following the Heckman procedure to correct for sample selection, and in our case the selection equation simply indicates whether or not the individual works. The equation for hours of work is estimated using a standard censored regression Tobit model.

In particular, we use this methodology to assess the contribution to income inequality of the following factors: returns to residing in an urban area; returns to education; returns to a salaried job; gender earnings gap; educational structure of the labor force; hours worked; and unobserved factors. We consider only the direct effect of these factors on hourly earnings—that is, we are not estimating the *total* distributional effect of changes in these factors as in a general equilibrium model. Rather, our approach corresponds to one of partial equilibrium.[10]

Although this methodology allows us to simulate the entire counterfactual distribution, we focus on a summary measure of income inequality, namely the Gini coefficient. The simulation of Gini counterfactuals is relatively straightforward for labor market returns. It consists of estimating individual labor income per hour using all parameter estimators of the equation 7-1, including the residual term ε_1, for a given base year but replacing the relevant β with the corresponding estimated β for the year of comparison.[11] Next, we multiply that by actual hours worked and by the number of weeks in a quarter, thus recovering quarterly

10. This limitation of the methodology is pointed out in Bourguignon and Ferreira (2005).

11. Observed Gini coefficient estimates are slightly different from those we reported previously in the chapter because to estimate the counterfactuals we restricted the sample to those observations with valid answers in the relevant variables for the estimation of our model.

income. Then, in order to get from individual earnings to household labor income per capita, we simply add the total earnings of all the household members and divide that total by the total number of members. To obtain total household income per capita we simply add nonlabor income per capita to the latter.

Estimating counterfactuals for education structure and unobserved factors requires a slightly more sophisticated procedure. For education structure, we cluster observations by location, gender, and age. We then replicate the distribution of years of schooling for a cluster in the corresponding cluster in the year of comparison, following the procedure described in Legovini, Bouillón, and Lustig (2005). For unobserved factors, we rescale the estimated residual of the log hourly earnings equation, multiplying it by the estimated standard deviation of that equation in the year of comparison and dividing it by the estimated standard deviation of that equation in a certain year.

Table 8-4 reports the average results obtained at the national level for three periods: 1997–2006, 1997–2001, and 2001–06. We use the two endpoint years alternatively as base year since the decompositions are path dependent and report effects as an average of the two.[12] The interpretation of the results is as follows: if the sign of the estimated effect of a particular factor on the Gini coefficient is positive (negative), it means that the factor was unequalizing (equalizing). The larger the absolute value of the effect, the more significant its effect on inequality.

Three factors played important unequalizing roles in relation to household income during the period from 1997 to 2006: returns to residence in urban area; hours worked; and returns to education. At the same time, three other factors pushed in an equalizing direction: educational structure; returns to experience; and unobserved factors. The gender earnings gap did not play a significant role in changes in household income inequality. Returns to having a dependent (salaried) job played a significant but opposite role in both post-reform subperiods, thus adding up to a negligible effect over the entire decade. We note that urban residence and educational structure played a strong role during the recession years (1997–2001) but a minor one in the growth period (2001–06). In contrast, hours worked played a significant role in the growth period. Generally, the evaluated factors work in the same direction for household income or individual earnings inequality, but the size of the effect can vary significantly.[13] The exception is returns to education, which reduced individual earnings inequality but slightly increased household inequality (possibly due to marriage sorting).

---

12. Tables reporting regression results for log hourly earnings equations in urban and rural areas, as well as tables reporting regression results for the selection equation of the Heckman estimation model and for the Tobit censored model are in our companion piece (Jaramillo and Saavedra 2009). Tables showing decompositions for each of the base years as well as the average effect also are found there.

13. Patterns are generally quite similar for urban areas, though the sizes of some of the effects differ. In rural areas we find some contrasts: educational structure does not play a role, but returns to education plays a significant and equalizing role. See Jaramillo and Saavedra (2009).

Social Policies

We have shown how different labor market factors have affected the dynamics of inequality. State policies also can affect welfare distribution, through two channels in particular. The first channel, which is indirect, operates through regulatory policies that seek to establish the set of incentives and restrictions for social action and specifically for economic interaction. The second channel is direct; it operates by transferring resources directly to targeted population groups through social programs. The transfers can be made through direct provision of services, such as education, health, or nutrition services, or through cash or in-kind transfers, as in the case of subsidized pensions or as part of social programs. Here we examine the role of social policies in producing inequality results.

Income redistribution is effected by transfers (social spending) and taxes. Countries active in redistributing income do so mostly by providing some segments of the population with goods and services besides what they would receive by contributing themselves through taxes and to a lesser extent by providing direct monetary and nonmonetary assets. In assessing how large that redistribution is in Peru, a joint analysis of taxes and transfers can shed some light on the role of public policies in the redistributive process and hence in inequality. Breceda, Rigolini, and Saavedra (2007) reports estimates of disaggregated social spending and taxation for several Latin American countries to asses how much is spent (the amount of resources devoted to the social system) and on how it is spent (coverage and distribution). Using disaggregated data for expenditures in education, health, direct transfers, and taxation across quintiles, adjusted to national accounts, they found that different expenditure patterns are supported by different tax patterns.

Average social spending per individual in a sample of Latin American countries corresponds to 10 percent of per capita GDP, which is significantly lower than social spending in the United Kingdom (14 percent) but similar to social spending in the United States (11 percent).[14] Peru spends an average of 6 percent of per capita GDP while Argentina, Bolivia, and Honduras spend twice as much (12 percent), although in Bolivia and Honduras absolute per capita expenditures are lower. In addition to showing significant differences with the United Kingdom in average level of social spending, Peru and most Latin American countries show a strong contrast in terms of pro-poor social spending. In Peru, social spending is slightly biased in favor of the rich; on average, social spending on the poorest quintile corresponds to 92 percent of social spending on the richest quintile, whereas the same figure is 233 percent in the United Kingdom. Peru seems closer to the U.S. model, which has a ratio of 107 percent.[15]

14. In order to correct for spending capability, we normalize social spending (which comprises education, public health, and direct transfers) and taxes by average GDP per capita in the country and by income quintile.

15. It should be noted that in this calculation public pensions are excluded, as it is nearly impossible to establish how much of current expenditures are plain transfers and how much are accounted for by the

Table 8-4. *Counterfactual Changes in Gini Coefficients at the National Level*

	2006–1997			2006–2001			2001–1997		
	Per capita total household income	Per capita labor household income	Individual labor income	Per capita total household income	Per capita labor household income	Individual labor income	Per capita total household income	Per capita labor household income	Individual labor income
Observed effect	−4.24	−0.20	2.08	−2.98	−2.68	−0.77	−1.26	2.48	2.85
Average changes									
1 Returns to residence in urban area	0.36	0.35	0.08	0.06	−0.14	−0.27	0.32	0.47	0.37
2 Education structure	−0.35	−0.54	−0.53	0.22	0.09	0.04	−0.53	−0.63	−0.57
3 Returns to education	0.13	0.04	−0.37	0.13	−0.06	−0.20	0.01	0.09	−0.18
4 Returns to experience	−0.11	−0.31	−0.71	−0.17	−0.43	−0.31	−0.23	−0.21	−0.74
5 Returns to dependent job	0.00	0.09	0.30	−0.21	−0.33	−0.11	0.20	0.43	0.45
6 Gender earnings gap	0.04	0.05	0.22	0.10	0.00	0.09	−0.02	0.07	0.15
7 Hours of work	0.17	0.38	−0.08	0.29	0.45	0.07	−0.11	−0.09	−0.18
8 Unobserved factors	−1.20	−1.72	−1.61	−1.51	−2.25	−2.02	0.21	0.40	0.29

Source: Authors' estimates based on data from ENAHO (1997, 2001, 2006 fourth quarter of each year).

As a consequence of lower levels of overall spending as well as lower progressiveness, spending for the poorest income quintile is lower in Peru (9 percent) than in a sample of Latin American countries, where it averages 9.9 percent, which is in turn similar to spending in the United States (10.4 percent) but lower than that in the United Kingdom (20.3 percent). Overall, Peru does not do especially well in redistributing income through the tax and transfer structure. On the tax side, revenues from personal income taxes are very low, and on the transfer side, expenditures are not pro-poor enough.

Nevertheless, behind this static picture are interesting trends that point to a Peruvian state that has increased its role in redistributing resources, albeit slowly. During the last decade, transfers to the poor in the form of nonmonetary transfers and public services increased; more recently, they increased in the form of monetary transfers. In fact, between 1997 and 2006 per capita public social expenditure rose from an annual rate of US$150 to US$206.[16] Growth rates in this aggregate were similar for the recession and growth periods. It is important to point out here that while these numbers are roughly suggestive of the redistributive effort by the state, they by no means prove that state actions have had the effect of reducing inequality; social programs can be progressive, regressive, or neutral with respect to their effects on income distribution. An incidence analysis, however, can clarify their role.

Table 8-5 allows us to assess the role that public transfers from social programs played in household income across the income distribution during the growth years (2002–06).[17] The first thing we note is the increasing role of nonmonetary transfers from social programs in household income across the distribution.[18] Second, we note that public transfers play a much larger role for the poorest households and that their importance has grown notably. Change was markedly pro-poor as transfers tended to grow faster for the poorest deciles. Two items, food and public health services, account for fully 90 percent of the transfers; however, their effects are contrasting. Food transfers are progressive while health transfers are more evenly spread across income quintiles, tending to favor the groups in the middle quintiles. Progressive transfers are one factor behind the reduction of inequality and the progressive role of nonlabor income.

Access to basic infrastructure services is an area in which the state historically has had an important role, either by directly providing access or by promoting

---

social security contributions made by each individual. Since almost everyone who receives public pensions belongs to the richest quintile, if those pensions were included here, the pattern of public expenditures would be definitively pro-rich.

16. The source for these data is ECLAC (http://websie.eclac.cl/sisgen/ConsultaIntegrada.asp).

17. It is not possible to break down transfers into their public and private components for previous years. We include only those components that are comparable across the household surveys. The two major exclusions are the typically regressive transfers from social security for health care and public education.

18. We note that these increases are observed in a context of increasing public expenditures.

Table 8-5. *Nonmonetary Public Transfers as a Percent of Household Income, Peru, 2002–06*

	National			Urban			Rural		
	2002	2006	Difference	2002	2006	Difference	2002	2006	Difference
Decile 1	7.2	13.7	6.5	11.6	16.2	4.6	6.5	13.2	6.6
Decile 2	5.4	10.9	5.5	5.6	9.3	3.7	5.3	11.5	6.2
Decile 3	4.3	8.7	4.3	4.2	8.0	3.8	4.5	9.1	4.6
Decile 4	3.9	6.5	2.6	4.0	6.0	2.0	3.8	3.8	0.0
Decile 5	3.4	4.9	1.5	3.5	4.6	1.1	3.2	5.6	2.4
Decile 6	3.3	4.5	1.2	3.3	4.4	1.1	3.3	5.0	1.7
Decile 7	3.6	3.6	0.0	3.8	3.7	–0.1	2.4	3.3	0.9
Decile 8	3.8	3.3	–0.5	3.9	3.5	–0.4	3.6	2.4	–1.2
Decile 9	3.4	2.9	–0.5	3.5	3.0	–0.5	2.4	2.0	–0.3
Decile 10	1.8	2.3	0.4	1.8	2.1	0.3	1.8	6.3	4.5
Average	2.9	3.7	0.8	2.8	3.2	0.4	3.7	6.7	3.0

Source: Authors' calculations based on data from ENAHO (2002 ad 2006).

private sector expansion into the poorer areas. We observe significant improvements in basic access during the last decade (see table 8-6 for related data). The first and most striking fact is the huge gap between urban and rural areas for any type of service. The good news is that the gap has decreased during the last decade for every basic service except telephone land lines because of the faster expansion of access in rural areas. Second, improvements have been greatest in sanitation services, which have expanded quickly in both urban and rural areas. In urban areas, improvements have been definitively pro-poor, with the largest gains occurring in the two poorest quintiles, while in rural areas they have been only slightly pro-poor, as services have expanded significantly for all income groups. The pattern is similar for electric service.

Finally, expansion of land line telephone services is essentially an urban affair, as coverage is very low for any income group in the rural area. In urban areas expansion has favored the middle groups (quintiles 2 to 5). It is worth noting that our analysis does not change if we look at mobile phone lines instead. On the whole, improvements in access to public services have been pro-poor and have tended toward reducing the gap between urban and rural areas. These findings are consistent with findings in Barros and others (2009), which concluded that Peru shows one of the fastest increases in coverage and reductions in inequality of opportunity in Latin America, driven in large part by improvement in sanitation and electric services.

In sum, it can be said that social policy played a positive role in reducing inequality over the last decade. Part of its effects manifest themselves through changes in labor market variables (such as expansion of employment opportunities and an increase in returns to salaried and self-employment) and therefore are captured in the microsimulation exercise presented previously. For example,

Table 8-6. *Access to Basic Services, Peru, 1997–2006*

	Urban areas			Rural areas		
	1997	2001	2006	1997	2001	2006
Electricity						
Quintile 1	0.80	0.82	0.89	0.09	0.16	0.29
Quintile 2	0.92	0.91	0.97	0.14	0.22	0.34
Quintile 3	0.94	0.95	0.98	0.26	0.27	0.40
Quintile 4	0.97	0.97	0.99	0.32	0.37	0.51
Quintile 5	0.98	0.99	0.99	0.52	0.46	0.57
Average	0.92	0.93	0.97	0.26	0.3	0.42
Sanitation						
Quintile 1	0.34	0.56	0.73	0.01	0.07	0.25
Quintile 2	0.58	0.74	0.85	0.02	0.13	0.35
Quintile 3	0.67	0.80	0.90	0.05	0.15	0.39
Quintile 4	0.77	0.87	0.95	0.16	0.23	0.41
Quintile 5	0.92	0.95	0.98	0.21	0.30	0.50
Average	0.66	0.78	0.88	0.09	0.18	0.38
Phone line						
Quintile 1	0.08	0.08	0.12	0.00	0.00	0.00
Quintile 2	0.20	0.16	0.31	0.01	0.00	0.00
Quintile 3	0.29	0.31	0.45	0.00	0.00	0.00
Quintile 4	0.47	0.46	0.61	0.00	0.00	0.01
Quintile 5	0.75	0.69	0.80	0.02	0.02	0.04
Average	0.36	0.34	0.46	0.01	0.00	0.01

Source: Authors' calculations based on data from ENAHO (1997, 2001, and 2006, fourth quarter of each year).

access to electricity in rural areas may affect opportunities for employment (both salaried and independent) in the agricultural processing industry, and greater access to sanitation may reduce morbidity rates and consequently reduce lost working hours due to illness of workers or their dependent children. Finally, another part of the effects may be independent of the variables included in our model and therefore may be captured by the "other factors" element.

The Role of Market Forces and Social Policies

Our decomposition exercise indicated that returns to experience, educational structure, and unobservable factors had an equalizing effect in Peru over the last decade, while returns to urban residence and hours worked had an opposite effect. Returns to education had an equalizing effect at the individual level (returns to skill at the worker level became less convex) but unequalizing at the household level (couple formation patterns turned the returns to education into an unequalizing factor). Here we explore the market and policy forces behind these factors.

Returns to education for individual workers in Peru during the 1990s increased sharply, in part due to trade liberalization, increased foreign direct investment, and the general opening of the economy. To be sure, that pattern was observed not only in Peru but across Latin America (Sánchez-Páramo and Schady 2002). Much of the GDP growth during this period involved new investment, which tends to incorporate new technology. That suggests that, as in other parts of the world (Acemoglu 2002), technological change in Peru was skill-biased. That pattern, however, has not persisted in the present decade. In fact, during the recent growth period (2001–06), individual returns to education have declined, particularly with respect to higher education (Jaramillo and Saavedra 2009). The structure of returns to education by educational level and the structure of the potential labor supply moved in opposite directions.[19] In fact, from 2001 to 2006, the potential supply of workers with postsecondary education increased faster than the potential supply of workers at any educational level. Since demand for workers at this level did increase, supply factors may explain the decline in returns to tertiary education after 2001. At the other end of the educational spectrum, workers with just primary education (the supply of whom has been shrinking), comprise the only group that has not seen its returns decline (in relative terms) during this period. Each of these findings supports the conclusion that market forces are behind the trends in returns to education for individual workers.

Changes in the structure of educational attainment of the labor force have played a positive role in the reduction of inequality over the last decade. In effect, during this period, the largest increase in relative labor supply can be observed among workers with secondary school education. The increase in the educational attainment of the labor force is the result of policies and household decisions made over the last four decades. Between 1970 and 2000, registration for basic education in public schools increased at an annual average rate of 3 percent, greater than the growth in the population at normative schooling age.[20] By 2005 the gross enrollment rate in primary education exceeded 100 percent of children at the normative age while that of secondary education topped off at around 90 percent (Cotlear 2006).

Nevertheless, public resources allocated to the education sector remained fairly constant over time. Constant real resources coupled with the increase in enrollment imply a reduction of public expenditure per student over time. It was only in the 1990s that public spending per student in basic education increased substantially, though not enough to catch up with its high point in the early 1970s or with contemporary levels in most of Latin America.[21] In that regard, it should

19. Potential labor supply refers to individuals older than 14 years of age.

20. According to official figures (Peru 2004), in Peru enrollment in public schools represented about 85 percent of total enrollment in 2003; in rural areas it was 98 percent.

21. From 1990 to 2000, annual public expenditure per student jumped from US$80 to US$135 at the elementary level and from US$124 to US$191at the secondary level. During the 2000s, public expenditures per student increased further, by 20 percent (Saavedra and Suárez 2002).

be noted that even though expansion of education clearly is an equalizing force, long-term deterioration of the quality of education reduces its equalizing power.

It is worth noting that Peruvian families have played a large role in financing their children's public education, contributing about one-third of total expenditures (Saavedra and Suárez 2002). As would be expected, family contribution totals are larger in the richer deciles; consequently expenditures in goods and services in public schools are higher in the richer regions of Peru. The resulting heterogeneity in resources across public schools tends to reproduce economic differences between social groups, thus betraying the role of public education as an opportunity equalizer. Recent evidence reaffirms that, despite expenditure inefficiencies demonstrated in all regions, the richest regions tend to have broader educational coverage, higher completion rates, and higher learning achievement rates. That is accompanied by higher public sector expenditures in those regions (Tam 2008). Exacerbating inequality is the fact that Peruvian public schools tend to be of lower quality than private schools.[22] In light of this information, it is not surprising that Peru's education system is one of the most unequal in Latin America as measured by learning achievement on international tests (Cueto 2006).

In sum, the progressive change in the structure of educational attainment in the Peruvian labor force has had to do with public policies to expand basic education and with the market-driven investment decisions of families that saw an opportunity to improve their children's prospects in life through education. The expansion of the educational system has been a key factor in the educational upgrading of the labor force. However, the expansion was not accompanied by an improvement in the quality of education, and it may well have entailed a reduction in average quality and increased inequity in the quality of education. Both facts are consistent with the long-term trend of stagnant productivity in earnings and high labor earnings inequality.

Average working hours for those employed declined during the recession period from 47.5 to 47 hours per week and remained unchanged during the growth period. In the case of women, however, there was an increase in weekly hours worked, from 42.3 to 43 over the span of the decade. Deciles 5 through 8 observed an increase in weekly hours worked by women in 2006 while the poorest (deciles 1 through 4) logged fewer weekly hours worked in 2006 than in 1997 and 2001. That pattern is, in turn, associated with women from the middle deciles putting in more hours of work on average, which, in turn, may be thought of as part of the long-term trend of increasing participation by women in the labor market. The fact that women in the middle deciles of the distribution are increasing their participation and hours of work suggests that growing demand for relatively skilled female labor is one factor in the overall trend of increased hours worked for

---

22. Calonico and Ñopo (2007) and Yamada (2007), which study returns to public and private education, find that returns to private education carry a substantial premium.

women. However, greater educational attainment, which increases the cost of not working, and institutional factors, such as changes in social norms, also may be influencing this trend.

Returns to experience declined from 1997 to 2006, with a slight increase between 1997 and 2001; subsequently there was a significant drop between 2001 and 2006, to levels below those of 1997. The overall decline occurred in the context of the demographic transition to lower rates of population growth. In effect, the Peruvian labor force is getting older because younger cohorts are smaller, a fact that is changing the shape of the age distribution of the employed labor force. From 1997 to 2006, the percentage of those aged 30 years or less declined 6 points, from 38 percent to 32 percent, while that of those older than 50 years increased 4 points, from 20 percent to 24 percent. Two other elements may also have played a role in the decline of returns to experience. The first is that better economic conditions in households allow youth to stay in school longer and become better prepared to enter the labor force. The second element is technological change. As we argued earlier, the period from 2001 to 2006 was characterized by a rapid increase in the investment rate, and new investment tends to incorporate new technology. That may favor demand for younger workers of the same educational attainment as older workers because younger workers tend to have incorporated the necessary new skills while older workers may have more traditional skills that have become obsolete in the new labor market. It seems, therefore, that demographic factors may play a role in the decline of inequality, in conjunction with market forces, because they may have served to drive down returns to experience.

Finally, returns to urban location reflect the gap in access to basic services between urban and rural areas that we demonstrated earlier. Our decomposition results for the recent growth period indicate a small equalizing role for the urban-rural earnings gap, which may be associated to improvements in rural infrastructure. Also during the recent growth period, mean income (both labor and nonlabor) increased faster in rural than in urban areas. The ratio of hourly labor earnings in rural to urban areas in 1997 was 0.48, while by 2006 the same figure rose to 0.53. Performance, however, was uneven over time within rural areas; average labor earnings in the rural coast increased much faster during the 2000s. As a result, the ratio of earnings in rural coastal Peru to earnings in the rest of the country rose to 80 percent by 2006, up from 62 percent in 1997. That is the result of large investment in the agro-industry of the Peruvian coast during that span.

Therefore, though we find evidence of improvements in rural areas, such as expansion of basic services and rising incomes, substantially reducing the inequality gap in urban areas will still be a high priority on the agenda of any equity-oriented economic reform program. Market forces still drive the concentration of productive activity and consequently of income generation in urban areas, where both essential and more sophisticated services are more readily available. By working toward closing the gap in access to infrastructure, social policies are moving in the right direction; however, a stronger and more sustained effort is needed to provide better opportunities for the rural population.

In sum, market forces, state policies, and demographics have each played a role in explaining changes in the income distribution. Market dynamics have kept returns to education on hold while, aided by demographic factors, they have also effected a decline in returns to experience. On the other hand, the education policies of the last four decades have played a key role in the expansion of access to basic education and the consequent rise of overall educational attainment of the labor force. Overall improvement in education quality in Peru has stalled, however, and inequity in the quality of education received probably has increased. From that perspective, education policies have not been successful in leveraging public resources to reduce overall inequality in educational opportunity. Finally, despite the recent spikes in rural labor incomes, particularly along the rural coast, the differences in earnings between rural and urban areas—which can be attributed to differences in human capital as well as in access to basic infrastructure and public services— are wide and persistent. Policies targeting those realms have served to reduce the gap, but much remains to be done.

Conclusions and Policy Implications

The current inequality in Peru has deep historical roots. Given those roots, over the last half century the country has experienced tremendous and rapid transformation. Broadened access to education and land redistribution may best illustrate the extent of the change that has occurred and has in effect transformed the Peruvian social landscape. Data on participation in electoral processes also suggest the increased democratization of Peruvian society. Nonetheless, we still find an unsettling degree of economic inequality and social exclusion in Peru.

Analysis of the evolution of inequality in Peru over the last four decades reveals four key findings. First, a review of the literature indicates a lack of comparable sources to link current household survey data back to any period before the 1980s. Quantitative studies that find a long-term declining trend in inequality therefore need to rely on indirect evidence, such as the notable expansion of formal education and the equalizing redistribution of land. Second, analysis of post-reform trends in inequality suggests that household income inequality has declined. That decline can be observed in the recession years of 1997 through 2001 (though it lacks statistical significance), and it becomes more accentuated and statistically significant in the growth period (2001–06). Third, nonlabor income has played the most important role in the reduction of income inequality during the period of analysis (1997–2006). Although labor income inequality at the level of individual workers declined, couple formation patterns rendered the effect at the household level nil. For the period 1997–2006, labor income inequality at the household level remained unchanged, increasing during the recession and declining in the growth period; in 2006 it was at a level similar to that of 1997. Fourth, disaggregating the analysis by geographical domain, we find that inequality levels examined were greater in urban than in rural areas and that the decline in inequality from 1997 to 2006 was larger in urban areas.

With respect to the noted decline in overall inequality between 1997 and 2006, decomposition analysis indicates that the key factors therein included changes in the structure of educational attainment of the labor force, the decline in returns to experience, and unobserved factors. We also note that hours worked and returns to being located in an urban area had an unequalizing effect. Changes in returns to education were equalizing at the individual worker level but unequalizing at the household level. Changes in the gender earnings gap did not play a significant role. Finally, returns to being salaried (as opposed to self-employed) played significant but opposite roles in the two post-reform subperiods: an unequalizing role during the recession (1997–2001) and an equalizing role in the growth period (2001–06). That adds up to a negligible effect over the entire decade.

We find a role for both state policies and market forces and even for demographics in mobilizing the above factors. Market dynamics kept individual returns to education on hold while, with the help of demographics, they effected a decline in returns to experience. On the other hand, Peru's education policies over the last four decades have been crucial to the expansion of basic education and the consequent upgrading of educational attainment of the labor force. At the same time, there exist important concerns about the decline in average educational quality and its possibly worsening distribution over the course of the last four decades. Finally, a wide gap in access to infrastructure seems to be behind the trend in returns to urban location, although in the period from 2001 until 2006 we find evidence of improvement. In effect, policies have tended to reduce the gap between rural and urban areas, but much more work remains to be done in that area.

Our findings suggest three specific areas for policy interventions in Peru. The first is educational quality. Results in international tests reflect low levels of achievement in both language and mathematics as well as large inequities, particularly between urban and rural areas. Given the current pattern of public school financing, the Peruvian educational system reproduces rather than ameliorates social inequities. While there is consensus on the need to improve the quality of education, there is less agreement on how to do so, and any strategy that the government adopts will have profound implications on the future dynamics of inequality. A strategy that targets those at the low end of educational achievement will produce more equalizing effects than one that focuses on simply improving average overall achievement. Opting for an equalizing strategy will likely mean providing more attention and resources to traditionally neglected rural areas as well as to the poorer segments of society in urban areas.

A second area for equity-enhancing policy intervention is support for entrepreneurship. A key target group is independent workers, who tend to have lower educational attainment and lower levels of productivity. Reducing barriers to the growth of microenterprises and small firms and promoting the growth of small and medium-sized enterprises (SMEs) through active policies can contribute to reducing inequality. The main problem in this area is that little is known about what types of policies work. Latin American countries have tried a number of policies to spur and support SMEs: reducing the bureaucratic burden, facilitating access to training and technical assistance, and offering microcredit, among others. Nevertheless, those policies have rarely been rigorously evaluated. A coordinated effort is needed to identify which specific policies have a better chance of working in different contexts.

Finally, it is clear that much work remains for policymakers interested in closing the gap in access to basic infrastructure services between urban and rural areas and, more generally, reducing inequality in opportunities in access to good basic services, such as education, health and justice.. Some of those services are public goods (such as roads) while others are privately supplied. In each case, public policy should help to ensure access. Aside from shifting the allocation of resources, that can be done by giving priority to investment in poorer rural areas and by promoting the provision of services by private firms or by public-private partnerships. It also is important to note here that differences between *departamentos* (political units equivalent to U.S. states) have been shown to be a major source of inequality. Peru's current political decentralization process may exacerbate those differences; devolution of responsibilities to local authorities does not necessarily imply more equity in the quality of public services, since the managerial capacity of local authorities tends to be lower in poorer regions. While centralized management ensures a certain homogeneity in the quality of public services across regions, poorer regions will likely end up worse off than richer regions whose authorities have greater managerial capacity. If decentralization is not accompanied by an effort to improve local capacities, inequity might even be exacerbated.

References

Abusada, Roberto, Fritz Du Bois, Eduardo Morón, and José Valderrama. 2000. *La Reforma Incompleta*. Lima: CIUP-Instituto Peruano de Economía.

Acemoglu, Daron. 2002. "Technical Change, Inequality, and The Labor Market." *Journal of Economic Literature*, 40, no. 1: 7–72.

Amat y León, Carlos. 1981. *Distribución del ingreso familiar en el Perú*. Lima: Universidad del Pacífico.

Barros, Ricardo Paes de, and others. 2009. *Measuring Inequality of Opportunities in Latin American and the Caribbean*. Palgrave Macmillan and World Bank.

Bourguignon, François, and Francisco Ferreira. 2005. "Decomposing Changes in the Distribution of Household Incomes: Methodological Aspects." In *The Microeconomics of Income*

Distribution Dynamics in East and Latin America, edited by François Bourguignon, Francisco H. G. Ferreira and Nora Lustig. Washington, D.C.: World Bank/Oxford University Press.

Bourguignon, François, Francisco Ferreira, and Nora Lustig, eds. 2005. *The Microeconomics of Income Distribution Dynamics in East Asia and Latin America.* Washington, D.C.: World Bank/Oxford University Press.

Bourguignon, François, Martin Fournier, and Marc Gurgand. 2001. "Fast Development with a Stable Income Distribution: Taiwan, 1979–94." *Review of Income and Wealth* 4, no. 2 (June): 139–163.

Breceda, Karla, Jamele Rigolini, and Jaime Saavedra. 2007. "Latin America and the Social Contract: Patterns of Social Spending and Taxation." Policy Research working paper 4604. World Bank.

Calonico, Sebastián, and Hugo Ñopo. 2007. "Where Did You Go To School?: Private-Public Differences in School Trajectories and Their Role in Earnings." *Well-Being and Social Policy* 3, no. 1: 29–52.

Cotlear, Daniel, ed. 2006. *Un Nuevo Contrato Social para el Peru.* Lima: Banco Mundial.

Cueto, Santiago. 2006. *"Educación y brechas de equidad en América Latina."* Santiago: PREAL.

ECLAC (Economic Commission for Latin America and the Caribbean). CEPALSTAT (http://website.eclac.cl/sisgen/ConsultaIntegrada.asp).

ENAHO (Encuesta Nacional de Hogares). 1997–2007. Lima: INEI.

ENNIV (Encuesta Nacional de Niveles de Vida). 1985, 1991, 1994, 1997. Lima: Instituto Cuanto.

Escobal, Javier, and Jorge Agüero. 1996. "Ajuste Macroeconómico y Distribución del Ingreso en el Perú." In *¿Cómo Estamos? Análisis de la Encuesta de Niveles de Vida,* edited by Gilberto Moncada and Richard Webb. Lima: Instituto Cuanto.

Escobal, Javier, Jaime Saavedra, and Máximo Torero. 1998. "Los Activos de los Pobres en el Perú." Documento de trabajo No. 26. Lima: GRADE.

Figueroa, Adolfo. 1990. "De la Distribución de la Crisis a la Crisis de la Distribución: Perú, 1975–90." Working paper No. 91. Lima: PUCP.

———. 1982. "El Problema Distributivo en Diferentes Contextos Socio-Politicos y Económicos: Perú, 1950–1980." Working paper No. 51. Lima: PUCP.

Gasparini, Leonardo, Mariana Marchionni, and Walter Sosa Escudero. 2005. "Characterization of Inequality Changes through Microeconometric Decompositions: The Case of Greater Buenos Aires." In *The Microeconomics of Income Distribution Dynamics,* edited by François Bourguignon, Francisco H. G. Ferreira, and Nora Lustig. Washington, D.C.: World Bank/Oxford University Press.

Glewwe, Paul, and Gillette Hall. 1994. "Poverty Inequality and Living Standards during Unorthodox Adjustment: The Case of Peru, 1985-1990." *Economic Development and Cultural Change* 42, no. 4 (July): 689–711.

Heckman, James. 1974. "Shadow Prices, Market Wages, and Labor Supply." *Econometric* 42, no. 4 (July): 679–94.

INEI (Instituto Nacional de Estadística) (www1.inei.gob.pe/web/aplicaciones/siemweb/index.asp?id=003).

Jaramillo, Miguel, and Jaime Saavedra. 2005. "Governability and Economic Performance in 1990s Peru." In *Political Crises, Social Conflict and Economic Development,* edited by Andrés Solimano. UK: MPG Books Ltd.

———. 2009. "Inequality in Post-Structural Reform Peru: The Role of Market and Policy Forces". Background paper prepared for the UNDP project *Markets, the State and the Dynamics of Inequality: How to Advance Inclusive Growth,* co-ordinated by Luis Felipe Lopez-Calva and Nora Lustig. (http://undp.economiccluster-lac.org/).

Legovini, Arianna, César Bouillón, and Nora Lustig. 2005. "Can Education Explain Changes in Income Inequality in Mexico?" In *The Microeconomics of Income Distribution Dynamics,* edited by François Bourguignon, Francisco H. G. Ferreira and Nora Lustig. Washington, D.C.: World Bank/Oxford University Press.

Perú. 1944. "Censo nacional de población y ocupación de 1940: resultados definitivos a nivel nacional." Lima: Ministerio de Hacienda y Comercio. Dirección Nacional de Estadística.

———. 2004. *Cifras de la Educación 1998–2003.* Lima: Unidad de Estadística Educativa, Ministerio de Educación.

Rodríguez, José. 1991. "Distribución Salarial y Educación en Lima Metropolitana, 1970–1984" *Economía* 14, no. 28 (Lima: Departamento de Economía – PUCP): 307–343.

Saavedra, Jaime, and Juan José Díaz. 1999. "Desigualdad del Ingreso y del Gasto en el Perú antes y después de las Reformas Estructurales" *Serie Reformas Económicas* no. 34. Santiago de Chile: CEPAL.

Saavedra, Jaime, and Pablo Suárez. 2002. "El financiamiento de la educación pública en el Perú: el rol de las familias." Working Paper no. 38. Lima: GRADE.

Sánchez-Páramo, Carolina, and Norbert Schady. 2002. "Off and Running? The Rising Demand for Skilled Workers in Latin America." Washington, D.C.: World Bank.

Tam, Mary. 2008. "Eficiencia técnica del gasto en educación publica en las regiones del Perú." Economía y Sociedad, no. 68: 50–64.

Webb, Richard. 1977. *Government policy and the distribution of income in Perú, 1963–1973.* Harvard University Press.

Webb, Richard and Adolfo Figueroa. 1975. *La Distribución del Ingreso en el Perú.* Lima: Instituto de Estudios Peruanos.

Yamada, Gustavo. 2007. "Retornos a la educación superior en el mercado laboral: ¿vale la pena el esfuerzo?" Documento de Trabajo no. 78. Lima: Centro de Investigación de la Universidad del Pacifico.

Contributors

Facundo Alvaredo
Oxford University

Ricardo Barros
*Instituto de Pesquisa Econômica
    Aplicada (IPEA), Brazil*

Guillermo Cruces
*Centro de Estudios Distributivos
Laborales y Sociales (CEDLAS),
Universidad Nacional de La Plata,
Argentina*

Mirela de Carvalho
*Instituto de Estudos do Trabalho e
    Sociedade (IETS), Brazil*

Gerardo Esquivel
*Centro de Estudios Economicos, El
    Colegio de México*

Samuel Franco
*Instituto de Estudos do Trabalho e
    Sociedade (IETS), Brazil*

Leonardo Gasparini
*Centro de Estudios Distributivos
    Laborales y Sociales (CEDLAS),
    Universidad Nacional de La Plata,
    Argentina*

Miguel Jaramillo
*Group for the Analysis of Development
    (GRADE), Peru*

Jaime Kahhat
*Department of Business Administration,
    College of Westchester, New York*

Luis Felipe López-Calva
*Regional Bureau for Latin America and
    the Caribbean, United Nations
    Development Program*

Nora Lustig
*Department of Economics, Tulane
    University*

Rosane Mendonça
*Universidade Federal Fluminense,
    Brazil*

Thomas Piketty
Paris School of Economics

James A. Robinson
Department of Government, Harvard University

Jaime Saavedra
Poverty Reduction and Equity Group, World Bank

John Scott
Centro de Investigacion y Docencia Economicas (CIDE), México D.F.

Index